Basics of International
Humanitarian Missions

Basics of International Humanitarian Missions

Edited by
KEVIN M. CAHILL, M.D.

A Joint Publication of
FORDHAM UNIVERSITY PRESS
and
THE CENTER FOR INTERNATIONAL
HEALTH AND COOPERATION
New York • 2003

International Humanitarian Affairs, No. 2
Kevin M. Cahill, M.D., series editor
ISSN 1541–7409

Library of Congress Cataloging-in-Publication Data

Basics of international humanitarian missions / edited by Kevin M. Cahill.
— 1st ed.
     p.   cm. — (International humanitarian affairs ; no. 2)
  Includes bibliographical references and index.
  ISBN 0-8232-2242-X (hardcover) — ISBN 0-8232-2243-8 (pbk.)
  1. Disaster relief.   2. Humanitarian assistance.   I. Cahill, Kevin M.
II. Series.

HV553.B38   2003
363.34′8—dc21   2002035324

Printed in the United States of America
03   04   05   06   07   5   4   3   2   1
First Edition

For Larry Hollingworth

CONTENTS

Acknowledgments   ix

Abbreviations and Acronyms   xi

Introduction   xv
    Kevin M. Cahill, M.D.

PART 1   1

1. Humanitarian Action in the Twenty-first Century: The
   Danger of a Setback   3
   Paul Grossrieder

2. Scope of International Humanitarian Crises   18
   Ibrahim Osman

3. The Language of Disasters: A Brief Terminology of
   Disaster Management and Humanitarian Action   35
   S. W. A. Gunn, M.D.

PART 2   47

4. Training for Humanitarian Assistance   49
   Kevin M. Cahill, M.D.

5. Teamwork in Humanitarian Missions   59
   Pamela Lupton-Bowers

PART 3   111

6. Humanitarian Ethical and Legal Standards   113
   Michel Veuthey

7. Rules of Engagement: An Examination of Relationships
   and Expectations in the Delivery of Humanitarian
   Assistance   142
   H. Roy Williams

PART 4   169

8. Humanitarians and the Press   171
   Joshua Friedman

9. The Sinews of Humanitarian Assistance: Funding
   Policies, Practices, and Pitfalls   200
   Joelle Tanguy

10. From the Other Side of the Fence: The Problems
    Behind the Solution   241
    Abdulrahim Abby Farah

Selected Web Sites   269

Chapter Notes and References   273

Appendixes   329

The Center for International Health and Cooperation and
    the Institute of International Humanitarian Affairs   337

About the Authors   339

Index   343

ACKNOWLEDGMENTS

THIS BOOK is made possible by the generous contributions of many individuals and organizations. All the chapters were written by colleagues who accepted the challenge of contributing to this book on short notice and for no honorarium because they shared my belief in the need to record their vast experience and knowledge for future humanitarian workers. Most authors had participated in the International Diploma in Humanitarian Assistance course offered by the Center for International Health and Cooperation (CIHC) in concert with Fordham University, the University of Geneva, and the Royal College of Surgeons in Ireland.

This book was supported, in part, by a generous grant from the Donner Foundation. Special thanks are due to Ms. Phaedra Annan, Rev. Joseph A. O'Hare, S.J., Mr. Saverio Procario, and the staff of Fordham University Press. The Executive Secretary of the CIHC, Renee Cahill, and Ms. Yvette Christofilis helped with editing and made a complex and difficult task a pleasure. Cindy McGinity graciously volunteered many hours to this cause.

ABBREVIATIONS AND ACRONYMS

AIDS	Acquired Immune Deficiency Syndrome
ALNAP	Active Learning Network for Accountability and Performance in Humanitarian Action
AI	Amnesty International
CAP	Consolidated Appeals Process (UN)
CDC	Centers for Disease Control
CERF	Central Emergency Revolving Fund
CHAP	Common Humanitarian Action Plan
CIA	Central Intelligence Agency
CIHC	Center for International Health and Cooperation
CIMIC	Civilian-military cooperation
CMR	Crude mortality rate
CNN	Cable News Network
CPJ	Committee to Protect Journalists
CRED	Center for Research on the Epidemiology of Disasters
CRS	Catholic Relief Services
CWS	Church World Services
DAC	Development Assistance Committee
DFID	Department for Foreign International Development (U.K.)
ECHO	European Community Humanitarian Office
ECOSOC	Economic and Social Council
EM-DAT	a comprehensive disaster database
EU	European Union
FAO	Food and Agriculture Organization
FTS	Financial Tracking System
HDC	Humanitarian Dialogue Center
HEWS	Humanitarian Early-Warning System
HIV	Human Immunodeficiency Virus
HRW	Human Rights Watch
IASC	Inter-Agency Standing Committee

ICC	International Criminal Court
ICJ	International Court of Justice
ICRC	International Committee of the Red Cross
ICTR	International Criminal Tribunal for Rwanda
ICTY	International Criminal Tribunal for the Former Yugoslavia
ICVA	International Council of Voluntary Agencies
IDHA	International Diploma in Humanitarian Assistance
IDP	Internally displaced person
IFJ	International Federation of Journalists
IFRC	International Federation of Red Cross and Red Crescent Societies
IHL	International Humanitarian Law
IIHA	Institute of International Humanitarian Affairs, Fordham University
ILO	International Labor Organization
IMF	International Monetary Fund
IOM	International Organization for Migration
IRC	International Rescue Committee
JDC	Joint Distribution Committee
MSF	*Médecins sans frontières*—Doctors Without Borders
NATO	North Atlantic Treaty Organization
NGO	Nongovernmental organization
OAS	Organization of American States
OAU	Organization of African Unity
OCHA	Office for the Coordination of Humanitarian Affairs (UN)
OECD	Organization for Economic Cooperation and Development
OFDA	Office of Foreign Disaster Assistance (U.S.)
OSCE	Organization for Security and Cooperation in Europe
POW	Prisoner of War
PVO	Private Voluntary Organization
RCSI	Royal College of Surgeons in Ireland
SCHR	Steering Committee for Humanitarian Response
SITREP	Situation Report
SOS	Emergency call: Save Our Souls

TRC	Truth and Reconciliation Commission (South Africa)
UNAMIR	United Nations Assistance Mission in Rwanda
UNDAC	United Nations Disaster and Coordination
UNDP	United Nations Development Program
UNEP	United Nations Environment Program
UNESCO	United Nations Educational, Scientific, and Cultural Organization
UNHCR	United Nations High Commissioner for Refugees
UNICEF	United Nations International Children's Emergency Fund
UNIENET	International Disaster Management Information Network
UNPROFOR	United Nations Protection Force (in Yugoslavia)
UNRWA	United Nations Relief and Works Agency for Palestine Refugees
UNFAO	United Nations Food and Agriculture Organization
USAID	U.S. Agency for International Development
VOICE	Voluntary Organizations in Cooperation in Emergencies
WFP	World Food Program / UN World Food Program
WHO	World Health Organization
WCC	World Council of Churches
WV	World Vision

INTRODUCTION

FORDHAM UNIVERSITY PRESS'S International Humanitarian Affairs series is launched with two practical volumes, *Basics of International Humanitarian Missions* and *Emergency Relief Operations*. The series will issue two to three books per year and will consider various aspects of a discipline that, while in some senses is as ancient as humankind, is nevertheless still in a stage of definition. Only in recent years has humanitarian assistance been appreciated to be a potent political and diplomatic tool, and also recognized as big business. What began at the dawn of existence as an individual altruistic undertaking evolved into a charitable vocation and is now recognized as a distinct profession.

The purpose or goal of Fordham University's Institute of International Humanitarian Affairs is to preserve the traditions and values of this discipline while also providing a framework for appropriate training and academic analyses. The book series directly complements, and draws from, the Institute's other programs and teaching courses. This international humanitarian book series is intended to provide practical volumes for use by professionals in the field as well as by students in a wide variety of academic departments. The multidisciplinary nature of international humanitarian relief will be obvious to any reader.

Humanitarian assistance, particularly in the midst of conflicts and disasters, is not a field for amateurs. Good intentions are a common but tragically inadequate substitute for well-planned, efficiently implemented operations that, like a good sentence, must have a beginning, a middle, and an end. Compassion and charity are only elements in humanitarian assistance programs; alone they are self-indulgent emotions that, for a short time, may satisfy the donor, but will always disappoint victims in desperate need.

The number and severity of humanitarian crises is rapidly escalating in our post-cold war era, where the perverse stability of East-West superpower politics can sometimes seem preferable to the chaos that now prevails in "failed states" that dot the world. Civil wars have largely replaced formal conflicts between nations. In World War I, 90 percent of those injured or killed were military combatants, while in modern conflicts, civilians account for over 90 percent of the victims.

International humanitarian laws, which were established to provide rules of war, are rarely recognized and are certainly not observed in civil wars. International laws and the Geneva Conventions were composed for an earlier era when state governments officially represented combatants. Now childhood warriors with AK-47s rule the roads, and clans use ethnic cleansing as a solution to borders that, according to one's own peculiar view, had been artificially imposed by a historical process they would never forget nor forgive. Today there are more internally displaced persons than international refugees.

In noncomplex emergencies such as floods or earthquakes, where a stable government exists, that government understandably expects to, and is responsible for, handling all relief activities. International assistance workers must accept the traditions and rules of functioning sovereign nations or invite confrontation and painful rejection. Aid offered without respect for the rights of an independent people will almost always result in counterproductive misunderstanding, damaging both donor and recipient.

But in complex humanitarian emergencies, security concerns and political decisions are an intimate part of any relief response. This volume, divided into four sections, presents some of the basic elements that need to be considered in both natural and man-made humanitarian crises. Companion volumes will offer more detailed coverage of specific aspects of humanitarian assistance.

Basics of International
Humanitarian Missions

Part 1

To build a solid edifice one must have a good foundation, a basic structure for growth and development. There are many reasons to begin any undertaking with a careful study of history. It allows us to appreciate the contributions of our predecessors and to offer a perspective so frequently missing in the flow of a current crisis. A historical approach permits us to introduce the traditions and values of our profession. And, maybe most importantly, it helps us avoid repeating the more egregious errors of past interventions. Only by accumulating solid data can better programs be developed. To communicate, especially in the midst of chaos, we must carefully define our methods and goals, constructing a new and accepted language to fit an evolving discipline. In this section, three acknowledged masters in the field of humanitarian assistance review the history of our field, recent statistics, and its vocabulary.

Current efforts in organized international humanitarian assistance are rooted in a noble past. The ethos of our discipline, and the codes of conduct that guide our actions, reflect the aspirations, as well as the failures, of our forebears. Paul Grossrieder, the Director-General of the International Committee of the Red Cross (ICRC), reminds us of the evolution of humanitarian action from ancient times to the modern day, and concludes with an assessment of the new challenges in the twenty-first century.

The number of calamities in our ever-shrinking world seems to inexorably expand, especially if one depends solely on television images, the "CNN effect" of immediate involvement in every disaster. Reality, however, and the rational plans to deal with that reality, depend on careful statistical analysis. Ibrahim Osman, the Director of Monitoring and Evaluation for the International Federation of

Red Cross and Red Crescent Societies (IFRC), has studied the data on international disasters for many decades. His chapter defines the scope of both natural and man-made disasters in the last decade of the twentieth century.

In response to any large disaster, many players will convene, representing varying backgrounds, cultures, nations, and tongues. An indispensable requirement for an appropriate humanitarian response is to agree on terminology, for without a common, accepted language, the efforts of disparate helpers may—in fact, usually will—add to the disaster. Dr. S. W. A. Gunn, who has authored a multinational dictionary for disaster and relief workers, contributes an essential chapter of common terms, and helped select the abbreviations, acronyms, and useful Web sites listed.

1

Humanitarian Action in the Twenty-first Century: The Danger of a Setback

Paul Grossrieder

Introduction

Humanitarian action as envisaged by Henry Dunant, the founder of the Red Cross Movement, is both simple—it is based on the natural human tendency to respect a fellow human—and original—Dunant wished to apply that common sense principle in systematic fashion, even in war.

A fleeting glance at the past will help us appreciate what was original about humanitarian action as conceived by Dunant; why it goes beyond good intentions or mere charity. Until September 11, 2001, there was no reason to believe that the international community would be tempted by a simplistic view of the world to roll back the concept of humanitarian action that was born with the Red Cross. I do not wish to indulge in facile anachronisms, but will retrace the development of humanitarian idea and action and highlight the challenges as well as the risks of the twenty-first century for humanitarian action.

Ancient Greece (Fifth Century B.C.)

War had limits for only some members of humanity. The extent to which the Greeks humanized war can only be understood in the light of their society's division into city-states, competition between which was natural and gave rise to regular conflicts in an attempt to establish which was the best. Fighting between cities of the same culture and the same religion was governed by unwritten rules *(agrafoi nomoi)*. The city that lost was always at a disadvantage, but the victor had to respect limits to its conduct with regard to captives. Those rules were not, however, a form of international law, as they applied only between Greek city-states; whereas, there was no limit to the acts of violence that could be carried out against the enemy in wars between Greeks and barbarians (non-Greeks).

Ancient Greece therefore witnessed the first, very partial endeavor to use rules of law to regulate certain conflicts between Greek city-states. Whether or not those unwritten rules applied depended not on one's condition as a human being, but on one's membership in Greek civilization.

RELIGION AND RESPECT FOR HUMAN BEINGS

On the one hand, all the world's great religions (primitive religions, Judaism, Christianity,[1] Islam, the religions of the Far East) recommend that their followers treat other human beings with respect; on the other hand, each religion is linked to a people, to a culture (or is imposed on others as a culture), and the notion of universality is therefore absent. In addition, violence is often a part of religious behavior, carried out to defend a god or a truth. In any event, it makes sense for every religion to consider itself the best, otherwise why believe? In most past and present conflicts, religious communities have identified with one of the parties to the conflict. In recent years, the conflicts in the Balkans have provided ample proof of this, but the same thing has happened in the eastern Democratic Republic of the Congo, in Sri Lanka, and in many other countries in conflict. It was therefore not religions that originated and promoted the founding ideas of humanitarian law, neither in the distant past nor in modern times.

CHRISTIANITY SINCE THE MIDDLE AGES: LOVE, COMPASSION, CHARITY

Since the Middle Ages and until the twenty-first century, the notions of love, compassion, and charity, and the activities based on them, evolved principally along two lines:

1. One tradition used love, compassion and charity to fight the established powers. In the face of the self-assigned privileges of the rich and powerful, men such as Francis of Assisi (twelfth century), Joachim de Flore (fourteenth century), and, later, Giordano Bruno (sixteenth century) branded those notions as weapons in defense of the poor and the underprivileged. In some cases, their struggles ended in social and political revolt.

2. In another tradition, represented chiefly by the institutional church, those notions were applied only in respect of the faithful who followed the right path. In that case, nothing took precedence over the established order; charity toward the poor was a means of maintaining that order and a requirement for salvation, but had no intrinsic value. It can even be said that this tradition substituted charity for justice. Charity was the pretext for not dispensing the justice that could undermine the power of the rich and mighty. This tradition's purpose was to maintain and uphold a political and social order that was unconcerned by equal rights and used charity to contain any hint of rebellion on the part of the lower classes. In that context, the idea of universal humanitarianism had no scope to develop.

The dichotomy between the two traditions prevailed throughout Western Christian culture until the nineteenth century and constituted the political *leitmotif* of that period.

THE PREMISES OF THE MODERN HUMANITARIAN IDEA

A Christian Exception: St. Vincent de Paul

In the seventeenth century, St. Vincent de Paul adopted a systematic approach to poverty in France, with a view to its eradication.

To that end, he established two structures, or religious orders: the Daughters of Charity and the Lazarists. St. Vincent de Paul's approach was original in that it tackled poverty as a social phenomenon and established structures to remedy it.

Unfortunately, the system was appropriated by Louis XIV, or more specifically his wife, Maria Teresa of Austria. St. Vincent de Paul's humanitarian endeavor was turned into "internment houses" run by the police, spelling a sad end to a pioneering humanitarian effort and protecting the hierarchical order of the time.

The Concept of "Humanity"

During that period—between the seventeenth and nineteenth centuries—Europe awakened to the revolutionary idea of a human being as an individual (Descartes, Spinoza, Kant, Marx, etc.). Whereas Christian charity as it had evolved in Western societies was compatible with social inequality, the modern concept of "humanity" considered every man and woman as equally "human." Without a doubt, the philosophical development of the concept of humans as individuals fostered the sociological advent of the demand that all men and women be treated equal, and hence the idea that any person, no matter what his social status, was entitled to respect without discrimination.

The First "Humanitarian" Operations (Late Eighteenth to Early Nineteenth Centuries)

1793: relief operation for French aristocrats forced to flee Santo Domingo during a slave uprising;

1812: earthquake in Caracas: the United States organized assistance by boat;

1821: aid for the Greeks (only) during their war against the Turks

Humanitarian action in time of war initially took the form of medical services provided by the armed forces for their troops.

Those who pioneered such services were Ambroise Paré (sixteenth century) and Baron Larrey (1766–1842).

The eighteenth century saw the conclusion of the first agreements between combatants for the reciprocal use of hospitals.

1743: Battle of Bethingen—agreement between the Marshall of Noailles (France) and Lord Sain (England)

1759: Seven Years War—agreement between General de Barail and Henry Seymour Conway

HENRY DUNANT AND SOLFERINO

The battle of Solferino in the Italian war of Unification (1859) marked a decisive moment in the modern concept of humanitarianism, thanks first to Henry Dunant and, subsequently, to the Red Cross in general and the International Committee of the Red Cross (ICRC) in particular. Dunant and the Committee of Five "invented" the principles that underpin humanitarian action to this day. They are based on three fundamental ideas:

The basic idea: a universal space, that of the victim, that respects the neutrality of the victims of war. Henceforth, aid would not be limited to one's own wounded but would be extended to all the victims. As Henry Dunant wrote in *A Memory of Solferino*: "The women of Castiglione, seeing that I made no distinction between nationalities, followed my example, showing the same kindness to all these men whose origins were so different, and all of whom were foreigners to them. '*Tutti fratelli,*' they repeated feelingly" (ICRC, 1986).

The second original idea: those helping the victims must be part of the same space, the space of humanity. Humanitarian agents help all the victims as members of one humanity. To give effect to this idea, an independent organization, untainted by any military or political commitment, was founded; it was the voice of humanity in the midst of armed conflict. It soon came to be called the Red Cross.

The third original idea: at a time when all man's laws apparently ceased to exist when fighting broke out, Henry Dunant created a space for a contract. Certain laws could be applied universally even in the heat of battle. International humanitarian law was born. In 1864, the States signed the Geneva Convention for the protection of the war wounded, an international treaty that defined a legal space for humanitarian aid.

Thus, Henry Dunant and the Red Cross laid the foundations of contemporary humanitarian action, which seeks to treat enemies *hors de combat* as equals in humanity.

Contemporary Periods of Humanitarian Action

World War I

Previously a legal and moral authority, the ICRC—and the entire Red Cross—had now to start taking action. The First World War was different from the wars of the nineteenth century in that it was total. It involved countries, economies, and populations on an unprecedented scale. The Red Cross was obliged to demonstrate that the principles and rules laid down in the law of war were applicable.

The ICRC went from being a moral and legal authority to an operational organization. Its main fields of action were prisoners of war, repatriations, and tracing activities. Forty-one delegates visited fifty-four prisoner-of-war camps. They repatriated a total of 700,000 prisoners; 1,200 volunteers worked at the International Prisoners-of-War Agency in Basel, restoring ties between prisoners and their families. Two million parcels were sent to prisoners.

In 1917, the ICRC was awarded the Nobel Peace Prize.

The Period between the Two World Wars

The first problem was *practical in nature:* what was to be done with the enormous infrastructure set up during the First World War? The fight against tuberculosis was one of the operations undertaken during this period. A Red Cross poster proclaimed: "Beat the Germans, beat tuberculosis."

There then arose a *political problem,* for after the First World War, pacifism became a force to be reckoned with (President Wilson, Treaty of Versailles, the League of Nations, the Briand-Kellog Pact). War was to be outlawed.

In order to deal with those two problems, the Red Cross organized itself into two international institutions. At the instigation of the President of the American Red Cross, the League of Red Cross Societies was established; it would be responsible for peacetime activities. The ICRC would specialize in wartime operations, and in humanitarian law and its dissemination.

During the same period, the Save the Children Fund (1919) and the United Nations High Commission for Refugees (UNHCR, 1921) were also established. Both organizations would deal with peacetime issues arising from war.

World War II

For the Red Cross, and in particular the ICRC, this war was marked by the questions and issues posed by totalitarian regimes (Bolshevism, Nazism).

Those regimes manipulated humanitarian aid for their own purposes. In 1921, for example, the USSR had demanded total control of the humanitarian assistance provided to the famine-stricken population of the Ukraine. Under the pressure of public opinion, the Western countries had caved in to its demands.

The Second World War also brought to light shortcomings in international humanitarian law. Specifically, it became apparent during the war in Spain (1936) that humanitarian law did not cover non-international conflicts. Nor did it afford protection to civilians in time of war.

Moreover, the totalitarian regimes, which rejected the international system of the League of Nations, also ignored humanitarian law.

The ICRC, for its part, strengthened by its success during the

First World War, approached the humanitarian issues of World War II as though they were a repetition of the first. It focused almost exclusively on prisoners of war. Blinded by its operational approach, concerned to safeguard its activities, the ICRC made the tragic decision not to deal with civilians or the Holocaust. There were, nevertheless, several heroic exceptions, the result of initiatives taken by certain delegates in the field. The most spectacular example was Friedrich Born, who saved an estimated 15,000 Jews in Hungary from the death camps.

The Postwar Period

After the Second World War and the horrors committed by the Nazis, the world felt the need to do all in its power to make sure such crimes were never again committed. In that atmosphere of widespread remorse, numerous associations were founded to help the populations of Europe, especially in the United States and among the religions communities (Catholic, Protestant, Jewish): the International Rescue Committee (IRC), Catholic Relief Services (CRS), Church World Services (CWS), the Joint Distribution Committee (JDC), CARE, Oxfam, to name but a few.

It was also during this period that most of the United Nations specialized agencies were founded; that the Geneva Conventions were renegotiated to include common Articles 1 and 3, and that the Fourth Convention, on the protection of civilians, was adopted. These new international instruments explicitly recognized that the ICRC was an "impartial humanitarian organization."

Finally, the Refugee Convention was adopted in 1951.

This was a heady period for humanitarianism, for society and public opinion were eager to correct the serious mistakes of the Second World War.

The Cold War and Humanitarian Action: The Limits Set by Ideology

The universal, independent, neutral, and impartial approach was severely tested by the growing ideological tension and deepening cold war between the East and West blocs. On the one hand, the Soviet Union did not agree to apply humanitarian law and its principles in the countries and regions within its sphere of influence;[2] on the other, the West included the law in its arsenal of weapons against the East bloc. All this took place against a backdrop of public will to do good.

During the same period, the widespread struggle for decolonization brought humanitarian organizations face-to-face with liberation movements and the peoples under their control. Generally speaking, the organizations belonged to one of two schools:

- those influenced by the analyses on inequality and anti-imperialism (F. Fanon, S. Amin);
- those guided by the position of American economist W. Rostow: that poverty fostered the spread of communism.

In the face of these global developments, of the rise and proliferation of liberation movements (the PLO, UNITA, the Sandinistas, RENAMO, etc.), how was the ICRC, the guardian of humanitarian law, to react? How should the law and practice be adapted to encompass these "new conflicts?" How could the basic principles and rules be recognized as applying to the victims of those conflicts? How could the ICRC contact all the parties? Obtain access to all the victims? These questions were the subject of protracted debate, and, in the end, the ICRC decided to adapt the law to the changed situation. That adaptation in no way signified that Henry Dunant's humanitarian principles were to be abandoned, but rather that their field of application was to be enlarged. The ICRC's decision resulted, in 1977, in the adoption of the Protocols additional to the Geneva Conventions.

At the same time, the "borderless" movement was launched as a different approach to the same issues. Doctors seconded to the ICRC by France during the Biafra war, deemed the organization's methods poorly adapted, too rigid and legalistic, too bound up with the authorities, and founded *Médecins sans frontières* (MSF) in 1968.

This new kind of humanitarian organization was set up to counter the ICRC, to circumvent the constraints of humanitarian law, which were seen as an obstacle to humanitarian action. Unfettered by diplomatic and legal considerations, MSF found it easy to be ironical about the timid approach of the Red Cross and the cowardice of the United Nations. It has covered interesting ground since then, for today MSF is one of the most fervent defenders of humanitarian law and has published a highly accessible handbook, the most complete manual for humanitarian practitioners in existence.

MSF and the organizations founded on the same model have a number of strengths and limitations. One of MSF's strengths is that it is a private association conducting private operations, which are therefore very independent and free. Its staff tends to go on brief but intense missions, and its operational policy is characterized by enormous flexibility.

In terms of limitations, MSF's political choices, especially during the early years of its existence, prevented it from being impartial (for example, in Afghanistan during the Soviet period, when MSF doctors sided with the *mujaheddin*). The covert nature of certain activities precluded the development of systematic, large-scale operations.

Things have changed now. MSF's methods are much closer to those of the ICRC, and the ICRC has followed in MSF's footsteps and adopted a more informal style. What remains particularly different is the duty to bear witness, by which MSF staff are bound, whereas ICRC delegates must follow a policy of discretion, chiefly in order to obtain access to places of detention and prisoner-of-war camps.

The 1980s: The Proliferation of Conflicts on the Periphery:
"Le Tout-urgence"

The wars of liberation were followed by what Jean-Christophe Rufin called conflicts on the periphery. These were waged within the context of a return to the Roman *limes* policy, in which "imperial" interests did not extend beyond the limits of a concentric circle outside which war and chaos were allowed to rage. This new form of conflict was contemporaneous with the "dissolution of the bipolar order."[3] The proliferation of bloody and spectacular periphery conflicts, involving little activity on the part of the superpowers (Sri Lanka, Ethiopia, Cambodia) signaled a return to urgency. Humanitarian agents played on the emotions and troubled conscience of people in the West. This period of absolute urgency had its downside, as well. Were we feeding the victims or feeding war? Certain leaders, such as Mengistu in Ethiopia in 1995, considered it judicious, for reasons of internal politics, to foment disaster.

After the Cold War: Humanitarian Action in Spite of Everything

The fall of the Berlin Wall sparked somewhat rash predictions that conflicts on the periphery would end and humanitarians would be out of a job. In fact, the number of regional and local conflicts rose (Afghanistan, Angola, Sierra Leone, Liberia, the Balkans). The anarchic and chaotic nature of those conflicts made them extremely dangerous and rendered humanitarian work hugely complex, as it became more and more difficult to have access to the victims for security reasons. This period was marked by the almost total withdrawal of external political support for local wars. As a result, armed movements replaced their political partners with economic partners and embarked on business activities, at times forming alliances with private commercial firms. They also started to exploit territory or to plunder the population. They became incredibly diverse in nature.

In those circumstances, the plight of the civilian population became increasingly perilous (witness the famines in southern Sudan and Somalia). The ICRC, UNHCR, and the nongovernmental organizations (NGOs) all mobilized to provide emergency aid on an unprecedented scale.

Enter the States: The Politicization of Humanitarian Action

That situation—the proliferation of local conflicts and the growing number of victims who suffered as a result—was compounded in 1990 when the states burst on the humanitarian scene. During the cold war, direct state intervention had been justified by the fight against "the other side." That justification wore thin after the fall of the Berlin Wall, and when the international community decided, at the behest of the Americans, to intervene in Kuwait, it invoked defense of the law. Those grounds soon proved insufficient. The concept of "peacekeeping," with its humanitarian veneer, was then advanced. Most "peacekeeping" operations had no clear political or military objective and in fact, troops were deployed for no purpose other than to facilitate the arrival of relief supplies for civilians or to bring in those supplies themselves. That is what happened in 1991 in Kurdistan (United Nations General Assembly resolution 688, 1991), and subsequently in Somalia, the former Yugoslavia, and Rwanda.

Those interventions were the tangible expression of the right to intervene. They were generally not well received by those concerned, who saw in them the risk of a new form of legal domination by the north over the south, by the rich over the poor. In practice, those so-called "humanitarian" interventions were not without political ulterior motives, and were thus selective.

Those interventions also served to heighten the confusion between humanitarian endeavor and military operations. In Kurdistan, the exclusion zones remain, no one knows for how long. In Somalia, the ambiguous mandate of the allied forces led them to become just another belligerent and resulted in their precipitate withdrawal. In Yugoslavia, international troops undertook humanitarian action while the population was decimated by a siege. In Rwanda, United Nations Assistance Mission in Rwanda (UNAMIR) was not allowed to bring in more troops and the genocide could not be stopped. Confining the blue helmets to a humanitarian role gave rise to confusion. "How long will our governments persist in their hypocrisy?" Claude Malhuret wrote in *Le*

Monde on August 20, 1992. "Incapable of deciding on a course of action, which they know public opinion demands, they instead get involved, to show that they are 'doing something,' in humanitarian assistance that does nothing to remedy the basic problem. How much longer will they try to make us believe that humanitarian action can take the place of political action?"

In reality, there is a wide gap between military humanitarian action and the principles promoted by Henry Dunant. In particular, confusion between what is military and what is humanitarian voids the principle that the victim and the humanitarian agent are neutral, which remains the *sine qua non* condition for the existence of a humanitarian space. The principle of neutrality cannot be implemented by soldiers, only by independent humanitarian organizations.

Post-9/11: The Risk of a Further Drift

The attacks of September 11, 2001, against the twin towers of New York's World Trade Center and the Pentagon in Washington, D.C., naturally represent a paradigm shift in international relations. They open a new phase in humanitarian action and present a major challenge to international humanitarian law.

Following the attacks, the United States decided to launch a "war against terrorism" that, to date, has taken the form of a war against Afghanistan and a pitiless international fight against terrorism and terrorists.

We are therefore faced with two different phenomena, even though they occasionally overlap. On the one hand, we have an international war in Afghanistan in which the Geneva Conventions, in particular the Third Convention, apply. On the other hand, another struggle of another kind is being carried out against an international network (Al Qaeda); the American administration calls this a "war against terrorism." It in no way resembles traditional warfare and raises entirely new issues for humanitarian law.

It goes without saying that we must first affirm that humanitarian law is applicable in the international, American-Afghan conflict, and that it must be implemented as closely as possibly to the terms of the Geneva Conventions.

Strictly speaking, however, humanitarian law is not applicable in the "war against terrorism." We are nevertheless entirely justified in wondering how to classify the situation. In principle, it is a kind of police operation, but President Bush did call it a "war," and the means employed to wage it are indeed reminiscent of war. In addition, the parties represent a break with tradition in that one of them is transnational and trans-state. But is that sufficient reason to remove this new kind of war from the purview of humanitarian law, whose specific aim is to help and protect the victims of war?

In any event, the first step is to demand compliance with the existing provisions of humanitarian law where they are applicable and to do everything possible to ensure that the law does not crumble under political pressure. At the same time, the possibility to act must be ensured. Lastly, humanitarians must ponder the new challenges and deal with them.

Today, as during the bleakest period of the cold war, there is a real and present danger that humanitarian law will suffer a setback, its principles subordinated to political interests. We must not allow that to happen, we must hark back to the origins of the law and ensure that the interests of the victims reign supreme.

CONCLUSION

The definition of humanitarianism and its history reveal an original notion dating from the Enlightenment and Henry Dunant: that humanity takes precedence over war, over politics, race, and religion. The concept of humanitarianism, moreover, has been incorporated into an international corpus of law. The principles must at all costs be preserved so that the victims can continue to be protected and assisted.

The twenty-first century has started with doubts about the law and the Geneva Conventions. Giving in to those doubts would be an unforgivable setback for humanity. Yes, we can become more professional; certainly, the different stages of humanitarian endeavor, from prevention to development, can be more fully integrated with one another. But the first requirement of human-itarianism is and will remain independence and freedom. All else is a matter of method, logistics, and the management of security constraints.

It would be disgraceful indeed if the twenty-first century laid open to question the principles laid down in the nineteenth, no-tably that humanitarian action aims first and foremost to restore man's lost dignity, with no economic or strategic ulterior motives.

2

Scope of International Humanitarian Crises

Ibrahim Osman

INTRODUCTION

THIS CHAPTER ANALYZES general trends in humanitarian assistance for natural and technological disasters for the period from 1992 to 2001, and for complex disasters from 1994 to 2001. The introductory section traces trends in both the number of people affected by disasters and the humanitarian assistance disbursed. In the first section, natural and technological disasters are examined according to the estimated number of affected people, total flows of assistance, assistance in relation to the estimated cost, and assistance per affected person. The analysis incorporates both time and regional trends in the flows of humanitarian assistance. The second section applies similar analysis to complex disasters. The third section compares the trends in humanitarian assistance for natural/technological and complex disasters, while the fourth section provides some concluding remarks. Data collection techniques, methodology, and definitions used throughout this chapter are provided in the appendix.

Figures on the number of people affected by disasters[1] appear to be exhibiting an upward trend. In 1992, an estimated 118 million people were affected by disasters (both natural/technological and complex), while an estimated 275 million were affected in the year 2000. These figures indicate an average annual increase in the number of people affected by disasters of approximately 11.2 percent.

Figures for humanitarian assistance for natural and technological disasters also exhibit an upward trend. At the beginning of

Figure 2.1

Time Trend in the Number of People Affected by Disasters

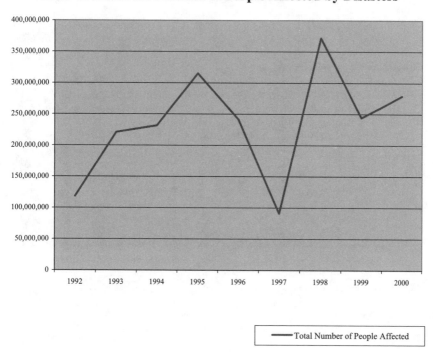

the period, 1992, an estimated value of contributions was U.S.\$235 million, compared to the end of the period (2001) estimated value of U.S.\$340 million.[2] Moreover, the end-of-period value slightly exceeds the mean value of U.S.\$321 million. Data for humanitarian assistance for complex disasters reveals a downward trend, however, with an end-of-period (2001) estimated value of contributions of U.S.\$1.695 billion, compared to the 1994 estimated value of U.S.\$2.131 billion and to the mean value of U.S.\$1.644 billion.

NATURAL AND TECHNOLOGICAL DISASTERS

Figures on the estimated number of people affected by natural and technological disasters appear to exhibit an upward trend,

Figure 2.2

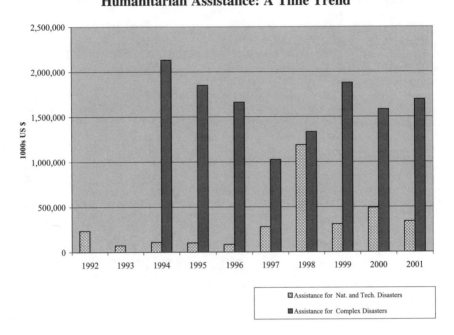

Humanitarian Assistance: A Time Trend

with an estimated 79 million people affected in 1992 as opposed to 170 million affected in 2001. Thus, the data indicates an 11.6 percent annual increase in the number of people affected by these types of disasters.

While the estimated cost of natural and technological disasters[3] rose fivefold during the period in question (with 1992 value of U.S.$2.86 billion and 2001 value of U.S.$14.294 billion),[4] humanitarian assistance rose at a much slower rate of about 45 percent (at the beginning of the period, in 1991, the estimated value of contributions is U.S.$235 million compared to the 2001 estimated value of U.S.$339 million). Furthermore, the average annual rate of growth of the estimated cost figures is more than eight times the average annual rate of growth of humanitarian assistance (4.95 percent estimated average annual rate of growth

Figure 2.3

Number of People Affected by Natural/Technological Disasters: a Time Trend

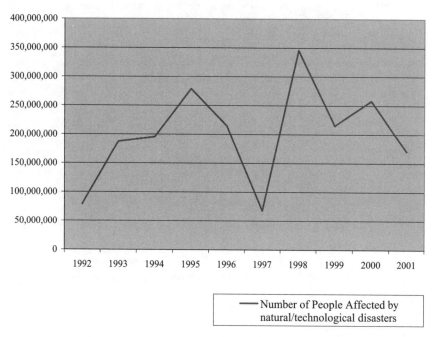

Number of People Affected by natural/technological disasters

of assistance as opposed to 44.42 percent average annual growth in cost).

Average annual assistance is highest for Asia (U.S.$126 million), followed by the Americas (U.S.$117 million), Africa (U.S.$51 million), Europe (U.S.$23 million), and Oceania (U.S.$5 million).

The highest level of assistance was recorded in 1998, and it was primarily directed toward the Americas and Asia. The assistance for Hurricane Mitch in Central America (October 1998) represents 21.92 percent of the total humanitarian assistance for natural and technological disasters chaptered by OCHA for the whole 1992–2001 period. Assistance for floods in China and Bangladesh (June and July of the same year) represents an additional 11.75 percent of the total recorded assistance.

Figure 2.4

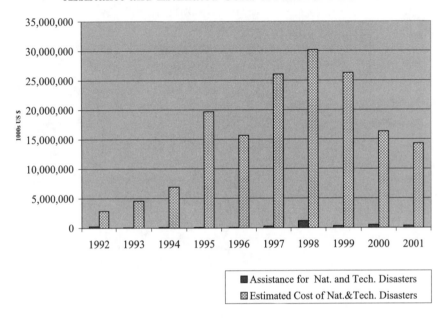

Assistance and Estimated Costs of Natural Disasters

■ Assistance for Nat. and Tech. Disasters
▨ Estimated Cost of Nat.&Tech. Disasters

The highest average level of assistance per affected person is in Europe (U.S.$76.78), followed by the Americas (U.S.$58.57), Oceania (U.S.$48.49), Asia (U.S.$39.47), and Africa (U.S.$39.34). Thus, the average assistance per affected person in Africa is just above a half of European average (55.22 percent) and about two-thirds of the average in the Americas (66.81 percent).

The highest average level of assistance as a percentage of estimated cost is in Africa (17.76 percent), followed by the Americas (15.79 percent), Europe (12.18 percent), Asia (10.74 percent), and Oceania (2.77 percent). However, figures relating to the estimates of material damage are likely to be positively related to the level of development, since not only the potential for material damage rises with development but also data collection techniques improve. Thus, it is very likely that the estimated costs of

Figure 2.5

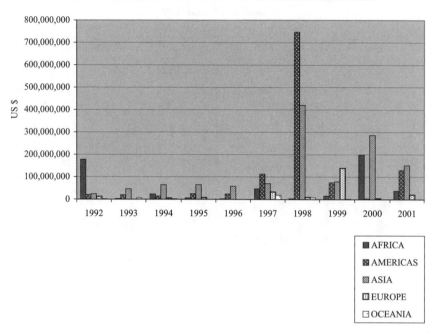

Natural Disaster Assistance Per Continent and Year

- AFRICA
- AMERICAS
- ASIA
- EUROPE
- OCEANIA

disasters in regions of lower development are understated, while the average level of assistance as a percentage of estimated cost in those nations are overstated.

The highest percentage of total humanitarian assistance for the period analyzed has been devoted to Central America (25.77 percent), South Asia (20.19 percent), East Asia (11.98 percent), and East and Central Africa (9.59 percent).

COMPLEX DISASTERS

The figures on the estimated number of people affected by complex disasters appear to be exhibiting a downward trend. In 1992,

Figure 2.6

Humanitarian Assistance for Natural Disasters Per Affected Person, by Continent and Year

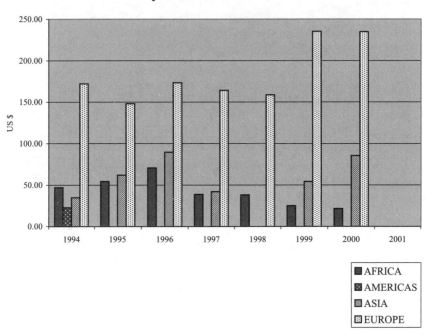

39 million people were estimated affected, compared to 21 million in the year 2000.

However, the estimated needs arising from complex disasters have been rising during the period analyzed (with the beginning of the period value of U.S.$2.663 billion, end-of-period value of U.S.$3.041 billion, and the mean of U.S.$2.663 billion). Nevertheless, the assistance has been falling, from U.S.$2.131 billion in 1994 to U.S.$1.695 billion in 2001 (the mean value being U.S.$1.644 billion). The annual average growth rate of estimated needs is 2.03 percent while the average annual growth rate of assistance is minus 2.93 percent.

The average annual humanitarian assistance is the highest in Africa (U.S.$804,946,930), followed by Asia (U.S.$485,394,409), Europe (U.S.$348,281,202), and Oceania (U.S.$50,068,036).

The average humanitarian assistance per affected person for

Figure 2.7

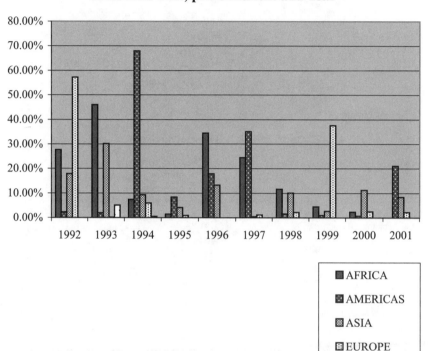

Assistance for Natural Disasters as a Percentage of Estimated Cost, per Continent and Year

AFRICA
AMERICAS
ASIA
EUROPE
OCEANIA

complex disasters is the highest in Europe (U.S.$183.75), followed by Asia (U.S.$61.31), and Africa (U.S.$42.24). Thus, the average humanitarian assistance per affected person in Europe exceeds that of Africa by over four times. Furthermore, while there appears to be an upward trend in the assistance per affected person in Europe, for Africa, that trend was positive during the period 1994 to 1996, but after that point there was a downward slide.

Average assistance as a percentage of estimated needs covered is highest in Europe as well (76.51 percent), followed by Africa (63.93 percent) and Asia (59.74 percent).

The highest percentage of total humanitarian assistance for

Figure 2.8

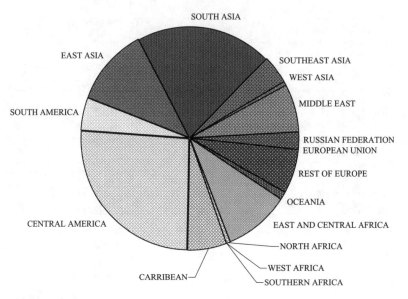

Breakdown of Humanitarian Assistance for Natural and Technological Disasters, by Regions

complex disasters during the period in question was given to the regions of East and Central Africa (36.25 percent), Europe (29.01 percent), North Africa (8.43 percent), and East Asia (8.15 percent).

Natural and Technological Disasters and Complex Disasters

A Comparison of the Trends

For the comparison of the humanitarian assistance for complex and natural disasters, we will use data for the period 1994 to 2001, as the figures for complex disasters are not available prior to 1994. The total assistance for complex disasters during the

Figure 2.9

Number of People Affected by Complex Disasters: a Time Trend

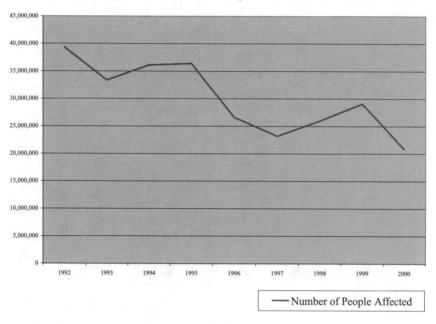

period examined was U.S.$13.159 billion, while the total assistance for natural disasters during the same period was U.S.$2.905 billion. Thus, the assistance for complex disasters exceeded assistance for natural disasters more than four and a half times (452.85 percent). During the period, the estimated cost of natural disasters exceeded that of complex disasters more than seven times (U.S.$155.347 billion for natural versus U.S.$21.308 billion for complex disasters).

Average assistance per affected person for complex disasters was U.S.$93.92, compared to U.S.$53.24 for natural disasters. Hence, the average assistance per affected person for natural disasters is estimated at 57.08 percent of that for complex ones.

Average assistance as a percentage estimated cost is projected to be at 11.85 percent for natural disasters, while the 66.28 per-

Figure 2.10

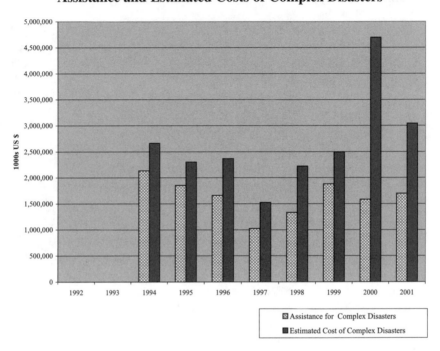

Assistance and Estimated Costs of Complex Disasters

cent of needs arising from complex disasters are estimated to be covered by humanitarian assistance.[5]

CONCLUSION

Humanitarian assistance for complex disasters exceeds assistance for natural/technological disasters for every category examined—total flows, assistance as a percentage of estimated cost/need, and assistance per affected person—and for every region. The highest percentage of total humanitarian assistance for natural/technological disasters has been devoted to Central America, while the highest percentage of total assistance for complex disas-

Figure 2.11

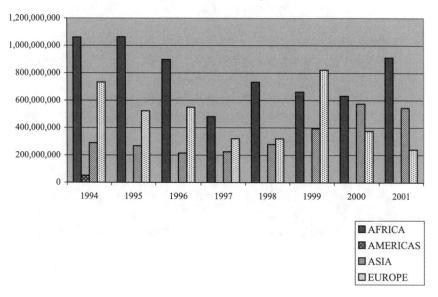

Assistance for Complex Disasters, by Continent and Year

ters went to East and Central Africa and Europe. The highest average level of assistance for natural/technological disasters per affected person has been recorded in Europe (U.S.$76.78) while the lowest was in Africa (U.S.$39.34). Figures for average level of assistance per affected person for complex disasters exhibit a similar pattern, with the highest observed in Europe (U.S.$183.75) and the lowest in the Americas (U.S.$22.55).[6] The highest average level of assistance as a percentage of estimated cost/need was recorded in Africa for natural/technological disasters and in Europe for complex disasters; however, as mentioned previously, estimated cost figures most probably have a downward bias in the case of countries with a lower level of development, in which case the average level of assistance as a percentage of estimated cost would exhibit an upward bias for those countries.

Figure 2.12

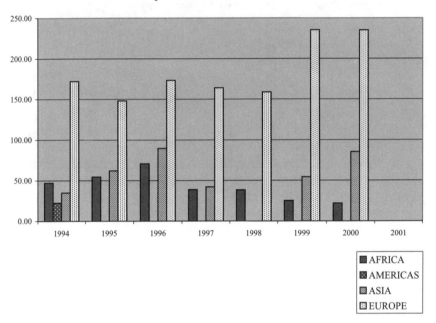

Assistance Per Affected Person for Complex Disasters, by Continent and Year

AFRICA
AMERICAS
ASIA
EUROPE

APPENDIX

I. Data and Methodology

Data has been assembled primarily from two sources—EM-DAT, a comprehensive disaster database compiled by the Center for Research on the Epidemiology of Disasters (CRED), and the Financial Tracking System (FTS) launched by the Organization for Coordination of Humanitarian Assistance (OCHA) on Relief-Web, the United Nations humanitarian Web site. EM-DAT contains core data on the occurrence and the effect of chaptered disasters, both natural and conflict in origin, compiled from various sources, including UN agencies, NGOs, insurance companies, research institutes, and press agencies. Figures on

Figure 2.13

Assistance for Complex Disasters as a Percentage of Needs Covered, by Continent and Year

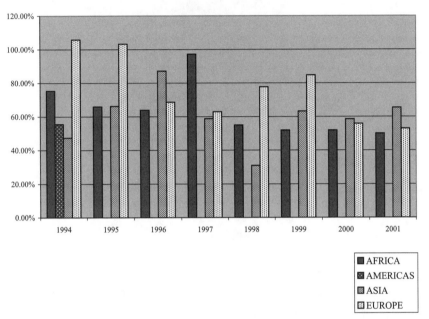

humanitarian assistance found on FTS are collected by OCHA from UN agencies, donor governments, and NGOs. More details on the data collection process are available on the respective Web sites. As this chapter tracks trends in humanitarian assistance, financial data was necessary, and only disasters for which humanitarian response has been chaptered by OCHA have been included in the analysis.

The exception is the analysis of total number of people affected by disasters. These figures have been taken from EM-DAT entirely.

It should be noted that data on the effects of natural and complex disasters is sketchy at best as there are no accepted standards or even definitions, and they could potentially differ greatly between sources. The figures should thus be regarded as indicative.

Figure 2.14

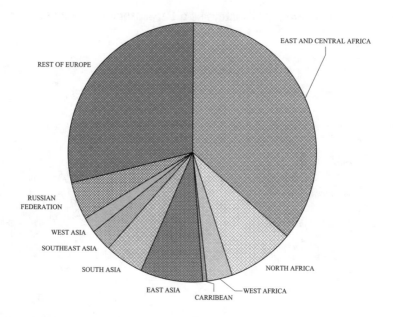

All figures have been transformed into 1996 U.S. dollars. Countries of disaster occurrence have been classified according to the continent and region. For complex disasters, figures that have been used for humanitarian assistance are total assistance that has been available within a given year, which might include carryover funds. There is a possibility that figures for percentage of needs covered by humanitarian assistance for complex disasters exhibit an upward bias, as surplus in one project does not necessarily cover the shortfall in another. However, as this chapter deals with the flows of disaster relief and not potential inefficiencies in its disbursement, percentage of needs covered was calculated as the ratio of total assistance available to the estimated needs.

II. Definitions[7]

A disaster is defined as a situation or event that overwhelms local capacity, necessitating a request at the national or international

Figure 2.15

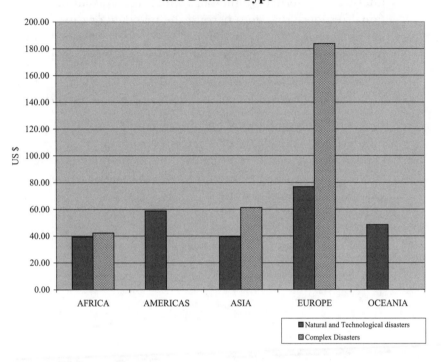

Average Assistance Per Affected Person, by Continent
and Disaster Type

level for external assistance. In order for a disaster to be entered
in EM-DAT, at least one of the following criteria has to be ful-
filled:

- Ten or more people chaptered are killed
- One hundred people chaptered are affected
- A call for international assistance; and/or
- A declaration of a state of emergency divided into following
  types:
  —Natural and Technological Disasters. In this category are in-
    cluded avalanches/landslides; droughts and famines; extreme
    temperatures; floods; forest fires; windstorms; insect infesta-
    tions; waves/surges; earthquakes; volcanic eruptions; indus-
    trial and transport accidents.

—Complex Disasters. A complex emergency is defined as "a humanitarian crisis in a country, region, or society where there is total or considerable breakdown of authority resulting from internal or external conflict and which requires an international response that goes beyond the mandate or capacity of any single agency and/or the ongoing United Nations country program" (Inter-Agency Standing Committee [IASC], December 1994).

Such "complex emergencies" are typically characterized by:

- Extensive violence and loss of life; massive displacements of people; widespread damage to societies and economies
- The need for large-scale, multi-faceted humanitarian assistance
- The hindrance or prevention of humanitarian assistance by political and military constraints
- Significant security risks for humanitarian relief workers in some areas

3

The Language of Disasters: A Brief Terminology of Disaster Management and Humanitarian Action

S. W. A. Gunn, M.D.

IF THE TOWER OF BABEL was a language disaster, disaster itself has a language. Whether act of God or act of man, disaster often calls for multinational assistance. The many governments, agencies, professions, and individuals from different parts of the world, representing different languages, specialties, religions, and cultures, yet all imbued with a humanitarian spirit of providing succor to the helpless, converge on the stricken land to help the victims, who are themselves of different language and background.

Communication among these different people and a certain understanding of the technical, administrative, and operational terminology of the many disciplines involved become paramount if the inherent difficulties of the disaster are not to be compounded by an overlay of communications disaster. In what often is a multidisciplinary operation, the physician has to understand the transport engineer, the meteorologist must be able to converse with the administrator, the volunteer with the EMS nurse, the planner with the journalist, the sanitarian with the nutritionist, the expatriate donor with the local government official, and the multitude of individuals whose normal life has been suddenly shattered by the earthquake, war, flood, refugee exodus, or the reactor accident.

If such understanding is essential in the field, it is becoming equally necessary away from the site of action: in planning board-rooms, lecture halls, statistical tables, press centers, and medical schools where disaster preparedness and humanitarian response increasingly are receiving attention. Indeed, it is heartening to notice that after many years of unplanned, ad hoc responses, di-saster planning is becoming more and more conceptual and sys-tematized and, with this trend, disaster medicine gradually is becoming a specialized field, within a broader humanitarian vi-sion.

All professions, techniques, and organized activities generate their own language, their specific terminology, and disastrology is no exception. Because it is relatively new and multisectoral in nature, its language is broadly based on evolving. In this chapter, I shall offer a small selection of terms to show its concepts, scope, organization, and operation. I have intentionally chosen terms that are predominantly outside the medical field, but which the emergency practitioner or prehospital nurse will encounter in the course of his or her disaster mission and will use in humani-tarian work.

Disasters: A Classification

Disaster: The result of a vast ecological breakdown in the relations between man and his environment; a serious and sudden event (or slow, as in drought) on such a scale that demands exceed available resources and the stricken community needs extraordi-nary efforts to cope with the situation, often with outside help or international aid.

Natural disaster: A sudden major upheaval of nature, causing extensive destruction, death and suffering among the stricken community, and which is not due to man's action. However, *(a)* some natural disasters can be of slow origin, e.g., drought; and *(b)* a seemingly natural disaster can be caused or aggravated by man's action, e.g., desertification through excessive land use and deforestation.

Man-made disaster: A disaster caused not by natural phenomena but by man's or society's action, involuntary or voluntary, sudden or slow, directly or indirectly, with grave consequences to the population and the environment. Examples: technological disaster, toxicological disaster, environmental pollution, desertification, conflict, refugees, epidemics, fires.

Complex disaster/Complex emergency: A major disaster or complicated emergency situation affecting large civilian populations, which is further aggravated by intense political and/or military interference, including war and civil strife, resulting in serious food shortages, epidemics, population displacements, pauperization, loss of human liberties, and significant increase in mortality, rendering the management of the situation very complex.

Man-conceived disaster: Distinct from man-made disaster, man-conceived refers to disastrous actions like genocide, death camps, ethnic cleansing, forced disappearance, pauperization, torture, and other acts against humanity that are obscenely conceived, cold-bloodedly planned, and indecently perpetrated with impunity by evil rulers, dictators, terrorists, or kleptocrats with the aim of inflicting maximum suffering, death, and destruction, in full violation of personal, social, and cultural rights of humanity. While the response to man-made disasters is scientific, humanitarian, and managerial, the response to man-conceived disasters must be through the International Criminal Court.

Disaster preparedness: The aggregate of measures to be taken in view of disasters, consisting of plans and action programs designed to minimize the loss of life and damage, to organize and facilitate effective rescue and relief, and to rehabilitate after disaster. Preparedness requires the necessary legislation and means to cope with disaster or similar emergency situations. It also is concerned with forecasting and warning, the education and training of the public, organization, and management— including plans, training of personnel, the stockpiling of supplies, and ensuring the needed funds and other resources.

Disaster management: The study and collaborative application by the various pertinent disciplines and governmental authorities of decision-making processes, management techniques, and resource utilization, to the entire process and different phases of a disaster, from prevention and preparedness to planning, immediate response, damage reduction, rehabilitation, reconstruction, and development.

Health: The state of complete physical, mental, and social well being, and not merely the absence of disaster or infirmity. Also, the state of an individual or a community free from debilitating conditions, demonstrating a reasonable resistance to diseases, and living in a salubrious environment.

Humanitarian medicine: While all medical intervention to reduce a person's sickness and suffering is in essence humanitarian, humanitarian medicine goes beyond the usual therapeutic act and promotes, provides, teaches, supports, and delivers people's health as a human right, in conformity with the ethics of Hippocratic teaching, the principles of the World Health Organization, the Charter of the United Nations, the Universal Declaration of Human Rights, the Red Cross Conventions and other covenants and practices that ensure the most humane and best possible level of care, without any discrimination or consideration of material gain.

International health: The study and systematic comparison of the multiple and variable factors that influence the health of human populations in different countries and different environments, and the resulting measures that need to be taken for its improvement.

Disaster medicine: The study and collaborative application of various health specialties—e.g., pediatrics, epidemiology, communicable diseases, nutrition, public health, emergency surgery, military medicine, community care, social medicine, international health—to the prevention, immediate response, humanitarian care, and rehabilitation of the health problems arising from disaster, in cooperation with other non-medical disciplines involved in disaster management.

CONCEPTS AND MANAGEMENT

Catastrophe theory: A mathematical and philosophical theory to explain and define transitional continuity whereby a disaster represents a brutal dynamic change in the forces present in natural, physical, or social phenomena.

Hazard: The probability of the occurrence of a disaster caused by a natural phenomenon (earthquake, cyclone), by failure of man-made sources of energy (nuclear reactor, industrial explosion), or uncontrolled human activity (overgrazing, heavy traffic, conflict). Some authors use the term in a broader sense, including vulnerability, elements at risk, and the consequences of risk.

Risk: The lives lost, persons injured, damage to property, and disruption of economic activity due to a particular hazard. Risk is the product of hazard and vulnerability.

Acceptable risk: The eventual loss and agreed conditions or degree of human, material, and economic damage that a country or community is willing to accept as tolerable rather than provide the necessary finances and resources to reduce such a risk.

Mitigation: Separate and aggregate measures taken prior to, during, or following a disaster with the view to reducing the severity of the human and material damage caused by it.

Vulnerability: The degree of loss from a potentially damaging phenomenon expressed in a scale from zero to 100 percent.

Assessment: Survey of a real or potential disaster to estimate the actual or expected damages and to make recommendations for preparedness, mitigation, and relief action.

Bioterrorism: Planning, threatening, using, or spreading of contagious disease organisms or toxins, e.g., botulism, anthrax, smallpox, or other viruses, as a terrorist tool or weapon.

Conventional arms: Arms or forces pertaining to a nation's non-nuclear, non-biological, non-chemical weapons, such as guns, tanks, battleships, aircraft, troops, etc. The opposite of arms/weapons of mass destruction.

Crimes against humanity: Crimes concerning the international community as a whole, committed in widespread and/or systematic manner, and/or on a massive scale, and/or on specified grounds, in war or peacetime. They include murder; genocide; extermination; enslavement; rape, sexual abuse, or forced prostitution; deportation; persecution on political, racial, national, ethnic, cultural, religious grounds; enforced disappearances; other inhumane acts of physical or mental injury; detention, imprisonment, or deprivation of liberty in violation of international law. Such crimes are punishable by the International Criminal Court.

Deportation: The unlawful and forcible transfer of a person, group, or population from its normal habitat; the forced transfer of children of a group to another group. This is considered a crime against humanity.

Disappearance/Forced disappearance: The arrest, abduction, forced detention, and cutting off communication of persons against their will, by or without the approval of the state or of a political organization, accompanied by refusal of the latter to acknowledge that abduction has taken place and denial of information on the fate of those abducted, thereby placing them outside the protection of the law. This is considered a crime against humanity.

Disarmament: The process of and regulations concerning the reduction of a military establishment to levels defined by international agreement.

Disaster epidemiology: The medical discipline, now extended to other fields, that studies the influence of such factors as life style, biological constitution, and other personal and social determinants on the incidence and distribution of disease, both under normal circumstances and in markedly changed disaster situations.

Embargo: An order forbidding certain activities, often accompanied with certain penalties or sanctions in case of non-compliance. Article 41, chapter 7 of the UN Charter provides for embargoes on a country that may pose a threat to peace, a breakdown of peace, or an act of aggression. Humanitarian goods such as food and medicine may be exempted.

Environmental pollution: Unfavorable changes and degradation of one or more aspects or elements of the environment by noxious biological, industrial, chemical, or radioactive wastes, from debris of man-made, especially non-biodegradable, products and from mismanagement and inconsiderate use of ecological resources.

Ethnic cleansing: New term for an age-old illegal and decidedly unclean policy with the aim of removing, through hatred, intimidation, deportation, killing, genocide, or any other form of force, certain groups or minorities within the country, in order to homogenize the national population, acquire land, pamper to extremist pride, and ensure control.

Genocide: Acts committed with intent to destroy, in whole or in part, a national, ethnic, racial, or religious group.

Guerrilla warfare: Literally "small war," which takes on a different meaning or interpretation according to whether it is justified or unjustified, a struggle for independence, liberation, resistance, or insurrection, destruction or subjugation. International humanitarian law, the Geneva Conventions, and United Nations instruments have difficulty in dealing with such situations.

Human rights: The inalienable rights of every human being, based on the recognition by all of the inherent dignity and equality of each person, as codified and guaranteed by the Universal Declaration of Human Rights and other international instruments.

Incident/Accident: Although different in meaning and consequences, these two terms are often used interchangeably in emergency management. Incident is a sudden, unexpected occurrence that happens by chance and is usually without very serious consequences. Accident is also a sudden, unforeseen event, but more serious, usually with some resulting damage, injury, or death.

Internally displaced person(s) (IDPs): Persons or groups of persons who have been forced or obliged to flee or to leave their homes or places of habitual residence, in particular as a result of, or in order to avoid, the effects of armed conflict, situations of generalized violence of human rights, or natural or man-made disasters, and who have not crossed an internationally recognized state border. According to established principles, these persons have the right to seek safety in another part of the country, to leave their country, to seek asylum in another country, and the right to be protected against forcible return or unsafe resettlement. But these are not refugees in the juridical sense.

Measures of effectiveness: In assessment techniques, the qualitative and quantitative criteria used to predict or correlate the value or measure of an organization or a system, such as disaster management. Such measures must be appropriate, measurable, sensitive, timely, cost effective, and meaningful.

North-South: A theoretical division of the globe into north, representing the developed, more affluent, technologically advanced, financially rich, healthy, educated, and stable countries; and south, with developing, poor, indebted, technologically retarded countries where mortality is high, health levels low, and education deficient.

Post-traumatic stress disorder: Delayed or protracted reaction to an exceptionally strong stressful event of catastrophic dimension, which can cause pervasive distress in almost any person, but more marked in some, following a natural or man-made disaster, combat, violent death, torture, rape, terrorism, etc. The onset may follow the trauma within a few weeks or at most six months. Typical symptoms include "re-living" or "flashbacks" of the event, "numbness" and detachment, fearful reminiscences.

Prisoner of conscience: Person imprisoned solely because of his/her political or religious beliefs, gender, or racial ethnic origin who has neither used nor advocated violence.

Prisoner of war: A member of the armed forces of a party to conflict; all members of armed groups and units that are under a command responsible to that party, and who have been caught and made prisoner by the opposing party in the conflict. Prisoners of war have rights and responsibilities defined by the Geneva Conventions. Guerillas also benefit from POW provisions.

Refugee: A person who is outside his country of origin and who, due to well-founded fear of persecution, is unable or unwilling to avail himself of that country's protection. Different official categories of refugees include: Convention refugee, de facto refugee, de jure refugee, mandate refugee, Protocol refugee, recognized refugee, refugee sur place, statutory refugee, environmental refugee.

The condition of being a refugee and refugee camps constitute a disaster. The problem comes under the jurisdiction of the United Nations High Commissioner for refugees.

Resettlement: Relocation and more or less orderly settlement, for temporary or permanent habitation, of refugees and other persons displaced from their usual place of residence.

Right to intervene: By international law, every state has absolute sovereignty over its national territory and its internal affairs, and no outside interference is tolerated. In view, however, of certain unacceptable injustices and totalitarian acts carried out by dictatorial regimes, in 1991, UN Resolution 688 introduced the concept of "right to intervene" on humanitarian grounds. Subsequent decisions have further codified the concept of the right to intervene, while some even extend this to a duty to intervene.

Sustainable development: Development based on decisions, processes, and actions that meet the present needs without creating undue burden on society or the environment, and without undermining the ability of coming generations to meet their own needs in the future.

Terrorism/Terrorist: Tem referring to various kinds of illegal acts of violence, such as bombing, setting fire, abducting, intimidating, killing, and other forms of illegal actions in order to create terror, panic, or submission among the public, state, or individuals. Intolerant regimes tend to accuse opposition actions as terrorism.

War crimes: During hostilities, crimes committed in breach of established customs and principles of international law or the laws of war. They include: *(a)* grave breaches of the four Geneva Conventions and their Additional Protocols, such as willful killing, unnecessarily excessive destruction; *(b)* other serious violations of the laws and customs applicable to international armed conflicts, such as targeting civilians, pillaging; *(c)* violation of laws concerning armed conflicts of not an international character, such as cruelty against those not taking part in the conflict; *(d)* other serious violations of laws in non-international conflicts, such as attacks on peaceful buildings. War crimes are considered as crimes against humanity.

Weapons of mass destruction: Offensive weapons whose destructive capability is derived from nuclear, chemical, or biological sources. Sometimes referred to as ABC: atomic, biological, chemical. Their use is prohibited by the UN and other international conventions. They are the opposite of conventional weapons or arms.

LAWS AND ORGANIZATIONS

Bilateral Cooperation: Technical cooperation or assistance by a donor country to a recipient country, through direct agreement between the two governments, without the UN or any other intermediary.

Geneva Conventions: The body of international agreements consisting of four Conventions (1949) and two Additional Protocols (1977) concerning the humanitarian treatment of victims of armed conflict, and put under the responsibility of the International Committee of the Red Cross. The first Convention regulates the care of the wounded and sick soldiers on the battlefield. The second is about the care of the wounded, sick, and shipwrecked in naval warfare. The third regulates the treatment of prisoners of war. The fourth is about the protection of civilians in time of war. Additional Protocols 1 and 2 ensure more humane considerations not only in international conflicts but also in national strife, such as the treatment of guerrilla fighters.

World Health Organization (WHO): The health arm of the United Nations aiming at "the attainment by all peoples of the highest possible level of health." The WHO coordinates efforts to raise health levels worldwide and promotes the development of primary health. Besides multiple public health programs and actions, it is engaged in disaster preparedness and relief both at its headquarters and in Geneva, Switzerland, and at six regional offices, and it coordinates the health sector of the UN involvement in major emergencies. The organization has compiled the Emergency Health Kit.

United Nations: The Office for the Coordination of Humanitarian Affairs (OCHA) mobilizes, directs, and coordinates the emergency humanitarian activities of the various UN agencies and other organizations. It has established the International Disaster Management Information Network (UNIENET), operates the OCHA warehouse in Pisa (Italy), and publishes studies on disaster relief and preparedness. In disasters and emergencies, OCHA dispatches field officers to the stricken site.

(Office of the) High Commissioner for Human Rights: The United Nations's central point for all human rights questions. Leads and stimulates human rights issues, responds to serious violations of human rights, investigates reports on their breaches, promotes human rights and strengthens national action in their favor, ensures that UN decisions on human rights are implemented, and the articles of the Universal Declaration of Human Rights are respected.

Biological Weapons Convention: United Nations Convention on the Prohibition of the Development, Production, and Stockpiling of Bacteriological (Biological) and Toxin Weapons and their Destruction, signed in 1972.

Red Cross: Red Cross, or International Red Cross, general terms used for one or all the components of the worldwide organization active in humanitarian work. The official name is The International Red Cross Movement, which comprises three components: (1) International Committee of the Red Cross (ICRC), acts mainly in conflict disasters as neutral intermediary in hostilities and for the protection of war victims. Guardian of the Geneva Conventions; (2) International Federation of Red Cross and Red Crescent Societies (IFRC), worldwide federation of the National

Societies, active in non-conflict disasters and natural calamities; (3) The individual National Red Cross or Red Crescent Society of every country.

SUMMARY

These are a few of some two thousand terms (see *Multilingual Dictionary of Disaster Medicine and International Relief*) that have been tested over many years in the field, in training programs, and briefing sessions, and are established as the standard terminology in disaster management and humanitarian service.

It is the author's conviction that in the difficult emergency situations of multilingual and multidisciplinary disaster action, the use of a commonly agreed vocabulary transforms a potential disaster of language into a commonly-understood language of disasters and lessens the Babelian confusion that often risks to hamper the most well-meaning, humanitarian, disaster response.

Part 2

As international humanitarian assistance grew at the end of the twentieth century, it became increasingly clear that mere sympathy and good will were inadequate responses. Complex emergencies required the involvement of many different disciplines. But there were no accepted training standards for the new breed of international humanitarian worker, and academia did not offer adequate courses or recognition for a new profession.

The development of the International Diploma in Humanitarian Assistance (IDHA) is offered as an example of an appropriate university-based training program, one properly rooted in the experience of a wide variety of specialists in humanitarian assistance. The IDHA is offered by Fordham University, the University of Geneva, and the Royal College of Surgeons in Ireland under the direction of the Center for International Health and Cooperation. The IDHA has become a standard training curriculum. It is now accepted by the UN, the International Red Cross, and major nongovernmental organizations. The chapter by the editor covers the essentials of the program.

All the contributors to the International Humanitarian Affairs book series are faculty members of the IDHA program. All were chosen because of their unique knowledge, unquestioned authority, and practical field experience in humanitarian crises that follow both natural disasters and armed conflicts.

The fundamental importance in a humanitarian crisis of effective teamwork—as opposed to individual efforts—is now fully accepted. But how does one build a team? Early in the IDHA course there is a strong emphasis on developing a cohesive and effective group. Pamela Lupton-Bowers, Chief of Training at the IFRC, details the team-building techniques she uses in the IDHA.

4

Training for Humanitarian Assistance

Kevin M. Cahill, M.D.

INTERNATIONAL HUMANITARIAN ASSISTANCE is a professional discipline appropriately influenced, as are the professions of medicine or law, by the loftiest ideals of civilized society. To help one's fellow human beings alleviate hunger and pain, give succor to the starving and homeless, unite ruptured families, and rebuild destroyed societies are the noble goals of humanitarian assistance.

But the sheer scope and extent of the human calamities that follow conflicts and disasters make individual efforts in such situations touching but ineffectual. Unless humanitarian assistance is carefully planned, coordinated, and delivered, with understanding and sensitivity, it often produces more harm and pain to victims and fragile communities; it also endangers and frustrates the very donors who wish to help.

One of the reasons for so much failure in the attempt to do good is a lack of training in the fundamentals of humanitarian assistance. Good will, or the desire to share in human tragedy, is simply not an adequate foundation. If timely and effective help is to be delivered, all participants must develop a common language, and this depends, to a great degree, on a universally accepted, basic standard of training.

Assistance workers must understand how complex humanitarian crises develop, what their potential roles are, and what skills are required when, as strangers, they become involved in traumatized communities where the normal supportive services of society have collapsed and entire populations become vulnerable dependents. Those who presume to offer help in such situations, who accept the privilege of providing life-saving aid, must be taught to appreciate the early warning signs of impending disasters so that prevention as well as reaction becomes part of their approach. They must learn from previous catastrophes, no two of which are identical, how to devise the most efficient, rapid, and flexible response to each challenge.

There are basic tenets, however, common to all disaster relief efforts. One must learn to be vigilant against the known dangers of inappropriate aid, to preserve, even in the midst of chaos, equanimity, humility, and respect that are the hallmarks of true professionals in every discipline. Humanitarian workers must learn to develop, and utilize, accurate tools to measure the extent of needs, and to evaluate the efficacy of aid programs. Only with a universally accepted vocabulary can they coordinate their efforts with other international agencies and especially with local authorities and leaders. They must properly plan programs so they can eventually depart and end their support without adding insult to existing injury.

Many factors mandate a change in the way humanitarian assistance workers should be trained. International relief efforts are now "big business" with profound diplomatic, military, political, and economic implications. Billions of dollars are spent annually on humanitarian assistance and the level is likely to rise in the twenty-first century. Yet until recently, there were no widely agreed upon training programs to certify the multiple actors in this critical discipline.

The International Diploma in Humanitarian Assistance (IDHA) is a product of the loss of innocence that followed the Somalia debacle in the early 1990s. It reflects a profound new appreciation of the dangers aid workers face and can create. My interest in the levels of training offered by different agencies was sharpened when I was asked to care for a young woman who had just been raped in Somalia in 1992. She had been sent into anarchy, armed with a pleasant morning's orientation program, and was led to believe that, somehow, if she caressed the starving babies, the problems of Somalia would be solved. No one told her that when societies collapse, people rob and murder and rape.

As I further investigated various training programs for international humanitarian workers, I discovered that even the largest international aid organizations offered mainly in-house courses of differing durations and quality. None offered a university diploma that could become part of a person's educational resume, a very useful credential as humanitarian workers change jobs and, often, organizations. The IDHA offered by the Center for International Health and Cooperation (CIHC), Fordham University, the University of Geneva, and the Royal College of Surgeons in Ireland filled that essential need. In the past five years, over 400 candidates have completed the program, received the IDHA, and now lead humanitarian missions and relief operations in every part of the world.

Young volunteers, as well as seasoned professionals, now frequently move from local and international relief organizations to national governmental services to the agencies and divisions of the United Nations, and back and forth. This movement of skills and personnel among organizations is both desirable and inevitable; it promotes cross-fertilization and should be encouraged.

However, this very mobility makes it imperative that there be a common foundation, an acceptable basic minimum standard of training. Brief orientation courses for humanitarian volunteers are obviously inadequate. There is a definite role for year-long Master's degree training programs for the committed professional, but they are hardly suitable for preparing large numbers of people urgently needed to serve in humanitarian crises, particularly in conflicts and disasters. Just as one would not consider sending a soldier into battle without basic military training, so also one must insist upon an adequate level of preparedness before permitting any involvement in complex humanitarian emergencies.

The CIHC developed a widely accepted curriculum that offers the necessary practical, thorough grounding in the fundamentals required for international humanitarian assistance. The IDHA course was devised after extensive consultation with colleagues from leading agencies involved in humanitarian work: the United Nations, the International Committee, and Federation, of the Red Cross, multiple governmental and nongovernmental organizations, and university-based experts.

An indispensable ingredient in making the IDHA program unique was the involvement of academia. It was critical that prestigious universities acknowledge practical humanitarian assistance training as a legitimate scholarly discipline worthy of an International Diploma. A careful, thoughtful curriculum, based on solid field experience, as well as academic analyses and research studies, could now replace the vague, emotion-laden ideological approach that characterized so many previous training programs.

Humanitarian crises cry out for an immediate response. The affected communities have obvious basic needs that must be met. Acute emergencies frequently become chronic situations that require a response capable of evolving from life-saving aid to rehabilitation and development; an adequate training curriculum must consider all these phases. Humanitarian crises can often be predicted and may be preventable, or their impact minimized, with appropriate foresight and planning.

Social, cultural, political, and economic forces influence crises and one must learn to appreciate, evaluate, and utilize these and other critical factors such as the local levels of health, education, and existing social service traditions. Health concerns in humanitarian crises are not limited to the control of communicable diseases or the obvious need to provide food, water, shelter, and emergency medical care in the midst of chaos. One must also be aware of the severe psychological stresses that result from and follow torture, rape, and displacement from the security of family and neighborhood.

Thus, a training course designed to prepare for an appropriate "humanitarian response" must have its foundation in a multidisciplinary approach involving and integrating personnel from a variety of backgrounds, including health, mental health, logistics, management, engineering, agriculture, communications, education, conflict resolution, advocacy, international humanitarian and human rights law, economics, politics, and diplomacy.

The IDHA course is purposefully intensive. It was constructed to simulate a humanitarian crisis, with long days of hard work and the forced intimacy of shared meals and dormitory accommodations. For twelve to fourteen hours a day, five and a half days a week for a full month, candidates participate in seminars and meetings, absorbing and discussing the views of an expert faculty, all of whom have had extensive experience in conflicts and disasters.

UN agencies and nongovernmental organizations (NGOs), working under personnel pressures in the field, can afford to assign candidates for training programs for relatively short periods in order not to disrupt their own operations. This was another practical reason we limited the IDHA to a month's duration, yet managed to provide over 200 hours of solid lectures and seminars to satisfy academic needs. Theory must be welded with experience if one is to train people for real crises. Since most IDHA candidates already had the opportunity to work in field operations, they bring their own insights and attitudes, and much of the learning comes from candidate interaction in debate and mock scenario exercises. A remarkable cadre of men and women who have lived through the hells of Somalia and Rwanda, of Liberia, Bosnia, and Chechnya, Afghanistan and Timor, have joined both as candidates and faculty for the IDHA courses.

In complex humanitarian emergencies, it is often difficult to identify any single paramount need. Throughout, the IDHA course fosters an appreciation of the myriad facets in humanitarian crises. The program encourages those who intend to provide help to do so with respect for the basic rights and dignity of those affected by such crises. The course, and the diploma, promote cooperation and dialogue among the critical triad: the international, governmental, and nongovernmental agencies on which international humanitarian assistance depends.

The IDHA program is rooted in an academic structure, which can establish and maintain standards, support research, evaluate interventions, and identify examples of good practice. The evolving discipline of humanitarian assistance must develop an essential institutional memory that should enable operating agencies to avoid the recurrent egregious failures and errors of earlier programs. Candidates are provided with basic textbooks, such as the International Committee of the Red Cross's *Handbook on War and Public Health,* my own *A Framework for Survival: Health, Human Rights and Humanitarian Assistance in Conflicts and Disasters,* and a CIHC-sponsored CD-ROM that has, on a single disc, over 1,000 fundamental documents on international law, the Geneva Conventions, et al.

The IDHA curriculum approaches humanitarian assistance by devoting the first week to disaster preparedness; identifying those economic and political forces that make nations vulnerable to collapse. The second week considers the many aspects of an emergency relief response. The third week is spent defining the steps necessary to rehabilitate fractured societies. In the fourth week, candidates reflect on personal protection, security, hostage situations, and how to deal with journalists from different media. Candidates learn how to devise appropriate exit strategies and, where possible, to develop a program that assures the critical transition from emergency relief to local development.

The faculty has steadily adapted our curriculum and teaching approach in response to the comments of IDHA graduates. For example, we have learned that there must be a balance between scheduled classroom lectures and protected time in the evenings for group discussions. Some discussions are introduced by keynote guest speakers. Topics may be chosen either from table 4.1, or students may suggest titles that they are particularly keen to discuss.

An important aspect of the IDHA program is to promote an approach of cooperation and teamwork rather than competition and individualism. On the first day of the course, the candidates are divided into syndicates of eight to ten persons each, chosen

Table 4.1 IDHA Discussion Topics

Week 1	Week 2	Week 3	Week 4
1. Humanitarian assistance—the price of international political complacency and inertia	1. Is an integrated multidisciplinary response an impossible deal?	1. Donor-driven humanitarian assistance—do funds meet needs or needs meet fund?	1. Institutional amnesia—inertia or impotence? To what extent do they exacerbate humanitarian crises?
2. Is the international community obliged to respond to each and every crisis?	2. Who should be responsible for independent research and evaluation in acute and chronic crises?	2. The aftermath of ethnic conflict—oblivion, justice, or revenge?	2. Advocacy and neutrality—a dilemma for international agencies, Red Cross and Red Crescent, and NGOs
3. Why is there a mismatch between need and provision of humanitarian assistance?	3. Central Africa—what would have happened if the world had done nothing?	3. Can the international community negotiate with key players if they have "blood on their hands"?	3. Humanitarian assistance—always positive?
4. For regional problems, can there be regional solutions?	4. Competition or cooperation: How can aid organizations optimize their effectiveness?	4. Child soldiers—what is the long-term impact on development?	4. How can we reconcile national security and human rights?
5. In the UN and its agencies—are there mechanisms of accountability and do they function?	5. Should refugees be kept in camps?	5. Is there a need for harmonization of refugee procedures and legislation? Can this be met?	5. Is distortion of reality acceptable in the interests of advocacy?
6. Is misappropriation and misuse of donor funds and resources inevitable?	6. Should professional registration be mandatory in emergency situations?	6. Forced repatriation—how do we respond? How should we respond? How can we respond?	6. Is the military logistic machine the best response to a humanitarian crisis?
7. Preventive diplomacy—cohesion through coercion?	7. Define the problems that must be expected because of existing political borders in the provision of humanitarian assistance?	7. Humanitarian assistance through partnership with host governments and services—rhetoric and reality	7. Is breach of national sovereignty justifiable in the interest of humanitarian action?
8. Is asylum seeking a lost cause?		8. How can we optimize opportunities for training of staff in countries afflicted by humanitarian crises?	
		9. Humanitarian action in situations of conflict—relief for victims or sustenance for perpetrators?	
		10. Interaction between expatriates and local staff	

so that candidates with different backgrounds and skills are forced to work closely together, as they would, in reality, during a humanitarian crisis. Each syndicate is assigned to one of the core tutors. There are usually five to six syndicates per course and an equal number of highly experienced resident tutors who carefully guide the candidates throughout.

Each syndicate chooses a chairperson and rapporteur, and the views of individual meetings are then discussed in weekly gathering involving the entire class and tutors.

As should be expected in an academic program under the auspices of three major universities, there is a persistent focus throughout the month-long IDHA on specificity, exact definitions, assessments, methods of quantifications, and measurements of effectiveness. Without these tools, only words and emotions prevail. It is easy to stress the need for training, but it is equally essential to recognize the obstacles to learning, the inherent prejudices of institutions and individuals even in times of great humanitarian need. In the IDHA lectures and seminars on politics, political will (or the lack thereof), basic human rights, ethical issues, and codes of conduct are recognized as integral parts of the humanitarian puzzle and must be addressed, and debated, in an academic setting.

Regardless of the candidate's background or aspirations, the IDHA curriculum is based on the premise that all humanitarian assistance workers must understand how political, as well as climatic and agricultural, forces might influence a crisis, and how essential, for example, basic logistics are in every undertaking. Adequate supplies, appropriate and thorough planning, and efficient application of resources are obviously preferable to emotional, haphazard attempts to quell a crisis.

Throughout the course, there is an emphasis on those most affected in humanitarian crises: women and, especially, children, too often the victims of preventable disease, too often lost or orphaned, frequently traumatized by seeing the violent deaths of family, even being forced themselves into conflict. Lecturers train the IDHA candidates in the best techniques to help reunite families lost in a massive flood of refugees, to help victims come to terms with the stress of national or clan collapse, personal injury, and family loss.

The IDHA curriculum also emphasizes the important role, and limitations, of the military during a humanitarian crisis. There is a continuous effort to promote coordination among the multiple actors that influence a humanitarian crisis. Individuals and organizations, each with their own viewpoints, interests, and even selfish agendas, must be encouraged, or even forced, to cooperate if overwhelming problems are to be resolved.

Finally, the IDHA course encourages all candidates to understand the bases of financial accounting, fundraising and dealing with donor fatigue, and to appreciate the scope and complexity of international assistance. How to assure adequate funding for humanitarian efforts, how to eliminate the wasteful, and demeaning, "begging bowl" approach to each crisis, and how to divide a finite fiscal pie so that all parts of the humanitarian triad can continue to contribute, are essential topics for discussion. The role of the media—for good or for ill—is also studied. In Rwanda and the former Yugoslavia, for example, the perverse use of the radio helped promote, even justify, horrible genocidal acts. Yet without media attention—the "CNN factor"—international leaders can, and do, conveniently ignore obvious famine and oppression.

All IDHA candidates are assessed throughout the course by weekly exams, tutorial reviews, and, in the final week, by written, oral, mock scenario situation, and syndicate presentation tests to satisfy the academic criteria required for a university diploma. Failures occur especially in candidates with poor attendance records or an attitude that prevents participation as a team member.

The signators of the IDHA diploma are the President of Fordham University in New York, the Rector of the University of Geneva in Switzerland, the Chief Executive of the Royal College of Surgeons in Ireland, and the President and Director of the Center for International Health and Cooperation. Several universities, including the University of Geneva, now offer up to a 40 percent credit toward a Master's degree to any candidate who has successfully completed the IDHA. The IDHA has been afforded full Copyright Protection by both the United States Patent Office and the European Union.

Further information on the curriculum and application process can be obtained from the following Web sites: http://www .cihc.org, http://www.idha.ch, and http://www.fordham.edu.

IDHA COURSE OBJECTIVES

1. To provide volunteers and professionals from a wide variety of backgrounds with a comprehensive insight into the needs of refugees and internally displaced people in acute and chronic settings and equip them with the awareness, understanding, and skills that are essential for effective service in a humanitarian crisis
2. To enable humanitarian workers to function effectively, both as individuals and members of a team, in acute and chronic situations of conflict and disaster
3. To promote cooperation and dialogue between international, governmental, or nongovernmental agencies involved in humanitarian action (assistance and protection)
4. To evaluate interventions and identify examples of good practice
5. To examine ways in which humanitarian crisis may be anticipated and prevented

5

Teamwork in Humanitarian Missions

Pamela Lupton-Bowers

Pamela Lupton-Bowers

THE IMPORTANCE OF TEAMWORK IN AN EMERGENCY OPERATION

THE IMPORTANCE OF TEAMWORK cannot be overemphasized in a humanitarian assistance operation. Groups of widely different people must work together at all levels: international technical support staff of many different disciplines must work with community groups responding to the immediate humanitarian imperative of saving lives and of organizing the logistics and distribution of aid. Then the interagency and government "teams" must orchestrate the whole event. When effective teamwork exists, people speak of uplifting experiences and of achievements beyond their expectations. They speak of a synergy that occurs in well-functioning teams that allows them to achieve more than the individuals themselves could have achieved. They speak of the experience as being life changing and rejuvenating.

When teams work well together, things are in synch, ideas flow, people are clear about what has to be done, they communicate openly with one another, they are comfortable with decisions, and they work in complementary harmony. An atmosphere of fairness and inclusivity reigns and team members respect and support one another. There is a sense of personal as well as team fulfillment and, most importantly, teams are effective.

Organizations in all disciplines favor more and more a work model based on teams. It's a model that favors cooperation, inclusiveness in problem solving, information-sharing, and collaborative action. Companies and organizations that promote and invest in teamwork generally agree that:

- Teams improve communication. They gather and share information as an essential part of their work.
- Teams achieve results that ordinary functional groups can't: a "product" in today's world is the result of a "process" of integrated events. There is too much to know for one person or one discipline. The combination of knowledge and ability can result in superior outcomes. A cross-functional team invariably knows more than a pyramid hierarchy ever can.
- Teams are more creative and more efficient at solving problems. Well-balanced and complementary teams combine multiple perspectives and create more innovative solutions.
- Teams achieve higher quality decisions. The essence of good decision-making is good leadership and appropriate process; in effective teams, both are shared.
- Teams increase quality and services. They understand purpose and goal and have the interpersonal skills to manage relationships.
- Teams mean improved processes. Effective teams are not hampered by bureaucracy; they identify obstacles and redesign processes to remove them, speeding up responses.
- Teams motivate and develop their members. Teams allow people with different kinds of knowledge, opinion, and approaches to work together. They learn together and grow together. Participation in such cross-functional teams strengthens and develops individuals and helps build the organization.

These results are no less desirable for a humanitarian mission than they are for a corporate business. Not all humanitarian relief workers share the belief that this model of teamwork is appropriate in a disaster relief situation. Some would argue that the conditions are unique and that the theories and practice of collaborative teamwork are not applicable. Others assume that the group dynamics involved will occur naturally without conscious effort to establish or maintain them.

We don't have time to deal with that. We are there to do a job; everyone knows what they have to do and they just get on with it. (Emergency relief unit leader deployed in several operations, Bosnia, Burundi, 1998[1])

This attitude is propagated, whether consciously or unconsciously, in disaster response training when topics such as interpersonal relations, stress management, and cross-cultural relations and teamwork are often relegated to minor positions in a technically full curriculum. It is not uncommon to see a module on teamwork awarded a slot of forty-five to ninety minutes in a one- or two-week program. This is totally inadequate for developing behaviors that ultimately can make the difference between success and failure of an operation.

The opinion expressed by the relief worker above might be considered, at first glance, to be admirable and one motivated by a clear commitment and drive to respond to the often-overwhelming humanitarian imperative. In the first hours and days of an emergency response, time is of the essence; the priority is saving lives, ensuring protection and sustenance and reducing the vulnerability of the people involved. But it ignores the reality that humanitarian relief teams are not different from any other team in that they are composed of different people with different perspectives, and they have a nasty habit of behaving like human beings, in that they have conflicting ways of thinking and doing things. Moreover, it ignores the fact that the relief team is not a hermetically sealed unit able to operate in isolation. They must operate with other actors, including not only other agencies, but also local communities and the beneficiaries themselves. More and more relief workers are reporting that while they are competent in their functional expertise, they are unprepared for and overwhelmed by the ambiguous and confusing situations on the ground, which they complain "get in the way of doing the job."

Unfortunately, under these conditions, relief managers, coordinators, and team leaders too often resort to command type or authoritarian leadership. Even when they "know better," the high stress of a disaster situation causes people to fall back upon preferred, comfortable behaviors. It's not difficult to see why when we look at the background of disaster organization. Historically, the dominant planning model for disaster response has been command and control, based on the "military model"[2] of emergency planning. This model is characterized by the assumptions of "chaos," which can only be eliminated by taking control. These assumptions lead to an organizational structure modeled on military structures. The assumptions being that "emergencies create a significant disjunction in social life which requires extraordinary measures to be put back in place" and that the "problems" are found in the "weaknesses" of individuals and social structures and that emergency planning should be directed at establishing control.

The belief is that a situation is suddenly so drastically different than "normal" time, that decision-making and authority need to be centralized, with precise planning and meticulous attention to detail. There is also the underlying presumption that spontaneous and unplanned behavior is dysfunctional, misdirected, and harmful. Communication lines are created "top down" with the belief that those at the top know what to do, and orders are issued at the expense of gathering information. The implications of this command and control model are that people cannot be trusted to obtain correct information, and that victims are passive and cannot help themselves. It is a paternalistic view of victims who need authorities to be decision-makers.

In such an organizational approach, the management style and team dynamic are naturally influenced and manifest as typical of command and control leadership. This in turn will influence the preparation of teams and leaders and determine the profile and competence of both. Admittedly, there will be some occasions when authoritarian management is perfectly adequate; too often though, this adopted style becomes habitual in circumstances and situations where it is no longer appropriate. And this can result in breakdowns between the actors and the very populations they seek to aid.

Several factors lead to the conclusion that different working models in emergency relief are needed.

LACK OF RESPECT REGARDING THE LOCAL POPULATION

Local agencies and staff liken traditional authoritarian style to imperialism and neo-colonialism; they are insulted by it, and the beneficiaries themselves tell us that it is not appreciated. It neither respects their wishes, their capabilities, nor their status. It simply doesn't recognize the capacity of the local population to contribute to the relief operation.

> In a series of journalistic interviews with victims of disasters, the American Red Cross discovered that authoritarian leadership was tolerated in the early minutes and hours of a disaster when lives and property were at risk. However, this type of management style was quickly considered inappropriate and unacceptable, and victims reported expecting to play a more involved role in their care and in the decisions being made about them. (Disaster Response Manager, Washington, D.C., U.S.A., 1999)

More Complex Environment

Disasters are becoming less routine and more expanding and emerging. There are a greater variety of vulnerable populations extending across sections of society and involving all levels, rich and poor. The stakeholders involved can include war lords, local and international media, military, armed guards as well as local communities, churches, and agencies. This demands a more sophisticated response and one that is able to respond to all the different actors.

Longevity and Permanence of Complex Emergencies

Both are increasingly distinctive features of relief operations, and agencies are seeking new models of operation that can cope with the crisis within the emergency and that include principles of "operationality in turbulence."[3] The situation in Gujerat is a perfect example of this. What started in January 2001 as an emergency response to a major earthquake evolved into long-term relief as reconstruction was hampered by the magnitude of the disaster, and has since had periods of renewed crisis as a result of the community disturbances and violence fourteen months later.

The Demand for a Higher-Caliber Humanitarian Worker

Large scale complex situations requiring an international response are dependent more and more on relief workers who are highly educated, skilled, and experienced. Gone are the beliefs that a technical relief worker need simply to follow clearly defined standard operating procedures to be able to function successfully in the pre-defined disaster situation. The whole playing field has less clearly defined parameters, which creates more unstable and changing situations. Relief workers need to be able to tolerate the flexibility and ambiguity of the arena in which they work. The technically professional relief worker cannot be considered truly professional unless he or she can effectively operate in a multidiscipline, multinational, multicultural team of workers. Naturally, such professionals resent authoritarian leadership for being overbearing and restrictive.

Sustainability and Continuity of Their Own Staff and Organization

The humanitarian relief field suffers a high turnover of staff. On the one hand, this is not too surprising as many relief workers approach the work as temporary or occasional. However, it poses threats to organizations if they lack professional career relief workers able to strategically manage their organizations and to be able to build on institutional memory and learning. Poor team leadership and interpersonal relations contribute to this drain of talent. While humanitarian organizations are cognizant of the risks to staff in conflict situations, more so as a result of the tragic deaths in recent years of humanitarian workers in Tchechnya, East Timor, Tanzania, and the current situation in the Middle East, there seems to be a reluctance to recognize the stress suffered by staff in day-to-day operations. The stress created by a dysfunctional working environment can have serious impact on the health of the humanitarian worker. We know this to be true from research in the general work environment; it is exacerbated many fold by the conditions in which the humanitarian relief workers find themselves. There is also the warriors' code of, "it's part of the job, we can handle it," which often denies workers access to debriefing psychologists, and this can contribute to accumulative stress syndrome and can cause serious and long-term effects on the humanitarian worker. The consequence of inappropriate management and poor interpersonal relations with supervisors and colleagues is a major contributing factor to this stress. In debriefing sessions, psychologists report that of the number of humanitarian workers deciding to leave the profession, a very high proportion cite unsatisfactory relations with managers or colleagues as a contributing reason.

> I went straight out to Macedonia; I didn't have time for a briefing. I didn't see my manager for several weeks. I went out as a driver and ended up coordinating a team. I had no experience for that. I had no support. I don't think I did a good job. I am completely burned out. I don't think I'll be going back. (First-time Danish relief worker returning from Macedonia, 2000)

AN ALTERNATIVE TEAM-BASED MODEL

Clearly a more sophisticated operational model is called for. Such a model needs to be based on:

- key characteristics of inclusiveness, coordination, and cooperation;
- the assumption that the capacity of the individual and social structure are not necessarily reduced;
- the reality that teams will include local community personnel: agencies, NGO's beneficiaries;
- the recognition that the most effective problem-solving and planning will include the local society in a participative process;

- the enhancement of coordination by common planning and re-hearsal activities;
- the understanding that the core of emergency planning should be toward building mechanisms, techniques, and facilities that promote inter-organizational coordination and common deci-sion-making.

The characteristics of such a model clearly demand a more cooperative and inclusive approach that match those of effective cross-functional, cross-discipline, and multicultural teamwork. An inherent assumption of this approach must be that the com-petencies of individual relief workers and, particularly, team leaders must include skills in facilitating these processes. Among some disaster relief workers there is still a reluctance, even em-barrassment, on the part of humanitarian agencies to give credit to this kind of training and preparation, but as we have seen, the consequences for not doing so are serious. On the other hand, there are real advantages in getting this right.

1. The overall success of the operation. Just as an organiza-tion's values and beliefs influence the actions and ethics of its people, so, too, does the structure, processes, and management style. By extension, both will influence the functioning of its teams on the ground and the overall perceived success of the organization.

2. Improved relationships and image with beneficiaries and local communities. A new profile[4] of beneficiaries "articulate communities of people used to power themselves," responds to relief personnel who provide prompt and effective services in a fair, respectful, and compassionate manner.[5] They reject the tra-ditional and essentially patronizing dynamic of the agency-bene-ficiary relationship that legitimizes an authoritative approach.

3. Improved potential for creating opportunities for capacity building. One of the great challenges of the relief operation is to exploit opportunities to share knowledge and capacity wherever possible and no matter how minimal. Skills associated with partic-ipative teamwork (facilitation, listening, participative decision-making, mediation, coaching, and guiding) are more relevant

for transferring know-how and building the capacities of the local communities and individuals.

4. Well being of their own staff and the strengthening of their organizations. Good team and interpersonal relations contribute to raising people's abilities to cope with stress. Stress is a common factor in the humanitarian world. Regardless of the presence or absence of conflict, the human tragedy associated with all disasters, the absence of family, friends, and the traditional support network, added to unfamiliar climate and conditions all contribute to increased anxiety and stress for any humanitarian worker. However, when humanitarian workers benefit from good leadership support, collaborative efforts on the part of colleagues, respect and recognition for his/her contribution, then the stress of the mission can be considerably reduced.

> In Abidjan when the violence was at its worst, the team spirit and relationship with our colleagues in other agencies was so good that we were able to handle the worst situations with a sense of humor and without being totally stressed. It would have been impossible to have survived without it. (Health coordinator, Congo, Brazzaville, 1999)

BUILDING THE TEAM

The International Diploma for Humanitarian Assistance (IDHA) program models its approach on the emergency relief situation. Groups of strangers are placed together within the first hours of arriving. They are organized into syndicate groups and expected to operate immediately as productive "teams." The majority of them do; a few do not. What is it that binds them? What helps to build the team? What prevents them and causes their failure? These are questions that are explored within the first day of the program, because when team formation is hampered, the entire outcome can be jeopardized.

A major contributing factor to whether a team is well functioning or dysfunctional is the underlying values and beliefs that motivate an individual to engage in humanitarian work, and will influence decision-making and relationships with colleagues and, especially, host communities and victims. Values and beliefs are fundamentally what humanitarian organizations are about. Religious organizations particularly, CARITAS, Lutheran World Service, World Vision, etc., have a clear mission to disseminate those values. Unfortunately, we can't rely on an agreed moral basis for modern humanitarianism; the principles guiding humanitarian agencies vary, sometimes quite widely, as we have seen in the case of *Médecins sans frontières* and the International Committee of the Red Cross. The entire humanitarian field is rife with the paradoxes of altruism.[6] Impartiality, long considered an essential of humanitarianism, was questioned during the Rwanda operations and in Bosnia. For many the concept of the "deserving poor" no longer held true, and many of the aid workers suffered from the deception. The ideology of an organization can be so strong that it will influence its organizational structure, resulting in a "missionary configuration."[7] This will naturally affect its style of operation, the profile of its workers, and its modus operandi. All this is to say that it is naïve to rely on only cognitive and behavioral approaches to establishing an effective team. Motives will influence the intensity with which individuals engage in the relief activity, and also determine how long they will persist faced with the attendant emotional stress and fatigue. The responsibility of the team leader is for the success of the operation and the well being of his or her team. The challenge is both to understand individual strengths and limitations and to consciously work toward common ground if the team is to jointly tackle the challenges ahead of it.

The teams in IDHA programs that form "naturally" display characteristics that are also evident in well-performing field teams.

Motivation—There is an immediate and agreed identification with the group and a common desire to succeed. More will be said about motivation and its challenge for the team leader later.

Rapport—There are conscious and overt efforts to seek common ground: experiences, place of birth, work locations, previous humanitarian experience, professional background, etc. And, less overtly but just as inexorably, searching out those who share beliefs and values.

Building rapport means being on the same wavelength as the other person, speaking their language, being completely in tune with the other person. Bandler and Grinder,[8] the authors of neuro-linguistic programming (NLP), discovered early in their work on the communication excellence of several notable therapists that, in order to communicate well, high levels of rapport had to be established. Their research also noted that when we are not in rapport, we continue to communicate; however, the messages we are sending may not be what we are intending. It is this fundamental of interpersonal communication that is at the heart of many of the problems of the team. Diversity can be both an opportunity for team strength; yet, at the same time, it can increase the potential for disjunction due to the misunderstanding of unintentional nonverbal signals (body language, gestures, expressions, tone of voice, etc.).

Neuro-Linguistic Programming is the study of human excellence. NLP is the observation of excellent communication skills and the description of them as models of behavior. It can be a powerful and practical approach to personal change.

Neuro refers to our nervous system, the mental pathways of our five senses by which we see, hear, feel, taste, and smell.

Linguistic refers to our ability to use language, and how specific words or phrases mirror our mental worlds. Linguistic refers to our "silent language" of postures, gestures, habits that reveal our thinking styles, beliefs, and more.

Programming is borrowed from computer science to suggest that our thoughts, feelings, and actions are habitual programs that can be changed by upgrading our "mental software." (Adapted from Andreas, Faulkner, et al. (1994))

Miscommunication can be exacerbated further by the customs and cultural mores rife in a multinational team, and by the fact of the team itself operating in a foreign environment. Culture, the combination of shared experiences, beliefs, and history, gives people their sense of self-worth, value, and world outlook. It is quite obvious to see that people who share a culture will find that rapport can be created immediately and subconsciously. We've all experienced that situation when we simply "click" with another person. We describe a "chemistry" that allows us to "be on the same wavelength" and to understand better what they are saying, and even what they may be thinking. This level of rapport can occur at a first meeting. You may discover that you have much in common: country of origin, place of birth, schooling or earlier work experience. You may have traveled to the same places, enjoy the same food, like the same music, read the same books, and share the same opinions.

This certainly doesn't mean to say that in order for good teamwork to occur everyone has to be the same. Far from it. Theories of team are founded on the opposite opinion: that the most effective teams are those that are composed of complementary members. Groupthink is just as potentially dangerous as conflict. But it does tell us that adding the cultural dimension to all other differences adds even more complexity to the challenge of creating effective teamwork.

> Since returning from the training, I am realizing more and more each day that the most important part of my job is establishing and maintaining good interpersonal relationships with my team and my counterparts in the region. When we do this, we can achieve almost impossible goals. (Humanitarian worker in Kazakhstan, 2001)

Although motivation and rapport give the group a good start, this process alone does not guarantee success. Group dynamic begins to dissolve and relationships fragment when processes such as appropriate procedures, relevant leadership, effective communication, and decision-making are not clarified. Also evident in effective teams is that members are willing to balance their own needs and expectations with those of the team and of other team members. They are able to some extent to suppress their personal needs for the greater good or for the development and support of a particular colleague. Individual team members recognize that even with superior intelligence or experience, the potential output of their efforts could not exceed that of the team in the given time frame or the circumstances. There can be no teamwork when individuals are simply out to prove themselves or to outshine their colleagues. "Prima donnas" don't do well in teams. Unfortunately, there are quite a few "prima donnas" in the relief world.

Male aid workers can be fiercely competitive and seem to gain greater pleasure from proving themselves (including the ability to devise theories and analysis) than helping those in need. (Tony Vaux, 2001, "The Selfish Altruist. Relief Work in Famine and War.")

The approach to achieve effective teamwork expressed in this chapter is founded on two basic truisms:

1. Teamwork is essentially all about understanding and working with people.
2. The outcome of team building exercises, apart from the direct goal of ensuring team achievements, must be to increase the individual's competence as a team worker. That is, the skills that they learn must be transferable.

With this in mind the approach considers:

- How people think. This has to do with cognitive preferences.
- How people act—the way they manifest these preferences in the way that they behave and do things.
- How self-aware they are of their cognitive and behavioral preferences.
- How well they recognize the differences in other team members.
- How willing they are to adapt to different thinking and behavioral preferences.
- How competent they are in behavioral flexibility. Do they have the skills and ability to act differently?

The outcome of the approach is to enhance team members' emotional intelligence. This involves improving interpersonal relationships and ensuring that team members acquire skills that permit them to operate successfully in other interpersonal and team situations. This intelligence includes the following:

- Know-what: the knowledge of what things should be done to allow a good team to work, i.e., goal setting, operating procedures, participative decision-making, etc.
- Know-how: the skills to be able to implement these actions
- Know-when: the judgment to know when things should happen and in what situation
- Know-who: the maturity to match different communication approaches and styles with different people's preferences and comfort levels

How People Think; How People Act

Cognitive differences have to do with how people perceive and assimilate data, make decisions, solve problems, and relate to people. The most widely recognized cognitive differences are those associated with right-brain/left-brain dominance. This distinction provides a useful impression about the radically different ways of thinking observed in people; although it's more metaphoric than physiological. Recent research reveals little current neuroscientific evidence for the phenomena;[9] yet, the popular psychology right brain/left brain distinction is readily accepted by many people.

Recent research tells us that evidence for hemisphere dominance and specialization is not as evident as was once believed. It appears that both hemispheres contribute to the holistic processing of faculties. Nor is one more important than the other. But in Western culture, the faculties associated with the left do take a more dominant position in our lives. We place less value and emphasis on those associated with the right. The highest material awards go to the logical rational thinkers; intuitive thought, spatial, and artistic creative processes are less appreciated. Whether neurological or culturally founded, this appears to be true.

Table 5.1

Left	Right
▪ Logic	▪ Recognition of patterns
▪ Reason	▪ Recognition of faces
▪ Mathematics	▪ Rhythm
▪ Language	▪ Visual images and depth
▪ Reading	▪ Creativity
▪ Writing	▪ Parallel processing
▪ Linear thinking	▪ Synthesis
▪ Serial crossing	
▪ Analysis	

When people assimilate information differently, they think about things differently. The way they think about things will naturally influence the way that they act. Some people "see" internal visions, but need to interact with others in order to "think" through problems. Others may "hear" their ideas, and prefer to reflect independently before presenting them to anyone else. Some people need to interact externally with their environment. These extroverts are likely to interrupt others, talk out loud, dominate meetings, and may overly influence decisions. In contrast, introverted types, by their non-expression, are underrepresented in meetings and often express frustration with their inability to influence. Analytical, logical types base their decisions on the empirical facts and evidence available, while more intuitive types rely on feelings, beliefs, and opinion. Abstract thinkers like to assimilate their information from a variety of sources and use divergent thinking patterns to evolve creative solutions; while more practical individuals prefer to have hands-on, experiential information with which to solve immediate pragmatic problems.

The first thing to emphasize is that these approaches relate to preferences and not to competencies—that is, a person's skills and abilities. People are able to operate in other ways, and often learn different behaviors than their preferential ones. However, it is also a fact that in an emergency situation, people resort to their most comfortable, preferred styles of behavior. The challenge for the team and the team leader is to build on these differences for the benefit of the team and not to allow them to create conflict between members. When differences are not understood, they are seen to be personal rather than professional. For instance, the "big picture" person requesting feedback on a report expects to get comments about the overall thesis and global view and is confused, even irate, to receive detailed comments about format, spelling, and punctuation errors. He assumes such "nit-picking" was done purposefully to insult and impose one-upmanship. Personality and work preference differences can be the cause of major dysfunction in a team.

The best and most objective way to assess differences is through specific diagnostic tools. Such tools can provide a more objective and detailed description of a person's preferences than the most observant manager. Many tools exist on the market:

- The Team Management Systems Index (TMS) examines work preferences and team role
- The Belbin Team Type Inventory (BELBIN) examines role preferences when working in a team
- The Myers Briggs Type Indicator (MBTI) is a personality inventory designed to help people understand themselves and their behaviors
- The Occupational Personality Questionnaire (OPQ) indicates

relevant personality characteristics across a wide spectrum of occupations

None of these measure ability in a specific area of work. They are mostly designed to encourage individuals to become more self-aware and to help them explore aspects of managing relationships and behavior. Most of them agree on several basic points:

- Preferences are neither good nor bad. They are simply different, and one or another may be more appropriate in certain situations than in others.
- Preferences emerge early and most stay with us throughout our lives, although certain experiences can persuade us to adapt and change. For instance, getting the opportunity to do something different and then receiving positive feedback about our abilities can cause us to modify our preference with regard to that behavior.
- Preferences are not rigid. Most of us have access to a variety of approaches, but find ourselves particularly attached to one or two key preferred ways.
- Preferences are not prescriptive of behavior, but descriptions of how individuals assess their own behavior.

The key to achieving good interpersonal working relationships is to raise awareness of the individual team members about their particular preferential styles. Initial team activities should focus on helping people to increase their understanding of how they operate, and the conditions in which they prefer to work. In an emergency relief situation, it is essential for team members to recognize differences early so that they can move quickly to being productive. It is vital for the team leader to understand the different styles of the team as well as his/her own. This is doubly important since adaptation of behavior can only occur with self-recognition, empathy for others, and a genuine motivation for change. Also true is that when people identify their own working styles, they also gain insight into the styles of others.

The team can use this information in a variety of ways to build team effectiveness:

- Creating team balance. A balanced team, in which all preferential styles are represented, tend to allocate work naturally among themselves. When this is not the case, leaders need to attend to the imbalance and identify ways of compensating for it. A team without any divergent thinkers may want to find one from outside of the team to give a different perspective to their creative problem solving.
- Matching work to work preferences. Detailed analysis of financial data is not the favorite task of everyone. Team leaders should match the task to the person who not only has the skills, but also enjoys doing it.
- Designing processes to capture everyone's contribution. This involves, among other things, information gathering from all relevant sources, managing the input of the talkative members, and creating space for the more reflective ones, ensuring that a period of innovative and divergent discussion precedes the convergent decision making and action planning.
- Tailoring communication. Recognizing different styles and matching the communication style to the receiver rather than the sender.
- Legitimizing honest constructive feedback. When the team recognizes the appropriateness of different behaviors, it is easier to convey when behavior is inappropriate or unhelpful.

The advantage of such tools is that they provide a language that depersonalizes behavior and reduces the threat of interpersonal conflict. People can disagree with the behavior and not with the person. Take the case, for example, of a desk officer in Geneva who was having difficulties relating to a field manager in his region. The field manager, in describing his decisions in a particularly sensitive area of the Balkans, would say things like, "Trust me. I have a feeling about this. I just know it will work." The desk officer, a highly practical, analytical decision-maker, was completely unable to understand or respect decision making that was not founded on clear, logical evidence and empirical facts. The conflict between the two was almost at the point of no return until each completed the TMS profile and understood their radically different approaches to decision making. They had other preferences in common: they were both extroverts and they both preferred a structured way of organizing. Their major differences were in how they assimilated information—one in a creative, divergent way and the other in a more pragmatic, convergent way—and in their decision-making. Once they understood these differences, they were able to depersonalize them and recognize their respective strengths. They also saw the validity and expertise in both ways of working, and they were able to establish a professionally successful relationship for the following two years.

The key to using such profiles is to understand that they are not prescriptive, but descriptive of the responses that the individual has provided at that particular point in time. Most psychometric tests rely on self-reporting; the behavior assumed may not correspond with what others observe. An invaluable complement to self-assessed questionnaires is feedback from others about their perception of the described behavior and their observation of actual behavior. The professional, nonjudgmental language employed in psychometric tests can help the team to provide constructive feedback.

In the absence of professional tools, a few simple questions can help groups to discuss their cognitive and behavioral preferences:

- Which type of people do you like to work with?
- Which people do you have difficulty working with?
- How do you make decisions?
- How do you think through problems?
- How do you create solutions?
- How do you organize your work?
- How do you decide what to do next?

Having people discuss their responses to these simple questions can provide a wealth of information about how they are likely to relate to people and to work.

FORMING THE TEAM

The discussion generated from the questions above is an essential part of forming the group dynamics that result in good teamwork. Good teamwork can naturally occur when people learn more about one another over time and are willing to be more open. But in an emergency situation, time is a precious commodity, and teams, after the immediate and almost automatic first hours and days of a response, must work quickly at establishing an effective working unit. The way to do this is to establish consciously standard operating behaviors. Relief workers are familiar with standard operating procedures. Standard operating behaviors are close cousins, and are the explicitly identified behaviors that a group agrees to perform by and to be measured against. They are essential if the team is going to be successful in working together. Standard operating behaviors are the essence of what psychologist B. W. Tuckman[10] called the forming of the team. Tuckman identified four stages of team formation through observing team progress. His resulting model of forming, storming, norming, and performing is commonly used in teamwork training. The terminology added below has been adapted and is more acceptable to multinational groups, which sometimes balk at the over-reliance on Western models and at jargon which is often impossible to translate. This does nothing to deter from the usefulness of the model.

Forming/Orientation

This phase involves getting to know one another—searching for understanding about purpose, goal, roles and responsibilities, turf. It is the stage of gathering information, analyzing, getting people on board. Learning about one another's skills—although sometimes surreptitiously or tacitly. It can also involve posturing by some and withdrawn observation by others. Forming can be a dangerous time; first impressions are made and sometimes never changed; alliances are created; power bases are sought. A major threat to team building is that some teams want to pole vault straight to performing with little concern or perceived value in the forming, storming, or norming. Unfortunately, there are no shortcuts to team building. Whether the team likes it or not, recognizes it or not, they need to orient themselves within in order to go through the stages.

Storming/Dissatisfaction

This period is identified by clashes of personalities, preferences, and work styles. There may be differences in interpretations, understanding of roles, etc. Competition and power-plays will be evident. There may be withdrawal, disengagement, resistance. The atmosphere is stressful, and the emotional energy of members of the team is spent on surviving the threatening team climate and trying to agree about the team goal and objectives. Storming is a necessary evil. It sometimes comes unexpectedly upon a team that thinks it knows itself, or in which the majority of team members have worked together before. Storming can reoccur with any subtle change of the team; the loss of a person, the addition of a person. Team leaders can help the team get through storming. It requires good leadership skills and an effective process for the exchange of opinion, ideas, and conflict. If such behavior is ignored during these early stages, it will come back to haunt the team. In the confined world of humanitarian aid, the team you failed to mature during this disaster may well be the one you will have to deal in the next one. Getting through this stage also requires some coaching on the part of the team leader. We have seen in the case of emergency disaster leaders that the typical profile does not predispose them toward the kinds of skills this requires. In some teams, another person takes on this nurturing role more naturally, and a mature leader will allow this to happen. The most important thing is that the team achieves a norming phase so that it can perform optimally. The team will respect the leader more if this occurs. If the team continues to storm, the leader, justly or otherwise, will become the focal point of their dissatisfaction and blame for the lack of coalescing.

Norming/Resolution

This stage occurs when understanding has been achieved about conflicts and misunderstandings. Agreements have been made about working culture, processes, decision-making, and team members have accepted or assimilated to the style of the team leader. Depending on the depth of the dissatisfaction, resolution may involve serious repair work on the part of the team leader and/or the team members, and may require the help of an outside facilitator. During this stage tensions will subside and defenses will be lowered. Team balance and complementarity will occur as one team member's strength will compensate for another's weakness. During this stage, it is essential to maintain some friction, but it needs to be "creative abrasion."[11] Creative abrasion is the intentional conflict of differing ideas that is essential to creative problem solving and for avoiding groupthink.

Performing/Production

This phase can occur when more emotional energy is being expended on the work than on surviving the team climate. The team has common objectives; members understand and agree on work culture; appropriate and effective communication networks are established; decision-making methods are agreed upon and respected. In short, everyone is performing and the team is results-focused. Performing can also be a period of great personal growth for the individuals of the team. There can be playful teasing, increased self-confidence, openness, and the honesty of constructive feedback. In the strongest teams, humor permits an almost painful honesty that allows the team to move quickly through dissension toward the successful achievement of its goals.

The disaster operation in its entirety can be described using Tuckman's stages:

- Initiation and mobilization: the phase during the "crisis or event" is forming and storming

- Integration: the early post "event" is the norming stage
- Production: the post-event phase is the performing stage

And just as in the case of the team, if the operation fails in the first two phases, it cannot hope to be maximally effective in production.

The result of the team failing to progress through the forming, storming, and norming stages is that the team members expend much of their emotional energy on surviving the internal climate instead of on the work to be done. When individuals are in a stressed state, they have reduced emotional strength for colleagues or beneficiaries. Team members become depressed and disillusioned. In the emergency relief situation, stress leads to more conflict, errors of judgment, lack of communication, collaboration, and the break down between individuals. It also results in the breakdown of individuals. Team members seek emotional support outside of the team. They resort to drink, sometimes to drugs, and to questionable and unsuitable sexual partners. This scenario is dangerous, not only for the individual, but also for the rest of the team. Such behavior brings disrepute to the organization and can cause serious security issues for all concerned.

ESTABLISHING STANDARD OPERATING BEHAVIORS

Typically the problem of a team failing to establish good teamwork is not a lack of "know-what." The problem, or more accurately the solution, to establishing an environment of effective teamwork is "know-how," that is, the "acting of the knowledge." Humanitarian relief workers are intelligent, knowledgeable individuals. Most of them had already experienced, at minimum, basic training in teamwork, and they are aware of the fundamental theory. Most of them are equally cynical, and do not simply accept a prescriptive list that purports to set out the operating behaviors for the mission. Another the contributing factor to dysfunctional teams is the assumption that because people know something, they will implement it. Simply providing a list to people will not ensure that their behavior will match it. The teams themselves should decide on their common standard behaviors. In this way, their lists reflect their experiences, and respect their understanding and beliefs about effective team performance.

Generating such a list is actually quite a simple process. The team is asked to describe what, in their experience, are the key factors that have contributed to good teamwork. Notice that this is a behavioral question based on experience and not a cognitive question based on belief or intellectual opinion.

For an international emergency team, this preparation can be done on a plane or in a waiting lounge. With larger groups, it naturally will require more facilitation and space. When your group is multicultural, the normal behaviors of the culture must be considered. Some team members from less open and individualistic cultures may need a little more support to contribute, but most individuals, whether they are from Bosnia or Tanzania, welcome the opportunity to shape the environment in which they must work when they are given the opportunity of doing so. The value of establishing operating behaviors is that much of the destructful conduct associated with storming can be reduced, or at least given legitimate process. The team has a chance to overcome hostility, overzealousness, intimidation, polarization, blaming, formation of "cliques," resistance, and unwillingness to compromise.

The following few techniques can help the team leader:

1. Encourage team members to relate to a specific and concrete past experience. This should be a pragmatic exercise, not a competition in theoretical knowledge. You know when people are speaking from experience; they use the past tense to describe events. When people are theorizing, they use conditional tenses, such as "should do," and the present, "good team work is. . . ." The list typically includes[12] good communication; respect for culture, differences, gender, linguistic level, time, experience, qualification; total contribution of everyone in the team; active listening; openness and frankness; common courtesy; common

goals and objectives; clear roles and responsibilities; leadership; good process; good decision-making.

2. Have individuals work independently for the first few minutes, asking them to write down their contribution. The whole point of this exercise is that people operate differently. And without process to manage input, the differences will begin to emerge and influence the dynamics of a group immediately. Preference and confidence in speaking out is a major distinction between Western expatriates and local team members. The more extroverted members of the team will immediately speak up and share their thoughts. Uncontrolled extroverts will take up a disproportionate amount of team talk and may well overly influence decisions. Permitting the time and space for individual reflection ensures that everyone has the chance to contribute.

3. Accept people's input verbatim. Write up what they say, exactly as they say it, unchallenged and unchanged. It is important that people feel that their input is being recorded accurately and is not being interpreted or misinterpreted by someone else.

4. Make sure you get everyone's input, especially the more introverted members of the team. When this is handled in an honest, genuine, and equitable fashion, it is amazing how much local experts will contribute.

5. Read and agree on the understanding of all recorded items This is great opportunity for the team leader and the team to begin to discover one another's preferences, as together they explore more precise meanings for the outputs collected, and they struggle for common interpretation and understanding.

6. Decide which behaviors are the most appropriate and commonly accepted ones for the team.

The benefit of this first step is to make expectations explicit. Teams are usually pleased that there is a great deal of common agreement about these key factors. The step of clarifying understanding is crucially important to the forming stage. Team members need to probe and ask one another what each of these terms mean to them. What is "respecting differences"? What does everyone mean by that? How do we do that? How do we manifest it in our day-to-day relationships? Once the team begins to get clarity and understanding, it can work toward an agreement of more precise behavior. This may sound like a lengthy ordeal, and many emergency relief workers may be shuddering at the prospect of "wasting" such time. Obviously, a team would not be undergoing such self-reflection when lives are at risk, when search and rescue is ongoing, or when bodies are still being recovered. But as we have seen that teams are engaged together long after the immediate response is over; disaster relief has a habit of continuing long after the initial emergency. Once the initial crisis is over, however, teams need to pay attention to their well being and operation. The process actually takes only a little time. Much of it can be carried out in the normal working procedure of the team. This particular exercise can be done in as little as thirty minutes for groups of five to ten. Larger groups of twenty to thirty will take about an hour to allow everyone to contribute and to analyze and to get broad agreement about the common behaviors. Admittedly, it may take a little longer than issuing direct orders. But the fact is that such team process is an investment that pays off in the reduction of time spent in future misunderstandings and conflict more associated with storming.

The characteristics or key factors associated with good teamwork can be categorized and presented in a standard three-component model.

What: Common Goals and Objectives

The "what" gives the team its purpose and legitimacy. It describes what the team has to do, what must it achieve:

- The common goal has to be agreed upon and accepted by all. It should be in line with the organizational mission and agree with other stakeholders and partners.
- Individual objectives develop out of this common goal. They are allocated fairly according to specific technical ability, skills, competencies, and capacity of each of the members. They should also take into consideration, where possible, individual style and preferences.

Figure 5.1

Three-Component Model for Describing Effective Teamwork

Who: People

This is concerned with the individual profile of each team member and how they are able to contribute. For optimal performance, teams must:

- Respect individual differences, cultures, preferential work styles
- Be aware of and put to use people's potential. There are many general activities that need to be accomplished in a team, above and beyond the individual technical contributions. It is impor-

tant for the team to know who are the accomplished negotiators, report writers, counselors, organizers, budget handlers, etc.

- Be empowered to achieve within their respective roles and as representatives of the team. Appropriate autonomy must be permitted and encouraged if the team is to operate optimally
- Have a leader skilled in adopting appropriate leadership style
- Last but certainly not least, pay attention to informal relationships. How will it celebrate success, how will it commiserate, how will it maintain energy and enthusiasm, how will it deal with stress?

How: Processes

These describe "how" the team will operate and describe how each member will contribute and participate. They need to include agreed upon procedures for:

Participation. How they will communicate with one another, with the team leader, with other teams and with external partners? How they will share information, status updates, and changing intelligence? How they will provide feedback to line managers, to external agencies as well as to one another?

Decision-making. There are different methods of decision-making, some are more appropriate than others. A key factor in the effective working of mature teams of professionals is that they have input into decision-making. This is referred to as participative decision-making (discussed below). This doesn't necessarily mean that everyone gets to make the decision, but that everyone's opinion is heard before the decision is made.

Contribution and performance. The team should agree upon the level of quality that they all aspire to meet. It is also valuable to make explicit and agree on the values and competencies that describe the way the team will operate. How will it deal with strong and weak personalities?

Progress. How will achievement be monitored and evaluated? How will your progress be measured?

FEEDBACK

It might be assumed that once standard operating behaviors have been established, team members will be able to moderate their behavior to match the agreed culture. Behavioral flexibility involves both the motivation and the ability to adapt. Inextricably linked with success in teamwork is the assumption that individuals are agreeable to change and that change involves learning new skills. Clear operating behaviors, and an atmosphere that encourages discussion and sharing of expectations, are necessary for members to be able to give and take timely, honest, and constructive feedback. To be most effective, feedback should be:

- **Ongoing,** so that it is a regular and natural part of the working style
- **Specific,** so that detailed examples are given of what happened and the impact it had. It's not enough to say, "Good job." You need to explain why you felt it was a good job, so that the person knows what to continue doing
- **Immediate,** so that the person relates the feedback directly to the behavior or incident
- **Both positive and negative,** so that feedback isn't associated with being reprimanded
- **Two-way,** so that it is legitimate and accepted that all members of the team, including the team leader, are open to feedback
- **Work related,** and directed at the behavior and not at the person. Always think about what the person did or said that you are responding to, rather than what you think the person is
- **Helpful and constructive,** so that the intention of your feedback is to help the person improve the behavior so they perform better, more effectively, more efficiently, or more diplomatically next time.
- **Given privately,** in most situations. Allow the person the opportunity to reflect or respond and to save face. People are generally less likely to accept feedback if they feel threatened, challenged, or humiliated.

Feedback can be given one to one, and can also be engineered into the processes to be solicited from the team as a whole. The following set of questions has been used by teams to gauge their satisfaction of the teamwork and of each individual's contribution. As with generating operating behaviors, it is helpful to have team members first reflect and respond to these questions independently and discuss them afterwards as team. Some or all of the questions can be used formally or informally to discuss the team's progress and performance.

Individual and Team Assessment

1. In what ways are you happy with the team's achievement? Why?
2. In what ways did the results meet your expectation? Why?
3. Did everyone contribute to the task? Who did not? How would the result have been improved with this contribution?
4. Was everyone's contribution sought?
5. How would you describe your contribution?
6. In future joint activities, would you want to modify your behavior? In what way?
7. Who led the process?
8. Was this a unanimous decision?
9. Was everyone happy with this decision?
10. In what ways was the leadership successful?
11. Did you have all necessary information? Whose input might have contributed to the success?
12. During meetings, did any members of the team talk more than any others?
13. How would you describe this "talk"? Be precise; was it informative, helpful, persuasive, assertive, unhelpful?
14. Did this influence the outcome of the team? How could you engineer more balanced input?
15. If you were an outside consultant, what advice would you give your team?

Based on this discussion, the team might revisit their operating behaviors and question their relevance. They might revise the behaviors to respond to the question: What are the optimum conditions and team dynamics essential for the success of our team?

A word of caution about feedback in emergency situations. People are often in a highly charged emotional state in the early phases of an emergency. They may be sleep deprived and stressed. In such situations, feedback will not be welcome and will frequently be taken as negative criticism. In the case of volunteers, feedback perceived in this way can reduce the relief workforce. Immediate feedback is difficult to give and more difficult to take in crisis situations. This is another reason for establishing standard operating behaviors or agreeing to common language to describe behaviors. The personal insult can be reduced when the person's behavior is being compared to standards already accepted. Another consideration is that feedback given to relief workers must also be aligned with the culture and values of the organization.

THE ROLE OF THE TEAM LEADER

The role of the team leader is to help the team progress through the stages of "forming" through to "performing," with the minimum of time spent in "storming" and the most efficient processes to assure the "norming" of the team. He or she achieves this by helping the team to clarify the key points of the team work model. Most teams will identify good leadership as a key criterion for success; however, in mature teams, it is acceptable for a person other than the team leader to take on some of the roles such as coaching and conflict resolution, if that person has superior skills in this area, the team accepts their role, and the "official" team leader is comfortable with that situation. This will not be an easy role for many relief team leaders to accept. Many of them are much more comfortable dealing with the analytical, practical, rational, and pragmatic issues of the situation. "Technical talk is specially comforting because it gives a feeling of solidity when all else is sliding into death."[13]

But the team can not be allowed to slide into death. And it is the role of the team leader to ensure that the team forms strongly enough to be able to withstand the stresses that it inevitably will be called on to deal with. The team leader can help the team through the forming and storming stages by helping clarify the various components of teamwork: the "who," the "what," and the "how." The team leader needs to:

- Get to know the individual members of the team, their strengths and their preferred style of working, and also to assure that team members get to know one another. The team leader must understand people's strengths and limitations. He or she needs to listen to and communicate with people in order to recognize how far they can be pushed and when they are approaching their danger zone.
- Be available and responsive to people's problems and be ready to counsel. He or she also needs to recognize the gaps and overlaps in work preferences, ensuring team balance and identifying opportunities for individual growth.
- Help encourage respect and trust among the team.
- Ensure understanding of the team's purpose and goal, and help the team to interpret the goals into achievable targets while encouraging them to reach their potential. Oversee the allocation of work to ensure achievement of the task and set examples for high quality achievements, both in task and relationships.
- Help the team to establish the processes that will permit them to communicate effectively, share ideas, make decisions, and deal with individuals who undermine the effectiveness of the team.

Leadership Styles

How, when, and with whom they use these skills is another part of the mosaic of team leadership. Based on experience, most managers express, and experts agree, that there are different leadership styles appropriate to different situations and different people. The most effective leaders exhibit a degree of flexibility that enables them to adapt their behavior to the changing and contradictory demands made on them. This ability is not evident or easily achieved by all managers. Take, for example, the East

European surgeon who could not be shifted from his position that the team leader held an authoritarian position that was not to be questioned. It was his job, he determined, to make the decisions for the team. He claimed that without such clear hierarchical leadership, anarchy would result. Of course he has a point, from the perspective of his profession (and we might even assume his cultural background). I'm sure most of us would agree that we would prefer the surgical team not to be debating and suggesting alternative interventions in the midst of a procedure, especially on our own person. There are times when undisputed leadership, and authoritarian control and command, are appropriate and necessary.

But consider the following example of a former military colleague, who recalled that as a commander of a patrol boat on the rivers of Vietnam, the only time he resorted to command and control leadership was when his ship was under fire, or in the vicinity of snipers. In those situations he did not expect it to be questioned or debated. Another trainer colleague, formerly of the Marine Corps of Engineers, admitted to numerous situations in which other members of his platoon were more qualified to lead than he himself. His role was to delegate leadership to the right person at the appropriate time.

I have witnessed teams both in training scenarios and in the field pushed to high levels of success by a driven, controlling leader. While the teams might initially express pride at their accomplishments, they also express reluctance, even fear, of being a permanent member of this individual's team. The new humanitarian worker is an independent, highly qualified, intelligent individual. In some cases, humanitarian workers will defer to a well-known and respected team leader, accepting a more authoritarian control. However, for the most part, uniquely task-focused team leaders who strive for immediate results at the expense of ignoring the emotional climate of the team do so at the risk of eventual burn out, disillusionment, and even break down of the team. This situation occurs even in short-term, transitory missions. Three weeks can be purgatory if the team spirit and environment is particularly unhealthy. The team then may go through a final, terminal stage of "mourning."

An extremely useful model for understanding and developing flexible leadership behavior is the Hersey and Blanchard Situational Leadership model.[14] In determining the best style to fit in any situation, there are four factors that must be taken into consideration:

- The leader: his or her preferred style of operating and personal characteristics
- The team: their preferred working, communication, and relationship styles
- The task: its objectives and constraints and parameters, technologies available
- The environment: the organizational values and beliefs, the organizational structure and culture, the external factors, the host country culture, political, economical, etc.

A real strength in leading emergency teams is to be able to match leadership behavior appropriately to the task and the vastly different people involved.

Situational Management or "Best Fit" Approach. Two of the fundamental distinctions used to describe managerial style are preferences for attention to people and relations, and attention to the task. And we've seen above that some people have preferences for behavior that is more task-oriented and others that are more people-oriented.

Task behavior is the extent to which leaders are likely to organize and define team members' roles, and to explain what activities each is to do and when, where, and how the tasks are to be accomplished. Task behavior is characterized by endeavoring to establish well-defined patterns of organization, channels of communication, and ways of getting jobs accomplished.

Relationship behavior is the extent to which leaders are likely to maintain personal relationships between themselves and members of the team by opening up channels of communication, providing socio-emotional support, active listening, "psychological stroking," and through facilitating behavior.

Leadership in this model involves varying combinations of attention to the task and relationship. Each quadrant in the model above describes a different leadership style.

High task, low relationship is associated with a "telling" communication and management style. The team leader gives specific instructions and closely supervises performance.

High task, high relationship is associated with a "selling" communication style in which the team leader explains decisions and provides an opportunity for clarification.

High relationship, low task is associated with a "participating"

Figure 5.2

The Hersey and Blanchard Situational Leadership Model

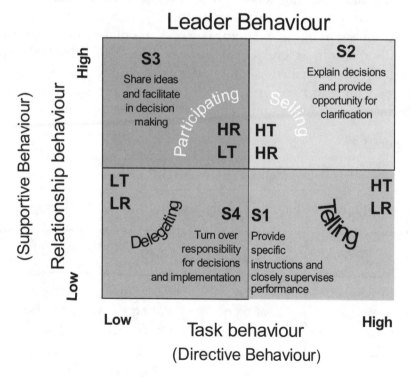

communication and management style in which the team leader shares ideas and encourages participation in decision-making.

Low relationship, low task is associated with a "delegating" style in which the team leader turns over responsibility for decisions and implementation to the team member.

The major factor in choosing the appropriate style is the "readiness level" of the team member. Readiness is determined or defined by the individual's ability to perform the task in terms of their capacity and previous experience (skill), and by the individual's perceived motivation for the task defined by their self-confidence and willingness to accept responsibility (will).

The distinctions are laid out on the model below, where it is clear that leadership styles S1, S2, S3, and S4 from Figure 5.2 are matched to the readiness levels of the team member as identified as R1, R2, R3, and R4.

Occasionally, team leaders in both relief and development situations only half jokingly assert that level 4 people should be the only ones sent out to the field. The reality is that no one is consistently at readiness level 4 in all situations. Even an individual who is generally described as a R4 performer will find him or herself faced with tasks never before performed and for which they have reduced confidence about their own abilities. It's important to

Figure 5.3

Follower Readiness

High	Moderate		Low
R4	R3	R2	R1
Able and Willing or Confident	Able but Unwilling or Insecure	Unable but Willing or Confident	Unable and Unwilling or Insecure

Follower Directed   **Leader Directed**

understand that the readiness label is not associated to the individual, but to their ability to perform a given task in a given situation.

The effectiveness of a leadership style is contingent on the situation in which it is used. And the style that a team leader adopts with a person will change according to the individual and circumstances. The style adopted must also be culturally sensitive. What works in Scandinavia may look weak and ineffective in Mexico.

If we go back to our Eastern European surgeon, one could assume that he would be an effective leader of a surgical relief unit where clear decisions and triage would mean life or death for victims. Without doubt, he would make valuable contributions in this role. However, he may not experience the same success in a more general leadership role. He would face difficulties in embracing the empowerment of his team or of sharing leadership. There are many disaster managers who are literally in their element in an emergency situation, and operate during the initial stages as well as you could expect anyone to operate. They are certainly the people I would want to have in charge if I were involved. But keep these people around too long and their style of management is neither appropriate nor appreciated by the teams on the ground. Blanchard calls these people "slot in managers."[15] Their style of directive management is ideal when people need strong leadership, but once you have competent people in place, or the emergency situation has subsided, the lack of flexibility in this type of leader can be abrasive, stifling, and demotivating. Additionally, to ask those managers to adopt a different style would be counterproductive. An organization would do best to use them in environments and for tasks that fit their style.

This is not necessarily a problem for the leadership of relief teams as long as:

1. The individual team leaders show mature self-awareness of their preferred style and the impact it will likely have on the team dynamics and team leadership
2. The managers concerned have some behaviorable flexibility and are able to adapt their leadership style to differing circumstances and people, or

3. Their organizations recognize their specific and limited skills and deploy them in appropriate situations for a specific amount of time, as in the Blanchard "Slot in Manager" concept

Figure 5.4 presents some of the external context factors that humanitarian workers recognize as relevant to identifying the contingencies and successful adoption of the situational model.

Communication Skills for Team and Team Leader. Essential to the ability of team leaders to successfully adopt a "best fit" approach to leadership is good communication skills. The most important of these is the ability to listen well, that is, to listen honestly, respectfully, and effectively. This means not thinking of other

Figure 5.4

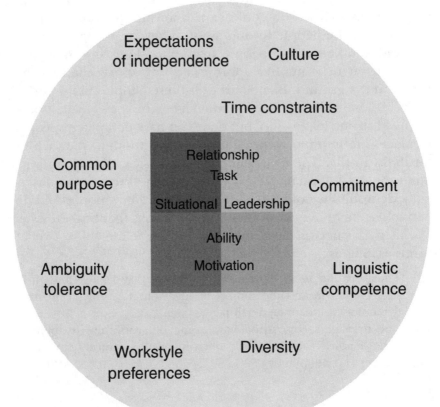

things at the same time, or handling other tasks (shuffling papers or checking your e-mail), or developing a rebuttal, or simply waiting for your turn to speak. The presupposition to good listening skills is that the listener is wise enough to recognize that there is value in what others have to say, and has the requisite skills involved in effectively doing so. The most eloquent presentation of listening I have ever seen is that encompassed in the Chinese pictograph meaning to listen. Students of communication skills could save themselves a semester's study by putting into practice the Chinese understanding of listening.

However, since knowing isn't doing, the art of listening, or "active listening" popularized by Carl Rodgers, fortunately can be deconstructed to a set of skills that can be learned by daily practice. People who want to be effective leaders and competent managers must begin practicing these skills every day. Listening to others and to one's self is part of the building blocks of self-discipline.[16]

- Listen for the content of the message. Make an effort to hear precisely what is being said.
- Listen for the feelings of the speaker. Try to perceive the speaker's feelings about what is being said through the way the message is delivered.

Figure 5.5

Ears
We have two ears and one mouth. We should spend twice as much time listening than talking

King
We should treat the speaker royally, with respect and honour.

Eyes
We have two eyes and should "see" what we hear by paying attention to facial expressions and other non-verbal signals.

Undivided attention
We should give the person our complete attention, putting aside all other distractions.

Heart
We should listen for emotion and "feel" what the person is saying.

- Respond to the feelings of the speaker. Demonstrate to the speaker that you recognize and understand the feelings being expressed.
- Note the speaker's cues, both verbal and non-verbal. Attempt to identify mixed messages and contradicting messages the speaker may be expressing.
- Reflect back to the speaker what you think you are hearing. Re-state to the speaker in your own words what you think the speaker said. Allow the speaker to respond to further clarify the message being sent.

The second most important skill for collaborative and cooperative leadership is that of being able to ask questions. Good leadership is the art of asking questions, not the science of providing answers. Effective leaders able to facilitate the leadership described here must have an arsenal of questioning techniques as part of their repertoire of skills. They must know the difference between different types of questions, and employ them judiciously, appropriately, and effectively.

Different types of questions:

- **Closed questions:** those that typically elicit a "Yes" or "No" response. For example, "Did it rain yesterday?" or requests a specific piece of information, "What time did it stop raining?"
- **Open questions:** those that open the door to information gathering and opinion. For example, "What happened?" "How does it work?" "How should we solve this?"
- **Probing questions:** different types of questions that can be used to probe into a topic deeper. They allow you to focus on learning more about specifics, such as people ("Who exactly was present at the meeting?"), or actions ("What exactly was done then?"), or locations ("Where precisely did the second aftershock occur?").
- **Leading questions:** like all techniques of communication, questioning can be used honestly or manipulatively. Leading questions can help a person to move in a particular direction; that is, away from a problem toward a solution ("Wouldn't it be good if we could start thinking about how to solve this now?"). But this can lead to presumption ("Isn't it when you're in a stressful situation that you miss details?").

The value of skillful questioning cannot be overestimated for the effective leader in adopting an inclusive and cooperative model of leadership. Without doubt, it's a complex balance of many variables. It requires a lot of discretion on the part of the team leader to be sufficiently flexible to meet the needs of the team and each of its members. The rewards, however, are huge when the team leader and the team get it right. And the potential for motivating teams beyond what they themselves thought possible is an exhilarating challenge.

Motivation of Individuals. Like all the topics discussed in this chapter, motivation is an extremely complex field in which years of research and volumes of texts[17] have been written. What is presented below is a kernel of certain considered fundamentals and the paradoxes that they present the team leader.

Theories of motivation suggest that most of us are continually seeking to increase our self-esteem and to enhance the concept we have of ourselves. We do this by searching for psychological success, which we experience if:

- We set a challenging goal for ourselves.
- We determine our own methods of achieving that goal.
- The goal is relevant to our self-concept.
- We achieve the goal.

For the leader of a team, it is enough to remember these key points about the motivation of individuals:

People like targets. Without something to aim for, work is just a job. The targets that people aim for should be ones that they themselves have accepted and, therefore, own as theirs. Wherever possible, the targets should be the sort that people can see for themselves, so they are not dependent on the views of others. Targets should be relatively short-term, less than six months, or else they are too far off to be real.

People like to feel good. When people feel good about themselves, they work better. People feel good when they succeed; that is, they meet their targets and are praised by people they respect.

It is easier to raise someone's standards by raising their targets and praising achievement than by criticizing them for their faults.

People are different. Different people want different things out of their lives and their work. Try to discover what people intrinsically believe is their relationship with the organization (their psychological contract) if you can; it may not be what you think it is.

As a team leader this leaves you with a set of paradoxes:

The motivation of the team cannot be ignored. It must be a high priority for both the team leader and the team members themselves. In disaster relief situations particularly, all team members must do what they can to encourage a positive climate in the team and to reduce the negative stress to a minimum. They must all, specifically the team leader, be aware of any changes in behavior among team members that might be indicative of stress,[18] and be prepared to deal with that either themselves or by seeking professional assistance.

Decision-Making. Two major factors that contribute to poor decision-making in crisis conditions are "groupthink" and the personality type of the decision-maker in response to the stress. Groupthink[19] is defined as being characterized by high cohesiveness and concurrence seeking and a striving for unanimity that overrides motivations to realistically appraise alternative courses of action. These in-group pressures lead to a deterioration of mental efficiency, reality testing, and normal judgment.

Contributing factors to groupthink include:

1. Internal or organizational
   —insulation of the group
   —lack of tradition of impartial management
   —lack of norms for procedures
   —homogeneity of members
2. External or situational
   —high stress from outside threats
   —low hope of solutions better than the leader's

Table 5.2

▪ Don't tell people what to aim for; it's better if they work out their goals for themselves.	▪ Do emphasize that they must work out some precise goals against which they can measure success or progress.
▪ Don't shout at people who make mistakes; paradoxically, it will make them try less hard.	▪ Do insist that they learn from their mistakes and they set new goals for next time; forgive the sinner but condemn the sin.
▪ Don't assume that everyone is like you; they may be there for quite other reasons.	▪ Do encourage people to be explicit about their psychological contract, what they expect to give and get from their work.
▪ Don't give only negative feedback; it either will diminish people's self-concept or their view of you.	▪ Do find every excuse to praise work well done; stroking is good for the ego, and a good ego makes a good contract.
▪ Don't trade promises for good work; it creates only dependent pigeons, and you will get locked into never-ending promises.	▪ Do make sure that people know when their work is good; create obvious signs of success/progress that people can read for themselves.

—fear to differ with the leader

—low self-esteem temporarily induced by recent failures, excessive difficulties in current decision-making, moral dilemmas, alternatives that violate ethical standards.

Factors affecting or characterizing impaired decision-making in crisis include:

- Short termism and lack of vision
- Over-desire for immediate action
- Procrastination as a result of search for more information
- Rigid cognitive preferences and reluctance for new information
- Low tolerance for ambiguity and uncertainty
- Low tolerance for complexity and deliberate reduction of the range of options
- Bias toward favorable factors, and rejection of opposing factors
- Over-reliance on past actions and decisions
- A tendency to seek familiar patterns, mental models, and scripts
- Diminished creativity
- Reduction of opposing views to personal opinions
- Lack of self-awareness and psychological motivations

It is clear that many of the factors above are symptomatic of the authoritarian and controlling leadership style.

The second factor that contributes to poor decision-making in crisis conditions is the personality style of the team leader or decision-maker.[20] Three leader personality types based on cognitive affective and interpersonal differences are frequently found in the ranks of leaders: the "compulsive personality," the "narcissistic personality," and the "paranoid personality." Paranoid personalities are found much less frequently, but extreme reactions of paranoid individuals under stress can have catastrophic consequences. It is not suggested that the humanitarian sector is littered with individuals who might be professionally identified as having serious personality disorders. Indeed, in many situations it is difficult to identify specific personality styles because healthy individuals have a capacity to call upon a broad array of psychological coping mechanisms or ego defenses rather than be limited to such a narrow defense as in the case of personality disorder. It's relatively easy to see in the descriptions below, personality styles that we have all seen and may even recognize in ourselves. Each type has a characteristic cognitive style that influences the quality of decision-making in crisis when exaggerated coping mechanisms are sometimes mobilized. Unfortunately for many in the humanitarian world, crisis becomes a way of life for even the most mundane of actions and activities. That level of crisis begins to justify the unacceptable leadership behavior described below.

The Compulsive Personality. Common in successful leaders. The core features of this type are organizational ability, attention to detail, and emphasis on rational process. They show a dominance of thinking over feeling and a need to keep strong feelings—such as anxiety and anger—under control. Crises, however, do not easily lend themselves to such orderly thought processes, and the compulsive leaders' logical preoccupation with detail may lead to their inability to see the "big picture" and nudge them toward indecisiveness. Under pressure to decide with incomplete information, and an inordinate fear of making a mistake, the compulsive decision-maker can become paralyzed and racked with doubt. Team members become providers of information but are excluded from the decision-making process. This paralysis can be avoided if there is a standard operating procedure for which the situation might fit, but will result in serious consequences when a unique situation is forced into a type it does not fit.

The Narcissistic Personality. Post claims that the upper levels of government and industry would be depleted if they were stripped of individuals with narcissistic personality features. While full-blown narcissistic characteristics could not sustain effective leadership positions, individuals with significant personality traits can, under pressure, resemble full-blown personality disorder. Narcissistic individuals are characterized by extreme self-centeredness, egocentricity, and self-absorption. They have a need for constant reassurance, self worth, and admiration. They are insensitive to the needs of others and have a tendency to exploit. They expect others to do what they want while regularly ignoring their rights and needs. Primary loyalty is for themselves, and they surround themselves with people who are uncritical and who protect them from discontent and criticism. In this way, the leader can be totally out of touch with reality. The narcissist will say things for effect, which will not necessarily reflect core beliefs. As a result, he may change judgments rapidly and reverse positions without qualm of conscience. Narcissists tend to overestimate the probability of success and this over-optimism can contribute to groupthink. They also attempt to use situations to enhance or protect their own reputation.

The Paranoid Personality. The essential feature of paranoid personality is pervasive and long-standing suspiciousness and mistrust of people. The paranoid is always expecting plots and enemies. This derives in part for the exaggerated need for autonomy. Paranoids are hypersensitive and easily slighted; they continually search for clues to confirm their suspicions and reject evidence to the contrary. The paranoid has predetermined conclusions. They are unwilling to compromise and fail to see the total context of a situation. They become hostile, defensive, and stubborn and any attempt to reassure them will likely result in anger. People tread lightly and carefully around the paranoid, walking on the proverbial eggshells. The psychologically healthy paranoid is able to abandon suspicions when confronted with new facts.

It is important to note that stress does not necessarily adversely affect performance, and that it is rare to come across people suffering from full-blown psychological personality disorder. But research shows that high stress can push individuals with these tendencies toward behavior that is difficult to distinguish at times from the full-blown case. This seems to be true particularly the case in people who are experiencing a situation for the first time.[21]

Both individuals and teams need to predetermine how they will cope with stress and how they will handle decision-making. Some people think they are coping well when they are actually just getting used to stress. Managing existing stress is not the same as dealing with the causes. Some humanitarian workers choose denial, others become workaholics; but this is frequently a preoccupation with the activity of work rather than the results. And then there are the typical and well-known, well-used short-term solutions like caffeine, cigarettes, alcohol, tranquilizers, and the wide range of prescription and nonprescription drugs.

Methods of Decision-Making.[22] Although current fashion occasionally underscores one or another of these approaches, there is no right or wrong way to decide an issue. The important thing is that the team decides in advance what decision-making method will be used. There should be no surprises. If members are apprised of the process, decision making can be a success. Even autocratic methods require the consent and blessing of all. Table 5.3 is a brief description of decision-making methods and the advantages and disadvantages of their use.

CONCLUSION

I hope the point has been made that there are serious consequences to poor teamwork and interpersonal relations in humanitarian relief work. Dysfunctional teams and below-optimum team relations put people, resources, and the success of the operation at risk. In terms of cost-effectiveness, organizations have to question the true impact of sub-optimal teamwork, both on the individual humanitarian worker and the overall success of an operation or program. The debate about appropriate team leadership style has to be reviewed in the light of the changing face of the humanitarian worker, the increasingly complex environment in which relief operations are staged, the expectations of the changing profile of the beneficiary, and the more equitable rela-

Table 5.3

CONSENSUS

Everyone airs their opinions. Discussion continues till you get an outcome. Compromise must be used so that everyone agrees with and commits to the outcome.

Advantages	Disadvantages
• Innovative, creative, high-quality decision;	• Takes a lot of time and psychological energy;
• Elicits commitment to implement;	• Time pressure must be minimal;
• Uses resources of all members;	• Can't respond to emergencies.
• Enhances future decision-making;	
• Useful for serious, important complex decisions.	

MAJORITY

Democracy in action. Team votes, majority wins.

Advantages	Disadvantages
• Simple;	• Often leaves alienated minority;
• Used when time is limited;	• Time bomb for future team effectiveness;
• When decision is not so important, or when 100% commitment is not essential;	• Important minority talents can be ignored;
• Closes discussion on issues not too important for the team.	• Commitment to decision is only partial;
	• Benefits of full team interaction may be lost.

MINORITY

Usually takes the form of a subcommittee that makes recommendations for action.

Advantages	Disadvantages
• Used when everyone cannot get together;	• Does not use all team talents;

Table 5.3 (continued)

• When time is an issue;	• Does not build broad commitment;
• When only a few members have expertise or experience;	• Unresolved conflict and controversy may damage future team effectiveness;
• When not every member needs to have 100% commitment.	• Not much benefit from team interaction.

AVERAGING

The epitome of compromise—haggle, bargain, cajole, and negotiate an intentional middle position. Letting members with the greatest expertise make the decision is almost always better than a group average.

Advantages	Disadvantages
• Extreme positions cancel each other out;	• Usually no one is happy with the result except the moderates.
• Better than "authority rule without discussion."	

EXPERT

Find or hire experts; listen to what they say and follow their recommendations.

Advantages	Disadvantages
• Useful when one person is obviously more superior than other members of the team;	• Determining the "expert";
	• Over-reliance on an individual;
• Useful when others accept expert and no need to bring others on board.	• Resentment or disagreement may result in sabotage and deterioration of team effectiveness;
	• Knowledge and skills of other team members are not used.

Table 5.3   (continued)

AUTHORITY RULE WITHOUT DISCUSSION

No room for discussion; predetermined decisions are handed down from higher authority.

Advantages	Disadvantages
• Applies more to administrative needs;	• One person cannot be the authority for everything;
• Useful for simple, routine decisions;	
• When team members lack the skills or information;	• Advantages of team interaction are lost;
• When the team members expect the team leader to make decisions (in some cultures).	• Zero team commitment on meaningful issues;
	• May result in sabotage, resistance, and deterioration of team effectiveness;
	• Resources of rest of team are unused.

AUTHORITY RULE WITH DISCUSSION

Known as Participative Decision-Making. Contrary to some understanding, does not involve abdication of responsibility.

Advantages	Disadvantages
• Gains commitment from all team members;	• Requires good communication skills on the part of all team members;
• Develops lively discussion on issues employing skills and knowledge of all team members;	• Requires a leader willing to make decisions.
• Is clear on who is ultimately accountable for the decision of the team.	

tionships expected of the humanitarian organizations by the host communities and governments.

When a team gets this challenge right they can survive almost any situation, regardless of the conditions or even the sensitive security in which they operate. The results of research in disasters are that many things take time to go wrong. Team leaders have the opportunity to make sure that the team does not go wrong and that it is sufficiently healthy and ready to cope with the onslaught of challenges it must face. The challenges should be external to the team, and they can meet them in cooperation and with collaboration.

Mature leaders must recognize that they do not have the expertise in all circumstances, and that the best they can do for the outcome and for the team itself is to have confidence in the team members and their ability to share the leadership of the team. Gone are the days of the omnipotent manager—if ever there was such a beast. Humanitarian organizations in development and capacity building struggle with implementing change in organizations that are petrified by hierarchical and authoritative structures where young, able members of the societies are prevented from rising because of the fear of competition from senior leaders. Yet how often do international relief groups emulate those same conditions as models? If we are espousing empowerment, sharing leadership, collaboration, and inclusivity, we must model these behaviors in our own leadership. We must also find ways of breaking the glass ceiling for local staff in contributing to humanitarian work, where too often the fact of being the expat delegate brings with it assumptions of hierarchy and power.

Robert Maddux[23] identifies "Ten Unforgivable Mistakes" for the organization and the team leader in creating the team:

1. Failure to develop and maintain basic management and leadership skills
2. Permitting poor employee selection and techniques
3. Failure to discuss expectations or establish goals that have been mutually set
4. Inattention to the training and development needs of team leaders

5. Failure to advocate, support, and nurture team-building activities

6. Preventing the involvement of team members in any activity where they could make a contribution

7. Failure to provide and receive feedback from the team

8. Allowing conflict and competition to get out of control, or trying to eliminate it altogether

9. Depending on someone else to recognize and reward the team and its members

10. Failure to send players who have not responded to coaching back to the B team

For effective and successful teamwork in relief operations, humanitarian organizations and individuals must ensure that they make none of these mistakes.

Part 3

Among the most important basics in humanitarian missions are the rules of law, of engagement, and of the rights of the victims. International humanitarian law has been codified to protect people in conflict as well as in peace. Refugees, the internally displaced, and especially the most vulnerable, women and children, have fundamental rights that are not negotiable by the powerful over the weak.

The rules of law, international conventions, and codes of conduct are considered by the highly respected legal scholar, Michel Veuthey. As help arrives in a conflict situation, various players compete, sometimes with the best of intentions, in organizing and delivering aid. H. Roy Williams, the President of the Center for Humanitarian Cooperation and former head of the U.S. Office of Foreign Disaster Relief, considers how the multiple nongovernmental organizations (NGOs) that respond to a humanitarian crisis relate to host governments, donors, international organizations, local NGOs, military, and press, as well as to the afflicted population.

6

Humanitarian Ethical and Legal Standards

Michel Veuthey

IN A GLOBALIZED and, nevertheless, chaotic world, there is a renewed need for ethical and legal standards,[1] especially regarding the fundamental guarantees of human dignity in today's armed conflicts.

International instruments of human rights and of international humanitarian law are not the only sources providing these fundamental guarantees.[2] International law is only one of the many sources of humanitarian standards. Legal mechanisms alone are insufficient to provide for an effective protection of fundamental human values.

There are many different approaches (such as spiritual, political, legal, and organizational) to the promotion of respect for fundamental human values in today's conflicts. Historical considerations, including spiritual and ethnic research,[3] could also be among the remedies for today's impasses.

We shall deal with the topic of "Humanitarian Ethical and Legal Standards" along the following lines:

1. Origins and Development
   —Spiritual Origin of Humanitarian Standards
   —Proliferation and Universality of Standards
   —Multiplication of Legal Mechanisms
2. Today's Impasse
   —Denial of Respect (Human Dignity)
   —Denial of Justice
   —Denial of Forgiveness and Reconciliation

3. Toward a Renaissance of Fundamental Humanitarian Values
   —Research Roots
   —Re-anchor in All Civilizations
   —Reaffirm Universality of Fundamental Values
   —Reinforce Existing Mechanisms
   —Reinvent Remedies
   —Re-activate the Network of Humanity
   —Rebuild Public Conscience

Origins and Development

Spiritual Origin of Humanitarian Standards

Limiting Violence in War in Order to Ensure the Survival of the Group.
Each civilization has formed islands of humanity inside which
certain rules limited violence by imposing restraints on the use
of force and an obligation of solidarity toward victims.

These religion-based rules were of two types:

1. A **taboo** by which it was forbidden to attack women and
children, to destroy temples or sacred places, to kill priests or
people in religious orders, as well as women, children, and el-
derly people belonging to the group. In the West, the Peace of
God *(Pax Dei)*[4] and the Truce of God *(Treuga Dei)*[5] were such
rules. The *Pax Dei* was a conciliar movement that began in southern France in the late tenth century and spread to most of Western Europe over the following century, surviving in some form
until at least the thirteenth century. It combined lay and ecclesi-
astical legislation regulating warfare and establishing a social
peace in the Middle Ages. By the 1040s, the Truce of God became the center of legislative action and aimed at restricting controlling feuds and private warfare by declaring Thursday through
Sunday days of peace. The Truce led to the emergence of public
institutions for the control of violence. The Catholic Church
tried to mitigate in some way the horrors of warfare in the Second Lateran Council (1139), forbidding the use of crossbow as
"deadly and odious to God." The Third Lateran Church Council

Figure 6.1

(1179) prohibited the enslavement of Christian prisoners of war. Others similar rules can be found in every religion. Some of these rules were more generous in so-called primitive civilizations than in today's international law.

2. The **Golden Rule,** which is found in several civilizations, not only in Judeo-Christian ones, and which can be resumed thus: *So, whatever you wish that men would do to you, do so to them.*[6]

These rules were set to ensure the survival of a group, and forbade behaviors that would have permanently endangered the group[7]. Indigenous people of all continents have aimed to avoid excesses that would turn conflicts into collective suicides. Customs of Melanesians,[8] Inuit,[9] and Nilotic peoples;[10] Buddhism,[11] Hinduism,[12] Taoism,[13] Confucianism,[14] and Bushido[15] in Asia; Judaism,[16] Christianity,[17] and Islam[18] in the Middle East; customary humanitarian law in Africa;[19] and mutual restrictions imposed by chivalry and military honor[20] in Europe contain examples of rules of "Life-Affirmative Societies," in which the main emphasis of ideals, customs, and institutions is the preservation and growth of life in all its forms.[21]

All these rules were aimed at precluding excesses that would turn clashes into anarchy and hence make peace more difficult to achieve. Thus, in article 6 of his *Perpetual Peace,* Kant wrote: "No State shall, during war, permit such acts of hostility which would make mutual confidence in the subsequent peace impossible."[22]

These barriers to violence and the notion of responsibility for others were valid, for the most part, only inside the group. Only on rare occasions were bridges allowed to be built between those islands of humanity, sometimes through individual acts of generosity.

Recognizing the Human Dignity of Every Human Being. Francisco de Vitoria (1480–1546), a member of the Dominican Order, is often considered the founder of Western international law. He believed in *jus gentium,* a universally valid "law of nations" established on the basis of natural law. Living at the time of the conquest of the Americas, Vitoria developed his teaching partly in the context of his discussions on the appropriate treatment of the native peoples of the New World.

Supported by Vitoria, Bartholomew de Las Casas (1474–1566) devoted himself to the defense of the Indians, against the ruthless exploitation and ferocious cruelty that they suffered under the Spanish conquerors.[23]

Building Bridges Among Civilizations. St. Francis of Assisi tried to open a dialogue between Christians and Muslims in 1219.[24] All of the world's great religious traditions today emphasize the intrinsic value of each individual human life, and in recent decades, religious communities have recognized their vital role in expressing moral outrage and taking actions to curb the types of inhumanity that people have, time and again, inflicted upon one another over the last century. Religious communities are, without question, the largest and best-organized civil institutions in the world today, claiming the allegiance of billions of believers and bridging the divides of race, class, and nationality.[25]

In the year 2000, the new millennium afforded an opportunity to bring to the United Nations a Millennium World Peace Summit of Religious and Spiritual Leaders, which sought to coordinate religious and spiritual leadership as a driving force for building tolerance, fostering peace, and encouraging interreligious dialogue among all regions of the world.[26]

2001 was proclaimed by the United Nations as "Year of Dialogue Among Civilizations." After the September 11 attacks, the United Nations Secretary-General stressed the need to reaffirm the rule of law, on the international as well as the national levels. Kofi Annan also denied the inevitability of a "clash of civilizations," and reasserted "our common humanity and the values that we share."[27] His report to the General Assembly[28] and the book *Crossing the Divide,* as well as the "Salzburg reflections"[29] and the "Declaration of Athens" ("The heritage of ancient civilizations: Implications for the modern world")[30] should be only the beginning of a much-needed dialogue based on equality and mutual respect.

Proliferation and Universality of Standards

International Humanitarian Law (IHL). International humanitarian law is usually defined as the set of principles and rules restricting the use of violence in armed conflicts, both to spare the persons not (or no longer) directly engaged in hostilities (wounded, sick, and shipwrecked members of the armed forces, prisoners of war, and civilians), and to limit the use of methods and means of warfare that causes superfluous injury (or excessive suffering, as in the case of *dumdum bullets* or with gas warfare[31]), or severe damage to the natural environment, or betrayal of an adversary's confidence in agreed-upon obligations ("perfidy").

The principle of the limitation of armed violence is reflected, in contemporary written law, in the Saint Petersburg Declaration of 1868,[32] as well as in Article 22 of the Hague Regulations of 1907,[33] which stipulates that: "The right of belligerents to adopt means of injuring the enemy is not unlimited." This text is taken up again, slightly reworded, in paragraph 1 of Article 35 ("Basic rules") of Protocol 1 of 1977: "In any armed conflict, the right of the Parties to the conflict to choose methods or means of warfare is not unlimited."

The terminology used to refer to international treaties may vary ("humanitarian law,"[34] "international humanitarian law applicable in armed conflicts,"[35] "laws of war,"[36] "law of Geneva,"[37] "Red Cross Conventions," "law of The Hague,"[38] "human rights in armed conflicts"[39]), but all seek the same objective—namely, to limit the use of violence in war.

Contemporary international humanitarian law is the moving balance between two dynamic forces: *the requirements of humanity* and *military necessity*.[40] It is also the sum of tragic real-life experiences that need not be repeated: military wounded and shipwrecked—and the humanitarian personnel taking care of them—must be rescued and respected; prisoners of war must be humanely treated and released at the end of active hostilities; and civilians not be killed nor harmed.

Each stage of the codification of international humanitarian law was the result of a post-war shock wave in public opinion and governments, a collective painful process of learning. These codifications occurred as follows:

- The battle of Solferino (1859)[41] between Austrian and French armies was the impetus for the First Convention, in 1864, protecting military wounded on land
- The naval battle of Tsushima (1905) between Japanese and Russian fleets prompted adjustment of the Convention on war at sea, in 1907, extending protection to military shipwrecked
- World War I brought about the two 1929 Conventions, including much broader protection for prisoners of war
- World War II led to the four 1949 Conventions,[42] an extensive

regulation of the treatment of civilians in occupied territories and internment, and decolonization

- The Vietnam War preceded the two 1977 Additional Protocols,[43] which brought written rules for the protection of civilian persons and objects against hostilities
- A worldwide campaign by governments, United Nations agencies, the Red Cross and Red Crescent Movement, and NGOs in a full partnership that stressed the human suffering and socioeconomic costs caused by anti-personnel mines and resulted on the total ban on anti-personnel landmines signed in Ottawa on December 4, 1997

Universality of International Humanitarian Law. The four 1949 Geneva Conventions are universally ratified. The two Additional Protocols are widely ratified, but still lack ratification by the U.S. and some other countries.

The 1907 Hague Regulations, which establish laws for conducting war on land, are considered part of international customary law since the International Military Tribunal of Nuremberg declared on October 1, 1946, addressing both signatories and non-signatories, that they were declaratory of the laws and customs of war.[44]

Humanitarian law has evolved from a law protecting only certain categories of individuals (from medieval knights to today's prisoners of war) to a set of provisions ensuring fundamental human rights guaranteeing the survival of civilian populations in wartime.

The International Criminal Tribunals for the Former Yugoslavia[45] and for Rwanda[46] broke down the distinction between international and non-international armed conflicts regarding the prosecution of war crimes.[47]

Humanitarian rules and principles are to be respected in all circumstances. This is especially important today, in the case of "collapsed states,"[48] "postmodern wars,"[49] and anarchic conflicts.[50] According to the ICRC's Commentary to the 1949 Conventions: "The words 'in all circumstances' in Common Article 1 of the four 1949 Geneva Conventions refer to all situations in which the Convention has to be applied, and these are defined in Article 2. It is clear, therefore, that the application of the Convention does not depend on whether the conflict is just or unjust. Whether or not it is a war of aggression, prisoners of war belonging to either party are entitled to the protection afforded by the Convention."[51]

The First Geneva Convention of 1864 had only twelve articles. The four 1949 Geneva Conventions and their two Additional Protocols of 1977 count more than four hundred and fifty provisions. One article summarizes international humanitarian law: Common Article 3 of the 1949 Geneva Conventions. (See the Appendixes for the full text of Common Article 3.)

The International Court of Justice (ICJ), in the Nicaragua case, considered Common Article 3 of the 1949 Geneva Conventions as "elementary considerations of humanity" binding all:

> The Court considers that the rules stated in Article 3, which is common to the four Geneva Conventions, applying to armed conflicts of a non-international character, should be applied. The United States is under an obligation to "respect" the Conventions and even to "ensure respect" for them, and thus not to encourage persons or groups engaged in the conflict in Nicaragua to act in violation of the provisions of Article 3. This obligation derives from the general principles of humanitarian law to which the Conventions merely give specific expression.[52]

Human Rights. The Preamble of the United Nations Charter states the determination of Member States "to reaffirm faith in fundamental human rights, in the dignity and worth of the human person, in the equal rights of men and women, and of nations large and small." Article 1, paragraph 3 defines one of the purposes of the UN as: "To achieve international co-operation in solving internal problems of an economic, social, cultural, or humanitarian character, and in promoting and encouraging respect for human rights and for fundamental freedoms for all without distinction as to race, sex, language, or religion." World

Table 6.1   The Law of Geneva

1. Geneva Convention for the Amelioration of the Condition of the Wounded and Sick in Armed Forces in the Field (First Convention of August 12, 1949)
2. Geneva Convention for the Amelioration of the Condition of Wounded, Sick, and Shipwrecked Members of Armed Forces at Sea (Second Convention of August 12, 1949)
3. Geneva Convention Relative to the Treatment of Prisoners of War (Third Convention of August 12, 1949)
4. Geneva Convention Relative to the Protection of Civilian Persons in Time of War (Fourth Convention of August 12, 1949)

Protocol Additional to the Geneva Conventions of August 12, 1949, and Relating to the Protection of Victims of International Armed Conflicts (First Protocol)
Protocol Additional to the Geneva Conventions of August 12, 1949, and Relating to the Protection of Victims of Non-International Armed Conflicts (Second Protocol)

War II and regional conflicts prompted the drafting of the United Nations instruments on human rights, disarmament, prohibition of terrorism and mercenaries, protection of the environment,[53] and of the rights of children.[54]

While instruments of international humanitarian law are normally applicable during armed conflicts, human rights treaties are based on a peacetime approach, yet their scope often overlaps, especially in regard to the fundamental guarantees they embody.

The universality of humanitarian standards can also be seen with human rights instruments:[55]

- The 1948 Universal Declaration of Human Rights (See the Appendixes for the full text of the 1948 Universal Declaration of Human Rights.)
- The 1948 Convention on the Prevention and Punishment of the Crime of Genocide
- Both 1966 Covenants (International Covenant on Civil and Po-

litical Rights and the International Covenant on Economic, Social, and Cultural Rights)
- The 1984 Convention against Torture and Other Cruel, Inhuman, or Degrading Treatment or Punishment
- The 1989 Convention on the Rights of the Child.

The universality[56] and indivisibility[57] of human rights was reaffirmed by the UN International Conference in Tehran in 1968[58] and by the World Conference of Human Rights in Vienna in 1993.[59]

The Advisory Opinion of the ICJ on Reservations to the Convention on the Prevention and Punishment of the Crime of Genocide, of May 28, 1951, confirmed that the prohibition of genocide is part of customary international law.[60]

The following regional instruments complement the UN instruments:

- The 1950 Convention for Protection of Human Rights and Fundamental Freedoms of the Council of Europe, signed in Rome;
- The 1969 Inter-American Convention on Human Rights, San Jose de Costa Rica;
- The 1981 African Charter on Human and Peoples' Rights;
- The Charter of Fundamental Rights of the European Union, signed and proclaimed by the Presidents of the European Parliament, the Council, and the Commission at the European Council meeting in Nice on December 7, 2000.[61]

Two regional instruments prohibit torture:

- The 1985 Inter-American Convention to Prevent and Punish Torture;
- The 1987 European Convention for the Prevention of Torture and Inhuman or Degrading Treatment or Punishment.

In addition to the first two "human rights generations" (civil and political/economic and social), new human rights—a third generation of "Solidarity Human Rights"[62] are under consideration at the United Nations and at regional fora, among which are:

- the right to development,
- the right to a healthy environment,[63]

- the human right to peace,
- the human right to health, and
- the right to food.

The "Declaration on the Right to Development" was adopted by the United Nations General Assembly in 1986.[64] The item has been regularly debated at the General Assembly since then.[65]

The "Human Right to Peace" was hailed by Federico Mayor, Director-General of UNESCO, as "a prerequisite for the exercise of all human rights and duties."[66]

The "Human Right to Health" is proclaimed in the World Health Organization's Constitution, as well as in Article 25 of the Universal Declaration of Human Rights, and in the 1988 Protocol of San Salvador.[67] The Secretary-General of the United Nations submitted a report to the fifty-eighth session of the Commission on Human Rights on "Access to medication in the context of pandemics such as HIV/AIDS."[68]

As for the Right to Food, the Preamble to the FAO Constitution sets "ensuring humanity's freedom from hunger" as one of its basic purposes. The World Food Summit in November 1996 reaffirmed the right of everyone to have access to safe and nutritious food, consistent with the right to adequate food and the fundamental right of everyone to be free from hunger, and gave a specific mandate to the High Commissioner for Human Rights to better define the rights related to food and propose ways to implement and realize them.[69] The General Assembly[70] and the Commission on Human Rights regularly examine this item. In September 2000, the Commission on Human Rights appointed a Special Rapporteur on the right to food.[71]

"Soft Law" Standards. Treaty law is not the only source of humanitarian standards. "Soft law" is also a source of humanitarian standards. One example is the adoption, by the International Conference of the Red Cross in Vienna in 1965, of the Fundamental Principles of the Red Cross/Crescent—humanity, impartiality, neutrality, independence, voluntary service, unity, universality.

Table 6.2   UN Instruments

Charter of the United Nations, adopted June 26, 1945

Convention on the Prevention and Punishment of the Crime of Genocide, adopted December 9, 1948

Convention Relating to the Status of Refugees, signed July 28, 1951

Protocol Relating to the Status of Refugees, opened for signature January 31, 1967

International Covenant on Civil and Political Rights, adopted December 16, 1966

International Covenant on Economic, Social, and Cultural Rights, adopted December 16, 1966

Convention Against Torture and Other Cruel, Inhuman, or Degrading Treatment or Punishment, adopted December 10, 1984

Convention on the Rights of the Child, adopted November 20, 1989

Regional Instruments

1. Africa

   Charter of the Organization of African Unity, adopted May 25, 1963

   Convention Governing the Specific Aspects of the Refugee Problems in Africa, adopted September 10, 1969

   African Charter on Human and Peoples' Rights, adopted June 27, 1981

   African Charter on the Rights and Welfare of the Child, adopted July 1990

2. Americas

   Charter of the Organization of American States, signed 1948

   American Declaration of the Rights and Duties of Man, signed May 2, 1948

   American Convention on Human Rights (Pact of San Jose), signed November 22, 1969

   Inter-American Convention to Prevent and Punish Torture, signed December 9, 1985

   Additional Protocol to the American Convention on Human Rights in the Area of Economic, Social, and Cultural Rights (Protocol of San Salvador), adopted November 17, 1988 (not yet in force)

3. Europe

   Statute of the Council of Europe, adopted May 5, 1949

   European Convention for the Protection of Human Rights and Fundamental Freedoms, signed November 4, 1950

   European Convention for the Prevention of Torture and Inhuman or Degrading Treatment or Punishment, signed November 26, 1987

Table 6.3   Fundamental Principles of the Red Cross/Crescent

HUMANITY

The Red Cross, born of a desire to bring assistance without discrimination to the wounded on the battlefield, endeavors—in its international and national capacity—to prevent and alleviate human suffering wherever it may be found. Its purpose is to protect life and health and to ensure respect for the human being. It promotes mutual understanding, friendship, cooperation, and lasting peace among all peoples.

IMPARTIALITY

It makes no discrimination as to nationality, race, religious beliefs, class, or political opinions. It endeavors only to relieve suffering, giving priority to the most urgent cases of distress.

NEUTRALITY

In order to continue to enjoy the confidence of all, the Red Cross may not take sides in hostilities or engage at any time in controversies of a political, racial, religious, or ideological nature.

INDEPENDENCE

The Red Cross is independent. The National Societies, while auxiliaries in the humanitarian services of their governments and subject to the laws of their respective countries, must always maintain their autonomy so that they may be able at all times to act in accordance with Red Cross principles.

VOLUNTARY SERVICE

The Red Cross is a voluntary relief organization not prompted in any manner by desire for gain.

UNITY

There can be only one Red Cross Society in any one country. It must be open to all. It must carry on its humanitarian work throughout its territory.

UNIVERSALITY

The Red Cross is a worldwide institution in which all Societies have equal status and share equal responsibilities and duties in helping each other.

Solidarity and compassion have always been widely expressed in both words and deeds in the most diverse cultures.[72] The Fundamental Principles are the result of a century of experience. Proclaimed in 1965, they bind together the National Red Cross and Red Crescent Societies, the International Committee of the Red Cross, and the International Federation of Red Cross and Red Crescent Societies.[73] They were imitated in many ways. The principle of neutrality has even become one of the core principles of organizations such as *Médecins sans frontières*.

The "MSF Charter"[74] also mentions the principles of impartiality, nondiscrimination, independence, and voluntary service. It stresses the right to humanitarian assistance.

Beyond institutional rivalries or humanitarian policy-making, such principles could certainly help humanitarian organizations in coping with constantly changing challenges.

Neutrality of the ICRC—or of MSF—has a different meaning from the neutrality of Switzerland or Sweden. It should be understood as the capacity of being available to everyone for service, the ability to assist and protect victims without discrimination, a tool not a virtue, enhancing the security of humanitarian workers and the sustainability of their action, more important in its perception by all actors than in actual practice, closely linked also to funding and access to victims.

Table 6.4   The MSF Charter

Médecins sans frontières, also known as Doctors Without Borders or MSF, offers assistance to populations in distress, victims of natural or man-made disasters, and victims of armed conflict, without discrimination and irrespective of race, religion, creed, or political affiliation.

MSF observes strict neutrality and impartiality in the name of universal medical ethics and the right to humanitarian assistance, and demands full and unhindered freedom in the exercise of its functions.

MSF volunteers undertake to observe their professional code of ethics and to maintain complete independence from all political, economic, and religious powers.

Volunteers are aware of the risks and dangers of the missions they undertake and have no right to compensation for themselves or their beneficiaries other than that which MSF is able to afford them.

In order to promote the complementarities of diverse humanitarian organizations, the implementation of the principle of neutrality could be interpreted in various nuances according to the needs of each individual situation.[75]

Other "soft law" texts could be mentioned as ethical standards, such as:

- The Code of Conduct for Law Enforcement Officials,[76] adopted by the United Nations General Assembly in 1979;
- The Code of Conduct for the International Red Cross and Red Crescent Movement and NGOs in Disaster Relief, developed and agreed upon by eight of the world's largest disaster response agencies in the summer of 1994;[77]
- The Sphere Project;[78]
- The Universal Declaration Of Human Responsibilities, proposed by the InterAction Council in 1997;[79]
- The People in Aid "Best Practices";[80]
- The Humanitarian Accountability Project;[81]
- Guidelines adopted by ecumenical aid agencies[82] and individual agencies such as the "Caritas International's Guiding Values and Principles"[83] and World Vision's Core Values.[84]

Professional ethics (Military,[85] Police,[86] Medical,[87] Media[88]) also strive for universality.

In 1999, the Secretary-General of the United Nations proposed the "Global Compact" to create a dialogue between business and civil society along nine fundamental principles, drawn from the Universal Declaration of Human Rights, the International Labor Organization's (ILO) Fundamental Principles on Rights at Work, and the Rio Principles on Environment and Development.[89]

Multiplication of Legal Mechanisms

The proliferation of standards is matched by the multiplication of implementation mechanisms for international humanitarian law or for human rights instruments or for both.

International Humanitarian Law Mechanisms. The mechanisms provided for in the 1949 Geneva Conventions on the protection of war victims are:

1. The States Party, which undertake to "respect and ensure respect" for the Conventions "in all circumstances."[90] "Respect" clearly refers to the individual obligation to apply it in good faith from the moment that it enters into force.[91] "To ensure respect," according to the ICRC Commentary to the 1949 Conventions, "demands in fact that the States which are Parties to it should not be content merely to apply its provisions themselves, but should do everything in their power to ensure that it is respected universally."[92] This collective responsibility to implement international humanitarian rules[93] often takes the form of bilateral or multilateral measures by States Party. Leaving aside the exceptional meeting provided for in Article 7 of Protocol 1 of 1977,[94] States Party to international humanitarian law treaties have used bilateral or multilateral meetings at the United Nations, the Non-Aligned Movement (NAM), regional organizations (OAS, OAU, OSCE, the European Parliament, the Council of Europe), as well as the Inter-Parliamentary Union (IPU), to manifest their concern that humanitarian law should be respected.[95] "In all circumstances" means in time of armed conflict as well as in time of peace, taking preventive steps, in the form of training[96] or evaluation,[97] and prosecution.[98]

2. The Protecting Power,[99] which was widely used in Europe during WW II[100] and much less therafter.[101] Additional Protocol 1 defines the Protecting Power in international humanitarian law as "a neutral or other State not a Party to the conflict which has been designated by a Party to the conflict and accepted by the adverse Party and has agreed to carry out the functions assigned to a Protecting Power under the Conventions and this Protocol."[102] The role of the Protecting Power is to maintain the liaison between two States at war, to bring relief assistance to the victims, and protection to prisoners of war and civilian internees.

3. The ICRC, which received mandates from the international community in the 1949 Geneva Conventions to:

- Visit and interview prisoners of war[103] and civilian internees;[104]
- Provide relief to the population of occupied territories;[105]

- Search for missing persons and to forward family messages to prisoners of war[106] and civilians;[107]
- Offer its good offices to facilitate the institution of hospital zones[108] and safety zones;[109]
- Receive applications from protected persons;[110]
- Offer its services in other situations[111] and especially in time of non-international armed conflicts.[112]

The First 1977 Additional Protocol adds two mechanisms of implementation:

- The United Nations, "in situations of serious violations of the Conventions or of this Protocol" (Article 89 of Protocol 1)
- The optional "International Fact-Finding Commission" (Article 90 of Protocol 1)[113]

To this day, none of these provisions (Articles 89 and 90 of Protocol 1) have been invoked.

The implementation mechanisms of international criminal law[114] was significantly developed as the United Nations Security Council established the ad hoc International Criminal Tribunals for the Former Yugoslavia and for Rwanda,[115] and with the sixtieth ratification of 1998 Rome Statute of the International Criminal Court[116] on April 11, and its entry into force on July 1, 2002. This is a milestone in the international community's fight to end impunity for war crimes, genocide, and crimes against humanity.

The International Criminal Court will be able to punish war criminals and perpetrators of genocide or crimes against humanity in cases where national criminal justice systems are unable or unwilling to do so. It is vital for the Court's effective functioning that the States Parties rapidly adopt comprehensive implementing legislation in order to be able to cooperate with the Court.[117]

Human Rights Mechanisms. Increasingly, human rights mechanisms, at the international, regional, and national level, deal with human rights as well as with international humanitarian law issues.

- The United Nations General Assembly (Third Committee), the Commission on Human Rights, the Sub-Commission on the Pro-

Figure 6.2

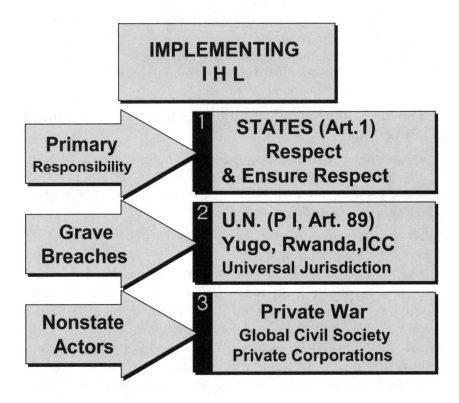

motion and Protection of Human Rights, the Human Rights Committee

- For the Americas: the Organization of American States Commission on Human Rights and the Human Rights Court
- For Africa: the African Commission on Human and Peoples' Rights, under the aegis of the OAU. The Commission was established in 1987 in Banjul, The Gambia. The Commission comprises eleven officials, each from a different country. They serve for renewable six-year terms, which governments cannot cut short. They also elect their own president and vice-president, and determine their own operational rules. The African Commission's role is more wide-ranging than that of its European counterpart, which is confined to handling complaints. Its mis-

sions also include promotion of human and people's rights and interpreting the Charter. The Commission may also develop and set out principles and rules for use by African lawmakers, and cooperate with other African or international institutions involved in rights issues. In 1998, the OAU adopted a Protocol on the Establishment of the African Court on Human and People's Rights, which is not yet in force

- In Europe: the European Commission, the European Court, the European Committee for the Prevention of Torture and Inhuman or Degrading Treatment or Punishment, all under the aegis of the Council of Europe,[118] as well as the relevant organs of OSCE[119] and the European Union[120]

Informal Mechanisms. In addition to the formal mechanisms of implementation of international humanitarian law and human rights, there is an increasing role for informal mechanisms at the international as on the national level:

- good offices,[121]
- media, (local, regional, and international),[122]
- NGOs such as Human Rights Watch[123] or Amnesty International,
- engaging non-State actors[124] to abide by humanitarian rules and principles,[125]
- civil society,[126]
- ad hoc independent monitors, agreed upon by all parties,[127]
- private diplomacy, including private economy (multinational as well as local),
- spiritual leaders,[128] including mediators such as the Sant'Egidio Community.[129]

TODAY'S IMPASSE

International Humanitarian Law finds itself in a deadlock today, despite the development of basic rules such as the 1977 Additional Protocols, whose Twenty-fifth Anniversary is being celebrated in 2002; the development of implementation mechanisms, such as the ad hoc Tribunals for the Former Yugoslavia and for Rwanda;

and the possibility of an International Criminal Court. This dead-lock may well lead us to the point where, with the fragmentation of humanitarian law, new islands of humanity will appear at the very moment that we think we have attained universality of humanitarian law and human rights.

Denial of Respect (Human Dignity)

In spite of starting with two peace conferences (The Hague, 1899 and 1907) and two attempts of establishing global intergovernmental security systems, the twentieth century was characterized by prolonged and extraordinarily devastating wars,[130] a century where the terms *genocide*[131] and *ethnic cleansing* were coined.

The impact of conflict on human lives, economic development and the environment has been devastating.[132] Today's conflicts (in Afghanistan, Bosnia, Burundi, Chechnya, Colombia, the Congo, Liberia, Rwanda, Sierra Leone, Somalia, to name just a few) provide a powerful illustration of the absolute necessity of protecting and bringing aid to war victims and, at the same time, the extreme difficulty of conducting humanitarian operations in a context of anarchy.

Peace, justice and development are linked as the Secretary-General of the United Nations reaffirmed for Africa:

> "Since 1970, more than thirty wars have been fought in Africa, the vast majority of them intra-state in origin. In 1996 alone, fourteen of the fifty-three countries of Africa were afflicted by armed conflicts, accounting for more than half of all war-related deaths worldwide, and resulting in more than 8 million refugees, returnees, and displaced persons. The consequences of those conflicts have seriously undermined Africa's efforts to ensure long-term stability, prosperity, and peace for its peoples."[133]

Unattended poverty leads to conflict. Unpunished crimes call for revenge. In Rwanda, the great needs are justice and cash, in that order.[134]

With so many tragedies happening today, one is struck by a feeling of predictability, the social equivalent of Greek tragedy, the feeling of a time bomb just waiting for the right moment to be detonated.[135]

Collapsed states bring entire populations back to the Stone Age, the only difference being modern weaponry. The new phenomena of the destruction of social fabric; the complete disappearance of any form of authority, except that of the gun; the denial of basic values; and the increasing chaos and anarchy are making conflicts more complex, the suffering of civilians ever more cruel, humanitarian workers and the international community more helpless.[136]

In the words of the psychotherapist Viktor Frankl, an Auschwitz survivor: "Since Auschwitz, we know what man is capable of. And since Hiroshima, we know what is at stake."[137]

Denial of Justice

Should justice for war crimes, crimes against humanity, and crimes of genocide be victors' justice, token justice, or selective justice? Despite the establishment by the Security Council of the International Criminal Tribunal for the Former Yugoslavia (ICTY) and of the International Criminal Tribunal for Rwanda (ICTR), and despite the entry into force in April 2002 of the Rome Statute of the International Criminal Court (ICC), most States Party to the 1949 Geneva Conventions on the protection of war victims make no meaningful use of the universal jurisdiction for crimes of war and grave breaches provided for by the 1949 Geneva Conventions. Important governments have yet to ratify the Rome Statute and enact national legislation.

For too many years, deserved attention was only exclusively given to war crimes, crimes against humanity, and genocide in Europe, while genocide was denied in Rwanda and elsewhere. Will there ever be a prosecution of the *génocidaires* in Cambodia? Virtually on the eve of the Milosevic trial in The Hague, the United Nations announced it could no longer be a party to the creation of a war crimes tribunal in Cambodia. After spending nearly five years in negotiation with Cambodian officials over a court that would try the surviving senior leaders of the Khmer Rouge, a genocidal communist regime responsible for the death of more than 1.5 million of its own people between 1975 and 1979, the UN concluded that officials in Phnom Penh did not and would not meet the basic standards for a fair trial.

One key matter of dispute involved the Cambodian government's attempts to preserve amnesty deals it worked out for key Khmer Rouge leaders.[138]

The prosecution of criminals of war and against humanity is still lacking in Cambodia, Liberia, and Sierra Leone, as well as in Guatemala. National courts only too rarely see cases of torts and liability for violations of humanitarian law and human rights.[139]

Denial of Forgiveness and Reconciliation

The ethics deficit[140] is not only in the denial of the fundamental dignity of others or in the denial of justice for too many victims of war crimes, crimes against humanity, and genocide. It is also to be seen in the excessive emphasis on an impossible justice, and on the denial of forgiveness and reconciliation.

The South African Truth and Reconciliation Commission (TRC)[141] was set up by the Government of National Unity to help deal with what happened under apartheid. The conflict during this period resulted in violence and human rights abuses from all sides. No section of society escaped the abuses.[142] The TRC was the result of a compromise settlement between one side asking for a Nuremberg-like trial[143] and the other side for a blanket amnesty. It was an original combination of African tradition ("ubuntu") and Christian sacramental approach ("penance").[144]

The Chairman of the TRC, Archbishop Desmond Tutu, in his foreword of the Final Report, quotes Judge Marvin Frankel:

A nation divided during a repressive regime does not emerge suddenly united when the time of repression has passed. The human rights criminals are fellow citizens, living alongside everyone else, and they may be very powerful and dangerous. If the army and police have been the agencies of terror, the soldiers and the cops aren't going to turn overnight into paragons of respect for human rights. Their numbers and their expert management of deadly weapons remain significant facts of life . . . The soldiers and police may be biding their time, waiting and conspiring to return to power. They may be seeking to keep or win sympathizers in the population at large. If they are treated too harshly—or if the net of punishment is cast too widely—there may be a backlash that plays into their hands. But their victims cannot simply forgive and forget.[145]

Less elaborate approaches of "Truth and Reconciliation Commissions" have been considered and experimented as tools of mending societies torn apart by war in Argentina, Bolivia, Bosnia, Brazil, Chad, Chile, East Timor, El Salvador, Ethiopia, Germany, Guatemala, Honduras, Northern Ireland, Morocco,[146] Paraguay, Peru, Philippines, Rwanda, Sierra Leone,[147] Uruguay, Zimbabwe.[148] It certainly is a painful process,[149] and a healing one, which should not be exceptional[150]

Toward a Renaissance of Fundamental Humanitarian Values

Research Roots

Renaissance literally means rebirth, renewal, return to the source. We need to research the roots of fundamental values in all civilizations in order to move beyond the superficial universality of legal instruments, too often perceived as imposed by Western powers, and poorly implemented in too many cases.

As the ICRC survey conducted in 1999 for the fiftieth anniversary of the 1949 Geneva Conventions demonstrated, the local spiritual values are often the only efficient, convincing factor, with which motivate the compliance with humanitarian rules in warfare.[151]

Re-anchor in All Civilizations

> The whole idea of compassion is based on a keen awareness of the interdependence of all these living beings, which are all part of one another and all involved in one another.
>
> THOMAS MERTON

Without losing the universality attained by the 1949 Geneva Conventions—and in especially Common Article 3—we need to re-anchor them in all civilizations in a new awareness of belonging, empowerment and interdependence, a renewed commitment to common humanity *(humanité commune),* and for the respect of common values *(patrimoine commun de l'humanité)* and objects indispensable to the survival of humankind such as water, food supplies, public health structures, cultural and spiritual treasures.

Reaffirm Universality of Fundamental Values

We need to underline the common values, to move beyond the twentieth century celebrations of the fiftieth anniversary of the UN Charter, of the Universal Declaration on Human Rights, of the 1949 Geneva Conventions, of the 1951 Convention on Refugees, etc., to reaffirm the universality of fundamental values.

There are divergences of opinion between American and European allies (on the death penalty, for example). There are differences of emphasis between civil and political rights on one hand and social and economic rights on the other. There are also differences of importance of individual and group rights.[152]

We therefore need to reaffirm a common core of human values, in discovering what makes them universal beyond cultural differences:

- The right to life
- The right to personal security and religious freedom
- The right to family life
- The right to health care, adequate nutrition, and shelter
- The principle of nondiscrimination

- The prohibition of torture, inhuman or degrading treatment or punishment[153]

Reinforce Existing Mechanisms

The international community of States Party to the 1949 Geneva Conventions should reaffirm their collective responsibility according to Article 1, common to all four Conventions and to Additional Protocol 1. According to this provision, "The High Contracting Parties undertake to respect and to ensure respect for this Convention in all circumstances." Should measures[154] be limited to diplomacy, adoption of resolutions, or rather the use of sanctions[155] and peace-enforcement operations in order to stop genocide and arrest war criminals? A number of Security Council resolutions, including those on anarchic conflicts, call upon all parties to respect international humanitarian law and reaffirm that those responsible for breaches thereof should be held individually accountable.

According to Article 89 of Protocol 1, "In situations of serious violations or the Conventions or of this Protocol, the High Contracting Parties undertake to act jointly or individually, in cooperation with the United Nations and in conformity with the United Nations Charter." This is a quite important provision, allowing for creativity and flexibility, as needed.

The involvement of the UN in the implementation of IHL took many forms including denunciations of violations of IHL in resolutions by the Security Council or the General Assembly (regarding "human rights violations in territories occupied by Israel," but also in Afghanistan, in El Salvador, in Guatemala, in the Iraq-Iran conflict, in the Gulf War, and even the dispatching of a mission to Iraq and Iran in 1985 to investigate conditions under which prisoners of war were being held, and, since 1992, in the former Yugoslavia[156]).

Ending the impunity of perpetrators of atrocities is a major challenge.[157]

The most important step taken by the UN in this context is the establishment of international criminal tribunals such as "The International Tribunal for the Prosecution of Persons Responsible for Serious Violations of International Humanitarian Law Committed in the Territory of the Former Yugoslavia." The Security Council established it in May 1993[158] for serious violations committed there since 1991. The Tribunal has competence on the following offenses: grave breaches of the Geneva Conventions,[159] violations of the laws and customs of war,[160] genocide,[161] and crimes against humanity.[162]

"The International Tribunal for Rwanda" was established by the Security Council in 1994. This is the first time that an international criminal tribunal has been established with respect to an essentially non-international conflict.

Those ad hoc Tribunals will need adequate resources and political support.[163] Their existence does not do away with the requirement in the 1949 Geneva Conventions for all States Party to see to the punishment of grave breaches wherever they occur, be it by government officials or warlords.[164]

The International Criminal Court needs to be supported. It is only one part of a system that would end impunity to the perpetrators of genocide, crimes against humanity, war crimes, and torture. Such a system could certainly contribute to deter people contemplating such crimes, to allow victims to obtain justice, and to support reconciliation efforts. States Party to the Geneva Conventions have been increasingly aware of their responsibility to respect international humanitarian law not only as individual States but also collectively. The awareness of their collective responsibility is a more recent phenomenon, resulting from the combined pressure of public opinion, the ICRC, and various human rights NGOs,[165] bilaterally or before United Nations bodies. This collective responsibility not only pertains to the enforcement of humanitarian rules, it is contributing to national stability and international security, preventing disorderly movements of populations, uprooting of displaced persons and refugees, and the spreading of uncontrolled violence around the world.[166]

Reinvent Remedies

We need to be more creative in applying remedies[167] to promote the respect of fundamental values in all situations.

Some remedies might include:

1. The reaffirmation of fundamental humanitarian rules, customs, and principles in a simple, easy to understand form, and translation into local languages;

2. Training of arms bearers (military, police, private security groups) in fundamental restraints of violence and essential humanitarian principles;[168]

3. Conducting international, regional, and local public opinion campaigns to promote fundamental humanitarian values[169] and counter hate campaigns;

4. Mobilization of public role models (such as artists or athletes) in close contact with local traditions who can influence leaders and public opinion at large;[170]

5. Including spiritual leaders in those campaigns, especially when religious and spiritual values have been used to fuel conflicts;[171]

6. Preparing the youth to recognize and defend the distinction between humanity and inhumanity through educational programs.[172] Reintegrate child soldiers into society;[173]

7. Learning from human rights[174] and environmental[175] activists to promote fundamental humanitarian values in order that, in the long run, humanitarian norms become a part of humanitarian consciousness;

8. Monitoring arms transfers, beginning with light weapons,[176] and promoting innovative disarmament approaches, such as "weapons for food" or "weapons for development";

9. Exerting better targeted bilateral and multilateral diplomatic, economic, and adequate military pressures against violators, in accordance with the UN Charter and international humanitarian law;[177]

10. Fully including the respect of fundamental human values in the framework of the maintenance and re-establishment of international security.[178]

Re-activate the Network of Humanity

We need to re-activate—or to create, when needed—a network of humanity carrying fundamental human values in all circumstances, and to maintain—or re-establish—the corresponding mechanisms on the local, national, regional, and international level.

The same fundamental values should be applicable in all situations of emergency[179] (armed conflicts and other emergency situations), reconstruction, development, economical growth,[180] peaceful settlement of conflicts, international, regional, and national legal cooperation. In all situations, the human person should be at the center, taking into account the spiritual dimension of all human activities.

Rebuild Public Conscience

> "Either we live together as brothers, or we perish as fools."
>
> THE REVEREND DOCTOR MARTIN LUTHER KING JR.

"Public conscience" was introduced in positive international law by the Martens Clause at the Hague Peace Conference in 1899. It was the result of a compromise reached at the Hague Conference to break a deadlock between great and small powers in Europe over the definition of combatants. In case of doubt, international humanitarian rules should be interpreted in a manner consistent with standards of humanity and the demands of public conscience.[181]

Humanitarian law is, at the same time, rooted in the history of all traditions of humankind, in all parts of the world, and is also very much part of our future, as one essential safeguard for our survival as a species. In the words of Jean Pictet, one of the founding fathers of contemporary humanitarian law, respect for humanitarian law is "necessary to humankind's survival."

In the words of Martin Luther King, Jr.: "The chain reaction of evil—hate begetting hate, wars producing more wars—must be broken, or we shall be plunged into the dark abyss of annihilation."

As the spiritual dimension was at the origin of universal fundamental human values, we now need to bring back the spirit of humanity into the letter of international humanitarian law.

7

Rules of Engagement: An Examination of Relationships and Expectations in the Delivery of Humanitarian Assistance

H. Roy Williams

Introduction

THE IMAGES of conflict and disaster are very much with us. We seem to fast-forward from one conflict to the next, virtually without a breathing space between events. It is close to inevitable that, sooner or later, there will be another humanitarian emergency in a place like Afghanistan, Kosovo, or Rwanda. Once more, the press will be full of accounts of impending crisis and unmet needs. Public officials will be pushing for action in an attempt to outpace the growing public sentiment for dramatic responses that it deems necessary.[1] In part, our greater awareness of these events is the result of an improved ability on the part of the press to reach and report from just about anywhere. In effect, the press—in the eyes of the public—frequently serves as a form of advance scout for the relief providers.

What can we expect of the humanitarians who will be responding? Who is going to do what and how successful will their efforts be? Will the response be managed in a coordinated manner? In short, how are the expectations placed on the shoulders of the relief community going to square with reality, and what is the basis for these expectations in the first place? Glaring instances of outright competition among relief providers are viewed with a mixture of surprise and frustration. What is the basis for the competitive behavior? Should it be expected? As the groups involved exist only to provide humanitarian assistance, there are expectations that cooperation in achieving this objective would be routine. This, unfortunately, is not often the case.[2,3,4]

In order to begin dealing with these questions, it is important to recognize that the community of relief providers is vast. It includes not only the thousands of nongovernmental organizations (NGOs) dedicated to providing assistance, but also International Organizations (IOs), such as the International Committee of the Red Cross (ICRC), the World Food Program, and the militaries from many countries. These groups function in different ways and under differing mandates and degrees of scrutiny. They do, however, meet in the same place: where the crisis unfolds. This chapter will focus on NGOs, their roles and performance in emergencies, and their interaction with the donors, IOs, the military, and the press.

It is also clear that in a crisis, issues concerning the political, military, and humanitarian actors involved may overlap. NGOs must often work with the military in order to accomplish their objectives and obtain the on-the-ground security required.[5] And the military must respond to the needs of the political leaders within their country of origin. These same political leaders will also influence the funding decisions that are so critical to the functioning of the NGO community.[6] It is, therefore, less and less possible to think of the resolution of the problems generated by a humanitarian crisis as being solely a matter for independent aid workers.

An Overview

NGOs carry a significant share of the burden of humanitarian response. The willingness to assume this responsibility, in some instances, represents the expression of a specific principle of action, as is the case with *Médecins sans frontières* (MSF). This organization has long been concerned with questions related to the neutrality of humanitarian action coupled with the right of humanitarian intervention.[7] Other NGOs, such as CARE and the International Rescue Committee (IRC), though interested in these questions, also embody a long history of direct service. Still others, typically smaller NGOs, while adhering to some of these principles of action, may also represent the expression of the need of local communities to respond directly to human suffering.

These smaller NGOs, for example, can be created at virtually any time. This is often the case where the goal is to accomplish particular, often short-term, objectives. Frequently, these smaller NGOs come into being without much awareness on their part of the collaborative arrangements under which larger NGOs attempt to operate. For example, there has been an extensive development of codes of conduct and standards of performance to which the more established organizations publicly subscribe. These distinctly different approaches can generate significant problems when communicating in the field and at the headquarters level.

There is a danger, therefore, in acting on the assumption that NGOs are more alike than they actually are. It also is important to recognize that their behavior on the ground is often very much related to the needs and expectations of others, including donors. This point will be discussed later in this chapter. Indeed, frequently, the funding that supports an organization will have a decisive effect on how it performs, and even on how it sees itself. Organizations that have little or no reliance on government funding, for example, will tend to be more independent in their performance and advocacy positions.[8] Organizations such as Oxfam and MSF, both with strong funding bases, have taken a position on issues of neutrality that renders them less likely to work directly with the military.

It is significant that groups working with NGOs, such as the UN system and the military, frequently take for granted the existence of an essentially monolithic NGO world. The reality is that such a world exists in name only. Understanding the significance of this is important to achieving effective and realistic operational and planning relationships.

The Individual and the Organization

To begin, it is abundantly clear that the highly motivated individual is at the heart of the work of NGOs. Being present at scenes of human tragedy places enormous demands on body and spirit. Facing up to being in close proximity to the "walking dead" of the famines in Somalia and Ethiopia requires a special kind of personal commitment. This is also reflected in the operational language of the individual aid worker, which relies heavily on terms such as *beneficiaries* and *victims*. Conversely, while the public language of the organization includes these terms, its operational discourse makes wider use of terms such as *making budget* and *fundraising strategies*.

Organizations, while wrestling with the same basic issues as the individuals they employ, do not carry emotional burdens or the level of motivation in the same way, yet their overall mission is aimed at incorporating the same objectives. Organization headquarters routinely engage in dialogues with a wider constituency than the ones concerning the individual staff member. This constituency typically includes donors, international organizations, the military, and the press. In addition, the corporate sector also may play a role.[9] In the face of responding to such a wide constituency, the element of survival becomes an organization's moving force. In a sense, this aspect of the culture of organizations is at odds with the behavior of its staff, whose objectives are more often directed toward the individuals and groups at risk.[10] It is also worth noting that in many cases, staff is hired in the field or at a location remote from headquarters. They frequently do not have the opportunity to learn much about how the organizations paying their salary actually operate. Yet, there is an automatic presumption on the part of the public that the individual and the organization necessarily have the same objectives in mind.

Individuals in isolation can have only a limited effect on the crisis with which they are confronted. This is generally understood. Only organizations can provide the necessary resources and overall support. What ensues, however, is the appearance of the contradiction within the very heart of the relief system, with highly motivated individuals being co-opted by the organizations that support their work, organizations operating under a very different set of imperatives.

The challenge for NGO leadership is managing both organizational concerns and individual motivations. Unlike the military, for example, where loyalty to the group is essential and includes the willingness to sacrifice all for its interests, the motivation of the relief worker is assumed to be based on a personal undertaking of a humanitarian mission. It is certainly not expected that this motivation will be subordinated to the needs of the organization. It is this motivation, however, on which the parent organization relies, and which the public takes for granted in its view of the system of humanitarian response.

This contradiction is generally apparent to the staff. Individual staff members often deal with this by separating their work on the ground from what goes on at the headquarters office. It is common to hear references to the gap between headquarters and the field.[11] What is usually referred to here is a difference in perspective. Unfortunately, the significance of this gap in perspective is rarely examined, and depending on where they are formed, staff impressions of the work of the organization will vary widely. The powerful sense of mutual reinforcement experienced by field workers loses its force when organizational priorities begin to overtake those of the individual.

Does this mean that the NGO community needs to acknowledge this reality and operate more like contractors than as vehicles for the work of highly motivated volunteers? One might argue that since NGOs have to compete in order to survive, this posture would make a great deal of sense. If, however, they were to follow the contractor model, this would necessarily change how they present themselves to the public and donors. It would also change the public's view of what humanitarian assistance is, and responding to a humanitarian crisis would have more of the aspect of a job to be done than the pull of emotional and moral responsibility. It is difficult to see how the overall effect of this would be positive. Certainly, the private donor would probably find contributing to this kind of effort far less rewarding. It would also change the fundamental relationship of leadership to staff. The mandates and charters of NGOs, at present, speak primarily to matters of principle and service. The contractor model is predicated upon efficiency. This represents a significant change in emphasis, even with the increased focus on performance, which will also be discussed below.

TRIANGLE OF RESPONSE: NGOs AT THE CENTER

It is apparent that NGOs are responsive to or influenced by a variety of actors involved with humanitarian response. I have attempted to depict this interaction in the diagram titled, "The Triangle of Response." Individual staff members are, to varying degrees, certainly aware of these influences. Their work and sense of mission is inevitably affected. The impact on the individual increases with the level of decision-making responsibility.

In "The Triangle of Response," an NGO is either influenced by or influences donors, the public and the press, international organizations, and the military. This influence is typically based on the presence, or potential presence, of the NGO at the disaster site. It is necessary for these groups to have either an NGO available to do the work on the ground or to speak to their sense of the issue. What ensues is a seemingly contradictory and paradoxical set of relationships.

For example, NGOs influence decision-making and public awareness through their often intensive advocacy efforts.[12] It is often the messages from the NGO community that make the difference in whether or not there is a humanitarian response of any kind. In so doing, they are the voice of conscience for themselves and the groups they represent. Sounding the alarm is one aspect of their responsibility, but this does not relieve them of reliance on outside support. The community, including donors, is aroused, but the forces motivating donors virtually guarantee the emergence of competition for the funds generated.

It is under these circumstances, however, that the considerable variety within the NGO world has something of an offsetting effect. Those NGOs with stronger private funding bases, such as MSF and Oxfam, can operate at a greater distance from the consequences of their own success in raising awareness. This does not mean that they always are necessarily in the best position to operate in a particular situation. They, too, must work within the community in order to be effective.

Influence of the Donor

NGOs in general are not self-sustaining. They do not generate profit from their work, so they must rely on funding support from a variety of donors, including the public. In an ideal world—from the point of view of the NGO—all such funding would be unrestricted. Decisions could be made without reference to the specific direction of the donor.

The reality is different. Public giving, as an example, is tied to the humanitarian nature of NGO work. But this means that the public has to be made aware of the work of the organization and of its special qualifications to perform as expected.[13] Marketing is required to get the NGOs' message across, and the more prominent the newspaper ad and overall exposure, the better.

A complicating factor in handling donated funds is that while givers are willing to pay for provision of direct service, they are far less willing to pay for maintaining the structural capacity required to deliver this service. The recent example of the American Red Cross following the events of September 11, 2001, illustrates the difficulties facing organizational leadership when handling contributions. In this instance, significant funds were initially set aside to be used for longer-term objectives, and the

Figure 7.1

Triangle of Response

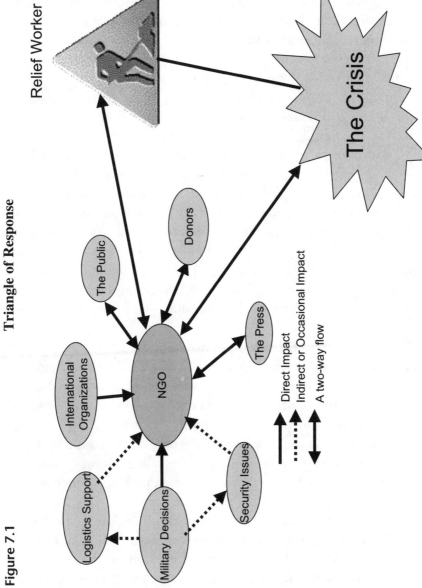

giving public was outraged with this unilateral interpretation of their intentions.[14]

Organizations must, therefore, create a diverse pool of donors paying for their different operational needs. This includes finding ways to generate funds not limited to direct support of programs. Accomplishing this involves extensive fundraising campaigns, which, by necessity, create an environment of active competition among NGOs for a limited number of potential givers. It is a competition that can easily spread and affect operations in the field.[15]

In addition, donors will often make funding decisions based on achieving a particular result. The concerns of their constituencies, including, in some instances, the press as well as political leadership, have to be addressed. Governmental donors described and reacted in different ways to the issue of shelter needs in Kosovo following the NATO bombing. This led to very public disagreements among the IOs and governments on the best way to approach the perceived problem. NGOs, as the implementing partners and recipients of their funding, were quickly drawn into the dispute.[16]

In a sense, therefore, competition among the NGOs can often be said to begin with the donor. This places the donor closer to the role of customer than disinterested supporter, and here we appreciate the notion of NGOs as contractors. Donors have their own priorities and needs and frequently choose funding recipients based on these. In addition, there are only so many donors in a position to provide the increasingly high level of funds required to deal with today's emergencies, making it necessary for NGOs to compete for available funds.

In short, donor expectations and public relations needs very quickly contribute to generating competitive behavior on the part of the NGO. These organizations often end up in the role of being the public face of the donor. As such, their performance in meeting donor expectations is closely scrutinized when considering the next contribution. This may be the case even when these expectations have little to do with the actual needs of the beneficiaries.

By contrast, the public and others expect the humanitarian actions of NGOs to be above the fray in all respects. As noted, the ability to respond in this fashion is far more characteristic of the individual than it is of the organization. To truly meet this expectation, organizations would require more independence than is typically available to them—that is, a source of unencumbered support.

Influence of the International Organizations

The United Nations family serves in a variety of capacities in the humanitarian arena. It has the responsibility of providing overall program direction as well as taking the lead in securing funds from governments. UN organizations also serve as a source of program funding for the NGOs working as implementing partners. NGOs have only a limited participation in the drafting and presentation of the Consolidated Appeals to governments, through which much of the area-specific funding is obtained. These appeals also determine the overall programmatic direction of the humanitarian response. They provide little funding, however, for other organizational requirements such as headquarters expenses. This brings about the need to make up the shortfall elsewhere.

Often, the UN is the only, or the major, source of program funding for a particular response. We saw this in the refugee camps in Tanzania following the Rwandan genocide.[17] Here, the NGOs were strongly influenced by the criteria of having independent resources established by the United Nations High Commissioner for Refugees (UNHCR). Sooner or later, the requirement of generating hard-to-obtain funds for program support affects the overall budget of an NGO. For public relations reasons, it often cannot afford *not* to be present at the site of a major crisis, even though being there can also create deficit spending. This approach to funding is another illustration of the lack of a coherent approach toward the real needs of NGOs on the part of the donor community. NGOs react in an equally disjointed manner in seeking financial support. This pattern of behavior contributes to the often-criticized self-promoting behavior displayed by many organizations.

Staff security is also another UN role, and will be discussed in subsequent commentary on the military as not an exclusive province of the United Nations. Here, the UN's relationship to NGOs is an incomplete and often ambiguous one, as the UN has only a limited responsibility to non-UN staff. Typically, security briefings will be organized by the UN, in some instances, in conjunction with the military. Security criteria will be established and shared, providing, for example, degrees of security alert status. Most of the time, this is done primarily for UN staff. The conflict in Bosnia, however, provided an example where the UN, through UNPROFOR, the United Nations Protection Force (in Yugoslavia), under a Chapter 7 mandate, took the lead in escorting NGO convoys. The UNHCR also established a countrywide communication system that established a very proactive relationship to the NGOs.[18]

It is clear, however, that NGOs have little influence on overall UN decision-making despite being major actors on the ground. While there have been improvements in this area, the relative absence of NGO involvement is telling.

*Influence of the Military**

The relationship of the military to the NGO community and its role in humanitarian emergencies is undergoing a steady evolution. The military is increasingly aware of the roles that NGOs play. The fact that the NGOs are more likely to be present before the military arrives makes it necessary to have some understanding of their structures and mandates. Coupled with this has been an acknowledgement of the specific strengths that NGOs possess,

---

*Editor's Note: This topic is also covered, in great detail, in the International Humanitarian Affairs Series companion volume *Emergency Relief Operations*.

strengths that increasingly have relevance to the missions of the military. There have been a series of exercises and briefings and the development of official publications such as Joint Publication 3-07.6, which is devoted to better acquainting the military with humanitarian organizations and their responsibilities.

As evidenced by the post-Taliban events in Afghanistan, there is a growing willingness on the part of the military to directly assume some of the traditional roles of NGOs, such as the support of small-scale community projects.[19] Also, the use of military aircraft to drop food/humanitarian daily rations in Afghanistan while beginning an extensive bombing campaign has attracted a great deal of attention and raised important questions on the appropriateness of combatants assuming this role.[20]

Typically, military capacities have been thought of in terms of lift capabilities, as in the large-scale provision of helicopter support following the extensive movement of Kurds to the mountains of Turkey during the closing stages of the Gulf War. We have also seen significant material support provided by or moved with the help of military units.

The broad question of security, and what is appropriate for a community dedicated to humanitarian neutrality, has presented serious difficulties for NGOs. There is little consensus within the NGO community on the proper attitude toward military involvement. It is often argued that the only proper role for the military is to provide logistical support, and that its participation in security-related issues should be essentially a passive one involving, for example, the circulation of security-related information.

These positions continue to be discussed and acted upon, and may well be in the process of becoming overtaken by post-September 11 events. We see in Afghanistan a much more proactive approach to providing humanitarian assistance where, much to the consternation of NGOs, a different model has emerged. We now see the military actively involved in so-called "quick-impact projects" designed to respond to immediate local needs.[21] These are being carried out without the involvement of the NGO community, which is typically associated with this kind of initiative.

This expanded model is apparently based on a conclusion that the NGOs, at the very least, need assistance in carrying out what is more and more seen as a shared humanitarian mission. The clear implication of this approach is that failing to resolve humanitarian needs can have political and military consequences, and attending to these problems is no longer the exclusive province of the humanitarians; hence expansion of the military's role is inevitable given its acknowledged capacities.

Influence of the Press and the Public*

The impact of the press on the thinking and behavior of NGO leadership has increased steadily over the past few years. This has been anything but a one-way relationship. As the press has achieved greater and greater access to disaster sites and areas of conflict, its use of information, frequently gathered with the assistance of NGO staff, has also increased. Technical progress in the area of satellite communication has greatly expanded the ability to report directly from the field. This combination of capacity to utilize and opportunity to obtain on-the-ground interviews with NGO personnel has enhanced the credibility of both the interviewer and the interviewee. The two sides have arrived at accommodations that serve both. The NGOs, in particular, have been able to move their concerns to the front pages of major newspapers. This puts enormous pressure on donors to support NGO proposals to address the now very public crisis.

NGOs have quickly recognized the expanded public relations options and opportunities for widening the audience for advocacy. States, in responding to the appeals and issues raised by the NGOs, have the problem of trying to ensure that their responses are not perceived by the public as, essentially, examples of political opportunism.

At the same time there is a debate within the NGO community regarding the extent to which humanitarian work is or is not in-

---

*Editor's Note: See also chapter 8, this volume.

fluenced by the needs of political decision-makers.[22] The difficulty for the parties on both sides of the question is apparent.
The NGOs often need the support of state donors to accomplish
their humanitarian objectives. The scale of what we have seen in
Rwanda and Kosovo, as examples, is such that private donors
would not have to capacity to meet the resource needs. On the
other side, states have few options apart from the NGOs in presenting their humanitarian face. It is noteworthy, in this regard,
that the military has been increasingly seen as one such option.
Some accommodation on the part of both sides in achieving
these respective objectives is required. Clearly, "humanitarian"
work has acquired a new and different level of importance.
Again, however, these opportunities both highlight serious concerns and serve as the basis for further competition.

The public and the press often have a virtually symbiotic relationship. They both expect independent and selfless behavior
from the NGO world. The public, however, has a more direct
basis for such expectations: it is part of the actual framework of
the NGO world. The dollars of individuals support NGOs, and it
is from the ranks of the general populace that the NGO staff
comes. Community groups will organize and launch themselves
as actors during a crisis. We saw this in Bosnia, with trucks driven
by volunteers from Scotland arriving with few plans, but considerable determination to be of assistance. The public sees the community as partners in a mission to overcome the impediments of
bureaucracy and an isolationist approach within their own societies. For its part, reporters often see the public as the constituency demanding the heightened awareness that they are charged
with providing.

One consequence of this interaction is that the expectations
of the public and the press often define the goals and objectives
of the NGOs. Organizations are in the position of having to respond, or be seen as having failed their professed purpose. If the
press reports the threat of an imminent humanitarian crisis, it
becomes difficult for an NGO to stand apart and openly argue
that there is little reason for its involvement. Saying nothing risks

criticism from its own constituency. It is here that we see the operative connections between donors, both public and private, the press, and NGOs.

Acknowledging this welter of influences upon individual NGOs is critical to understanding their behavior, and assessing how realistic are the assumptions made about their performance.

NGO CONSORTIA: A WAY OUT?

There is an impression that NGO consortia such as the International Council of Voluntary Agencies (ICVA), the Steering Committee for Humanitarian Response (SCHR), and InterAction have, as part of their mandate, the responsibility and the capacity to coordinate activities in the field—in effect to take the rough edges off the relationships between NGO members and the other members of the humanitarian community. It is a legitimate expectation, given the complexities of humanitarian operations, and to a limited degree, this is sometimes realized. But this view derives more from the needs and assumptions of donors and various cooperating groups, such as the military and international organizations, than from the charters or capacities of these consortia.

In order for consortia to truly coordinate their members' efforts, it must have the power to direct them. However, NGOs join consortia for a range of different objectives, including the need to be part of a recognized group, thereby gaining leverage in pushing donors and governments to be more proactive in dealing with humanitarian issues. By comparison, international organizations and the military are generally more willing than are NGOs to operate in a coordinated manner. Their internal dialogue seems more open to consensus as evidenced in the issuance of consolidated appeals during emergencies. Individual NGOs, on the other hand, are frequently noted for postures of isolation and insisting on being identified for their unique approach or level of accomplishment.

Nonetheless, the burden of hope for achieving a more organized process is often placed on the shoulders of the consortia. This follows from the assumption that joining a group implies the surrendering of some degree of autonomy. In reality, the charters and mandates of these umbrella structures do not specifically address the issue of coordination during the humanitarian response to a crisis. In addition, cooperative behavior in the field in the absence of personal understandings is something of a management issue. It requires specific prior agreements between organizations and the ability to enforce them. Here we will review some examples of major NGO consortia and support institutions.

The International Council of Voluntary Agencies (ICVA)

ICVA's objectives are threefold: to promote dialogue and information exchange among member NGOs, Geneva-based humanitarian agencies, and governments; to improve coordination[23] and standardization of humanitarian principles and practice among its NGO network; and to facilitate NGO advocacy, including institutional and governmental capacity building. Thus, ICVA seeks to act as "catalyst," "facilitator," and "broker" for interagency networking, collaboration, and policy-making initiatives.[24]

ICVA has an international membership that includes many national NGOs, which makes direct political leverage more difficult to achieve. ICVA looks to facilitate communication and information exchange between NGOs and international agencies and has paid particular attention to including southern NGOs in its membership.

InterAction

InterAction is the largest consortium of U.S. NGOs. Its mission is "to enhance the effectiveness and professional capacities of its members engaged in international humanitarian efforts." Representing over 160 NGOs, InterAction seeks to encourage "partnership, collaboration, and leadership among its members as they strive to achieve a world of self-reliance, justice, and peace."[25] Members undertake to adhere to the Private Voluntary Organization Standards, which promote fiscal and programmatic transparency and accountability. The standards are intended to increase the institutional credibility of members to their donors and the general public, without detriment to NGO autonomy and individuality. It is this insistence on autonomy and individuality that militates against functional coordination.

Steering Committee for Humanitarian Response (SCHR)

The Steering Committee for Humanitarian Response is a small consortium with limited membership, formed out of a desire to improve interagency cooperation. Much of SCHR's activities have been devoted to representing a group of NGOs before UN decision-making bodies. It is composed of the Chief Executive Officers from nine of the largest humanitarian agency networks (CARE International, Caritas Internationalis, ICRC, IFRC, International Save the Children/Alliance, Lutheran World Federation, MSF, Oxfam International, and the World Council of Churches), with one of these serving as Secretariat in Geneva. SCHR has a permanent invitation to attend Inter-Agency Standing Committee meetings. It does not maintain a formal mandate or charter, however. In addition to its "club" of CEOs, SCHR also sponsors a policy group, which spearheaded the Sphere Project in 1996 and continues to pursue other advocacy issues.[26]

VOICE

Since its inception in 1992, Voluntary Organizations in Cooperation in Emergencies has drawn its membership from over eighty European NGOs. In addition to improving interagency linkages, its mission is "to make an effective contribution to the framing and monitoring of humanitarian policy" at the level of the European Union.[27] Like ICVA, VOICE focuses activities on promoting information exchange and advocacy through its network membership. A major difference, however, lies in the VOICE emphasis on NGO issues as they relate to the EU programming and funding. In addition to acting as a consultant on humanitarian standards and efficacy of interventions, the VOICE charter mandates representing NGO concerns to the European Union and facilitating NGO access to the EU Council and European Community Humanitarian Office (ECHO). An example would be their work in assisting NGO communication with ECHO during the revision of the Framework Partnership Agreement.

In looking at some of the major consortia, we see some striking similarities, as well as differences, in the expectations of the membership. There is, however, an overlap of membership in these consortia, suggesting that the reasons for joining transcend the question of shared purpose or values.

NGO SUPPORT INSTITUTIONS

NGOs rely on more than their own internal capacities to improve the quality of service delivery. Additional interagency structures are dedicated to the issues of best practices and accountability, and we can observe a clear overlap in some of the objectives of these groups. In part, this arguably is indicative of the range of approaches and choice of emphasis within the NGO community; it also reflects the preferences and concerns of donors. Individual performance, once little discussed, has become one of the leading issues for the humanitarian community. The potential effect on beneficiaries, individual relief workers, and their parent organizations suggests that the realities of involvement in complex emergencies have moved well beyond the ritualized paying of lip service to humanitarian rhetoric.

People in Aid

The People in Aid Code of Best Practice was first developed in 1996 as the product of an informal collaboration between British

Table 7.1

Representative Mandates and Selected Membership of NGO Consortia

	SCHR	InterAction
Mandates	No formal mandate or charter	Increase NGO fiscal and programmatic accountability, particularly to donors
	Represent NGO interests to IASC	Encourage partnership within NGO network while mantaining organizational autonomy and individuality
	Address humanitarian advocacy issues through policy group	Promote broad-based advocacy through standing committees
Membership	CEOs from international NGO networks	U.S. private voluntary organizations
Overlapping NGOs	CARE International Caritas Internationalis Int'l Committee of the Red Cross Int'l Federation of the Red Cross Lutheran World Federation *Médecins sans Frontières* International Oxfam International World Council of Churches	American Jewish Joint Distribution Committee American Red Cross Action Against Hunger USA Adventist Development & Relief Agency Int'l CARE U.S.A. Catholic Relief Services Church World Service Concern America Concern Worldwide Doctors of the World U.S.A. Doctors Without Borders U.S.A. International Rescue Committee Jesuit Refugee Services/U.S.A. Mercy Corps International Oxfam America Save the Children U.S.A. World Vision U.S.

Table 7.1 (continued)

ICVA	VOICE
Improve information exchange between NGOs, IHAs, and governments	Improve information flows and humanitarian advocacy within NGO network
Strengthen NGO network through promotion of humanitarian principles and field practice standards	Facilitate NGO interface with EU and ECHO programming and funding
Foster advocacy skills among NGOs	Consult on humanitarian practice standards and represent NGO concerns to EU and ECHO
Varied, but with particular emphasis on including southern NGO membership	European NGO membership
ActionAid Adventist Development & Relief Agency Int'l American Jewish Joint Distribution Committee ASF-Dansk Folkehjaelp CARE International CARE U.S.A. Caritas Internationalis Church World Service Danish Refugee Council Dutch Relief and Rehabilitation Agency InterAction Int'l Committee of the Red Cross Int'l Federation of the Red Cross International Rescue Committee Jesuit Refugee Services International Lutheran World Federation *Médecins sans Frontières* International Medecins du Monde World Council of Churches	ActionAid Action Contre le Faim Adventist Development & Relief Agency Int'l ASF-Dansk Folkehjaelp CARE International Caritas Belgium Caritas France Caritas Germany Caritas Netherlands Caritas Spain Caritas Sweden Comite Internacional de Rescate Concern Worldwide Danish Refugee Council Dutch Relief and Rehabilitation Agency Lutheran World Federation Médecins du Monde International Mercycorps Scotland Oxfam Belgium Oxfam U.K. Save the Children Fund U.K. World Vision Austria World Vision Germany World Vision Netherlands World Vision Finland World Vision Ireland World Vision U.K.

and Irish relief agencies. British relief workers, who had participated in the humanitarian intervention following the Rwandan
genocide, felt that "there must be as great a duty of care to employees as to potential project beneficiaries" on the part of aid
organizations.[28] Unlike the Sphere Minimum Standards in Disaster Response, which recommend technical guidelines for service
in the field, or the IFCR Code of Conduct, which outlines NGO
behavior in accordance with humanitarian principles, the People
in Aid Code frames a standard of policy and management support to the volunteers and employees of humanitarian agencies.
The code's seven principles, ranging from an institutional commitment to "best practices" to responsible budgeting of field
staff, are expressed in specific indicators that can be subject to
monitoring and evaluation. People in Aid asserts that its code,
unlike others, is applicable to both relief and development organizations.

Active Learning Network for Accountability and Performance in Humanitarian Action (ALNAP)

ALNAP was established in 1997. It seeks to "encourage self-criti-
cism and learning" in the improvement of humanitarian practices and accountability. To achieve these objectives, ALNAP has
categorized its activities as "network," "programmatic," and
"interest group." Included among its network activities is the
sharing of humanitarian reports, evaluations, and "lessons
learned."[29] Programs include training in monitoring and evaluation of humanitarian action. Interest-group activities are pres-
ently allocated to case and consultation studies of complex
emergency programs. ALNAP currently assists forty-nine full
member organizations from the United Nations, bilateral and
multilateral donors, the Red Cross network, NGOs, and independent and academic consultants. Its leadership is composed of a
Steering Committee of Representatives from each sector
throughout its network.

The Sphere Project

The Sphere Project[30] was created by a humanitarian community troubled by the 1994 events in Rwanda. The increased demand for humanitarian relief was seen as exceeding the capacity of the system to respond, making the quality of relief delivery suffer. Following the 1996 report produced by the Joint Evaluation of Emergency Assistance to Rwanda, members of the SCHR policy group, with a letter of support from Kofi Annan, began a multilateral, NGO-driven process directed toward producing a humanitarian charter and technical standards in the management of humanitarian assistance. The Humanitarian Charter outlines the rights of persons affected by disasters, based on international humanitarian law, refugee law, and human rights conventions. A set of Minimum Standards and key indicators are the triggers for determining if technical needs are being met in the field.

The Sphere guidelines were intended to increase NGO operational transparency and accountability, both to donor organizations and to the beneficiaries of humanitarian interventions. While the first phase of the Sphere Project was largely driven by northern NGO consortia (SCHR and InterAction, with significant input from ICVA and VOICE), efforts were also made to include southern consultants and perspectives in the technical guidelines. The second phase of the project—dissemination and implementation of the handbook—continued to practice diversified donor funding and interagency collaboration. Phase three includes additional training objectives and agency incorporation of standards, as well as an evaluation of the Sphere Project, which is scheduled to be complete by 2003. The current edition of the Sphere Humanitarian Charter and Minimum Standards in Disaster Response references over 600 contributors, and a second edition is to be made available in September 2003.

PULLING IT ALL TOGETHER

In looking at the crossover in membership in the preceding chart, it is apparent that many of these structures offer similar

skills and areas of technical assistance. In addition, their governing principles are often identical, or at least complementary. A
reasonable conclusion would be that there is an abundance of
support available to NGOs, with numerous opportunities for
cross training and exchange of experience. The reality is that
these opportunities are not routinely taken advantage of or made
available to staff.

The NGO community has had opportunities to strengthen its
performance by drawing on the variety of resources available
from the consortia. These, more often than not, have been a lost
opportunities. Yes, the tools are there, but the means of incorporating them into the routine behavior of the implementing agencies are apparently lacking. In addition, there is limited
awareness at the level of NGO decision-makers of the availability
of these resources. Their responsibility, as noted earlier, is to a
different level of organizational imperatives. There is also apparent skepticism as to the overall value of these tools when viewed
in the context of the often-overwhelming needs on the ground.
There is no question that much of the work of the humanitarian
community is indeed extremely time-sensitive. It is debatable,
however, if this is an absolute deterrent to finding ways to incor-
porate more of these resources and those of supporting structures into daily operations.

That is not to say that individual NGOs have not performed
admirably; however, assuming that the frequently large number
of NGOs responding to a crisis can be "coordinated" usually
proves disappointing. The mandates of these consortia can quite
reasonably raise expectations of a far more organized and professional response than has been evident during recent crises. On
the other hand, the donor community and others concerned
with these issues have been content to let the system organize
itself, while at the same time demanding that it behave in a more
"coordinated" or "cooperative" manner.

Summary Observations

The expectations placed upon NGOs, and the humanitarian
community in general, are based upon assumptions of indepen-

dence that are not supported by the realities of their relation-ships with donors, the international community, the military, and the press. Each group, in differing ways, influences the perform-ance of NGOs in the field. The mandates of these organizations speak to a presumed independence that, we have asserted, exists only in limited fashion.

Further, it follows that the widespread and unorganized growth of the NGO community in the face of these influences has substantially compromised its ability to carry out its mission to alleviate suffering. Counterproductive competition and unco-ordinated performance are inevitable consequences. We have seen how this behavior plays into the hands of some of the groups creating the crisis, as was seen in the camps in Zaire in the aftermath of the Rwandan genocide. Donors and others have contributed to this situation by making self-serving or equally un-coordinated funding decisions, sometimes based on overt politi-cal objectives. The actions of donors serve to reinforce NGO behavior that is contrary to what is expected from humanitarian entities.[31] Yes, there are contributing factors, but it is the survival imperative of the organization that is central to this outcome.

What is the answer? The organizations that make up the NGO community are not likely to voluntarily go out of existence, thus reducing the number of players and the need for competitive behavior. Nor are they likely to surrender decision-making re-sponsibility to the consortia of which they are members, in order to reduce the effects of competition. Furthermore, the groups at the various points in the Triangle of Response are also not in a position to radically change their relationship to humanitarian operations, with the possible exception of the military.

If NGOs were no longer considered nonprofit entities but con-tractors, and had to compete for monetary support, they would soon, in Malthusian fashion, be reduced in number. There are some who feel that this would produce a more productive and better-performing workplace by reducing some of the conse-quences of having too many actors on the ground. The cost of this approach, however, is high. The entire character of assistance would change, and with it the nature of public support. There are many who feel that some organizations have already begun to work as contractors, but it is certainly not the way the community operates as a whole. I think it is evident that some of the more laudable aspects of the community would be lost if the relationship of NGOs to the public is drastically changed. There is a connection to the generosity of the human spirit that is expressed in the spontaneous creation and dedicated volunteerism of NGOs, and this is essential to maintain. Creating primarily contractual relationships would not allow for its expression.

Alternatively, it is argued that there should be enforceable mechanisms governing the performance of the humanitarian response community, managed by some form of centralized authority. After all, there already are codes and standards, with a broad range of NGO signatories that generally discourage the objectionable behavior cited. We see the value of the guidelines developed by the Sphere Project and People in Aid, for example. Is it not in the best interest of the donor community, and most importantly of the beneficiaries, writ large to find ways to see them more rigorously applied? This would not eliminate the broader impact of politically motivated funding decisions, but it would ameliorate their impact on the ground, motivating NGOs to function in a more neutral and transparent manner.

Also, the consortia have more in common than they have in opposition. The process of communicating this typically becomes the topic of scattered meetings or less than systematic attempts to share information and resources. Doing this in a proper manner takes the dedication of resources and careful planning. It may well be in the interest of donors to display more willingness to support this.

To go back to the beginning: the NGO community all too frequently presents a face that is confusing to its outside supporters and may well force them to turn to other, less traditional actors or approaches. The fundamental responsibility of NGOs is to those they were created to assist. This is the impression shared both outside and inside the system. It is essential that the community find ways to look at itself with the "terrible honesty" required when change is needed. The dialogue between the political, military, and humanitarian elements involved with emergency response is expanding. The full and open engagement of the humanitarian community is required, if the outcome is to benefit those in need.

FINAL THOUGHTS

We have been addressing how NGOs work together and what are some of the impediments facing greater cooperation—cooperation that is more consistent with the expectations of outsiders, and produces a more effective response. Assuming that the behavior of donors is as described here, there is little reason to expect a marked change in their approach to funding decisions. Public giving of major proportions will, in all likelihood, continue to be related to the media exposure of a particular crisis. Given this, it cannot be expected that NGOs will be able to exert independence such that they can avoid operating within their organizational constraints.

It has been taken for granted that the operative word for describing NGO efficiency is "coordination." The reality of the "Triangle of Response" suggests that it is far more reasonable to look for modalities of "cooperation;" modalities that don't expect an unlikely outcome from the realities of working within a frequently-competitive humanitarian funding environment.[32] Maintaining effective cooperation is best performed by entities without the program responsibilities that might otherwise draw them into a competition for funds. The provision of a neutral venue for planning and discussion of resource allocation would greatly assist the emergence of joint undertakings at both the headquarters and field level.

The NGO community has much to gain by looking seriously at ways to overcome some of the inherent impediments to more successful relief operations.

Part 4

In this final section, three highly respected experts discuss *(a)* the relationship between humanitarian workers and the media; *(b)* the critical need for, and some of the problems in, funding international humanitarian programs; and *(c)* the oft-forgotten view of the recipient of aid.

The role of the media in a humanitarian crisis is enormous. The written, spoken, and visual media, particularly in this era of instant communication, bring distant disasters into our homes, and influence the response of governments as well as of individuals. Joshua Friedman, a Pulitzer Prize-winning journalist with vast experience in international crises, presents the positive, and potentially negative, results of media attention during disasters. He also offers his own "rule of the game" for humanitarian workers dealing with the media.

During her tenure as head of Doctors Without Borders in the U.S.A., Joelle Tanguy raised annual donations to that NGO by tenfold. She has had to deal with an urgent need for funds to sustain essential programs while recognizing the inherent dangers for the freedom and flexibility of independent organizations that receive substantial aid from government sources. Her chapter closely examines current funding policies, practices, and pitfalls.

The views of local government and populations may not mirror those presented by Western aid providers. Abdulrahim Abby Farah, long-term UN Undersecretary General for African Affairs and a former Somali diplomat, details, in a moving chapter, the privileges of indigenous people even in the midst of crisis.

8

Humanitarians and the Press

Joshua Friedman

INTRODUCTION

THE QUESTION of media relations has been one of the mainstay preoccupations of InterAction, which was founded nearly twenty years ago to pull together the efforts of private voluntary organizations in the United States. InterAction convenes periodic fora where journalists speak to humanitarian workers about how the media works.

I have been on several of these panels. At an early one, a woman from a small organization got up in the back of the room with a question: Why didn't the press report on all the good works her group does? she asked testily, enumerating a number of accomplishments that sounded fairly routine to me.

People in the news business know that news is about something new, something out of the ordinary, something unique. But this earnest humanitarian obviously didn't know that. Short of launching into a quick course on how the media works, I really didn't have an answer for her.

But that's what this chapter is about. I finally have an opportunity to give an answer—a quick course on how the media works, what constitutes news, how news judgments are made and how journalists and humanitarians can interact productively. After covering wars, humanitarian disasters, and international diplomacy for many years for *Newsday,* I have developed some ideas about this.

Journalists and humanitarians have an intimate relationship—so close, in fact, that they often rub up against each other painfully, causing resentments on both sides. It's almost a form of sibling rivalry. They share some of the same problems. Especially in the last dozen years since the collapse of the Soviet Union, the world has been awash in comprehensive humanitarian emergencies that threaten to overwhelm both.

In my course on International Reporting at the Columbia University Graduate School of Journalism, I encourage the students to lean heavily on humanitarian organizations. In many cases, this is the best way to get off the beaten path when doing a story—for logistical and research help, to discover authentic community leaders, and avoid official spokesmen. "Don't reinvent the wheel," I tell them ad nauseam.

Private voluntary and nongovernmental humanitarian organizations have already solved many of the problems the students will face when they become journalists overseas—communications, transportation, lodging, health, and reliable local contacts. They have already figured out local customs, politics, and disputes.

I warn my students that the pressure to get the story leads some irresponsible journalists to play fast and loose with information that could put humanitarians and the people they work with at great risk, especially in anarchic, violent situations. Journalists must understand how to report the story without endangering them.

I caution students that some humanitarian groups are so driven to get good publicity that they try to manipulate the press. This rarely works, and then only in the short-term. Journalists are proud to have built-in "BS" detectors. At the slightest whiff of manipulation or exaggeration, they back off. In fact, journalists are a very touchy group with an arcane code of ethics and voracious needs that must be satisfied immediately.

Journalists are taught that it is wrong to provide favorable publicity in exchange for favors. In humanitarian disasters this can be very touchy. Sometimes the only way to get to a remote crisis spot is to be taken there by a humanitarian organization. Along the way, journalists might be given food or lodging. Good journalists aggressively try to reimburse the organization for its costs with money—never publicity.

There must be an understanding that there is no quid pro quo. I tell my students to practice a quality that former New York Governor Hugh Carey boasted of when asked about an apparent conflict of interest. He quipped that he had "monumental ingratitude."

I understand why humanitarian organizations feel they need publicity. They face growing responsibilities, but feel public support and funding is shrinking. In the United States—at least until the September 11 terrorist attack on the World Trade Center and the Pentagon—public interest in problems overseas has dropped. As a result, U.S. political and financial support for the United Nations has waned.

This is not the only bad news. Alarmed by long-term circulation decline and a more recent decline in advertising, the American press has also been losing interest in covering foreign humanitarian disasters, diverting resources instead to celebrity and personality features they think will attract readers and viewers. Just months after September 11, the bump in newspaper circulation the attacks caused began to evaporate and, with it, the increased press interest in overseas stories that didn't describe a direct threat to American service personnel, or readers and viewers themselves.

How the Press Works

How a story gets into a newspaper or magazine, or onto television or radio is probably a mystery to those not involved in the process. It's a sort of an industrial process. The product moves along an assembly line at an inexorable pace that cannot be interrupted. At daily newspapers, the editors must have information in printable form down to the presses by a certain deadline to get the publication printed and onto trucks in time to have it delivered in the morning. Radio and television news staffs must be ready to broadcast before the program is scheduled to go on the air. Wire services must get stories to their clients well before these deadlines. Hanging over all of them are the competing fears of being scooped if the stories are too late, or going public too quickly to prevent faulty reporting, which, at the worst case, could prove to be very expensive.

As the information moves relentlessly down this assembly line, journalists at the home office and out in the field adhere to rigid protocols and schedules that should be understood by humanitarians who want to influence the news.

Every morning at a designated time, editors meet to consider stories they might want to print or broadcast. The editors present ideas to each other from variety of sources: proposals from reporters who have been in touch before the meeting; stories the competition has already done; stories the editors have seen on reports from wire services such as Associated Press or Reuters; communications from public relations people sending press releases or calling by phone. Anything happening overseas is generally handled by the foreign editor who, at a large outfit, has a staff, or, if it's a small outfit, is juggling foreign news by himself or herself, along with other areas.

What are the editors looking for in a story? In simple terms, they're looking for news—something out of the ordinary, something that causes the reader or viewer to think: "I didn't know that" and to want to relate this information to someone else. But this is very general. It can be complicated because different publications or broadcasters have different ideas about who they want to reach. *The New York Times, Wall Street Journal,* and the *Washington Post,* for example, think they are writing for opinion-makers and decision-makers. They assume their readers already have a certain level of knowledge. Smaller papers often look for a more local angle, assuming readers will get the big picture from the big papers. Wealthier regional papers like *Newsday* try to combine both approaches. Local television news operations look for local news, leaving the big story to the networks.

After the meeting, assigning editors from the foreign desk get back to reporters to discuss what they will work on that day, that week, or long-term. In mid-afternoon, there is another editorial meeting to come up with a fairly rigid schedule of what stories will appear in the next edition or program. Later in the afternoon, unless they are covering a major breaking story, the reporters must meet deadlines and send in their copy, or send in the video or audio. The story gets processed by the editors, first on the foreign desk and then at a more general desk, before being sent to the printing press or made ready for broadcast. In the case of a longer feature story, the process can take days, weeks, or even months.

The time pressure on the editors is crushing. Not only do they have to make their deadlines, but they also have to make sure that the stories are both comprehensive and accurate. You can imagine how much time they can devote to considering a press release from a humanitarian group about the wonderful things it is doing—very little to none.

Reporters start out their careers being assigned generally to all sorts of stories. As they gain experience, they're assigned to beats with responsibility for geographic or substantive areas. Unfortunately for humanitarians, there isn't really a "humanitarian beat." Those stories usually fall to foreign correspondents, who work out of the aerospace and large capital cities, or a "fireman" like me, who are sent out with little or short notice to cover breaking stories overseas. In the trade, this is called "parachuting into a story," and there's always controversy whether the parachuting fireman will be able to provide nuance and background because the story is so new to him.

It's a kind of a truism among editors that reporters overseas get paranoid about what is happening to their stories. First of all, they are working under very difficult conditions, sometimes dangerous, often without enough sleep. Secondly, there is some truth to those fears. With recent technological advances, editors have many alternative sources of information other than the reporter. They often see the same event live on CNN and can read instant coverage of it from wire services and other media moving stories over the Web. Powerful institutions like the White House or the Pentagon can try to influence the editors by briefing reporters covering them with information that could influence their reaction. Sometimes editors will not take a humanitarian crisis seriously until reporters based in Washington, D.C., report back that the administration is taking it seriously. An example is the long-neglected famine and anarchy in Somalia that suddenly burst into the news in late 1992 when the Bush administration finally decided it merited attention and sent troops to protect humanitarians trying to deliver food aid.

So the reporter is scrambling around out in the field, trying to advance the story beyond his or her competitors, frantically trying to gather accurate information before the deadline to send it in. That's why the worst thing humanitarian workers can do is to try to manipulate the journalists or not tell the full story. This just gets the journalists nervous, and he or she moves on quickly. Journalists can be spooked easily by an approach that doesn't smell ethical to them. In the United States, journalists are supposed to be objective and not cover stories in which they have an emotional investment. For this reason, many journalists will not join or support organizations they might someday be covering. Some journalists will not even register with a political party.

Another key factor in understanding the media is understanding the rules of interviewing—or rather, understanding it the way the journalist does. Phrases like "off the record," or "not for attribution," or "deep background" have specific meanings that help both journalist and interviewee develop an upfront understanding about the ground rules of the interview. This prevents later recriminations about whether journalists endangered local or unsuspecting humanitarian workers by identifying them by name. You should discuss very frankly with the journalist how you want to be identified publicly. Diplomats and government officials often insist, for example, that the journalists agree to identify them only as "a government official" or "a Western diplomat." It's my own belief that journalists have an obligation to bring this up when they're dealing with naïve people who have no experience with the press.

Accurate facts are the currency of journalism. You must tell the truth. If there's a fact that cannot be disclosed, the interviewee should say so. To give the reporter some understanding of the situation without having certain facts published, say, "it's off the record." If a fact is disclosed but the source doesn't want to be associated with it, just say that it's "not for attribution." A "deep background" source of the information understands that reporters will strictly protect his/her identity. But never lie. Once a journalist is burned, he or she will never go near that source again.

KUKES—PARACHUTING IN

In the spring of 1999, I covered the kind of humanitarian crisis that I've been talking about. For months, the Clinton administration had been threatening Slobodan Milosevic with military action if he did not stop mistreating ethnic Albanians who made up the majority of the population of Kosovo, the former Yugoslavia province just north of Albania. The standoff finally led to confrontation, and NATO began bombing Serbia to force Milosevic to comply. Refugees began to flee into Albania and Macedonia with horrific tales of Serbian atrocities.

I was at *Newsday's* UN bureau in New York a few hours after the NATO attack had started when I got a call from the foreign editor, telling me to get to Albania and start filing stories as soon as I could. How I carried out this assignment is an illustration of the interplay between journalist and humanitarians.

If this had been an assignment to go somewhere unfamiliar, I would have found a PVO or NGO working there and asked for the best travel route, the best places to stay, any health problems I had to be aware of, the names of some reliable local contacts, and a quick briefing on the situation there. This approach has been really helpful to me in the past. When I covered the African famine, for example, the UN development program and UNI-CEF put me in touch with local representatives who were terrific. I tell my students to do this by going to the Web sites of InterAction or ReliefWeb, a site of the UN Human Rights Coordinator, to find which groups are working in the country or region they want to visit.

This time, I didn't have to do any of that. I'd been to Albania several times in the previous few years. Usually, the trip was not difficult—an overnight flight to Rome and then a quick plane trip to Tirana. But I knew it wouldn't be so easy this time. I wrote a brief description for *Newsday* about how I managed to get myself set up:

"Because NATO warplanes were flying every night over Kosovo, just north of Albania, all commercial flights into Tirana had been canceled. I would have to take a ferry across the Adriatic to Albania from the southern Italian city of Bari. But flights to Bari were canceled as well. I pulled my stuff together and flew to Rome, then to Naples, where I rented a car. Tired and jet-lagged, I raced at about ninety miles per hour (Italian speed limits seem relaxed) to Bari, just in time to catch the night ferry to Albania.

"Finally, I could relax. My friend, Fron, an Albanian refugee who had grown up in New York, was already in Tirana. He was going to pick me up at the ferry and we were to drive up to the Kosovo border together. (I try not to travel alone in situations like this.) As the hydrofoil ferry raced across the Adriatic, we passed warships carrying cruise missiles. Close to midnight, the ferry pulled up to a dark dock. No Fron.

"I hitched a ride to Tirana and called Fron. He thought I had missed the ferry. I found a hotel room and got a few hours of sleep. The next day, Fron found a driver (Orema, who had been the driver for the last communist dictator) and a translator (Artan, who was really a historian) for me. Remembering my experience covering refugees of the 1984 Ethiopia famine, I insisted we pack the trunk of Orema's Mercedes with bottled water and food, and we set off for Kukes, on the border with Kosovo.

"The road to Kukes had been built by the Italians during

World War II. It hadn't changed much since then. The journey of about 150 miles took nearly all day. Barely more than a narrow, rutted track, the road crept across snow-covered mountains. There were no barriers to the deep, sheer ravines just inches from the pavement. Tractors, trucks, buses, and cars were carrying thousands of refugees in the other direction. We became increasingly alarmed at the refugees' depressed and shocked appearance. Memories of the Ethiopian famine flashed through my sleepless, groggy mind.

"I had one priority—find a bed and a place to eat in Kukes, and start filing stories. That wasn't so easy. Kukes was an isolated frontier outpost. There were only a handful of hotel rooms. But Fron managed to find the Adriana, a little pension (small hotel) with seven rooms. We had arrived just ahead of the explosion of journalists and international aid workers who rushed in a few days later. By the time I left Kukes nearly two weeks later, journalists were sleeping on the Adriana's floors.

"What I wanted most at the Adriana was a room facing south. Without a southern window, I could not reach *Newsday* with my satellite telephone. Ten years ago, going somewhere like Kukes meant being out of touch with the paper for days. The satellite phone, about the size of a laptop, has changed reporting from remote areas, making it possible to call from anywhere in the world to anywhere in the world.

"I put the satellite telephone on the window ledge. Using a compass, I found one of four Inmarsat satellites that sit more than 22,000 miles above the equator. A few seconds later, I was talking to the desk in Melville, Long Island. Now I could start working.

"The days flew by. My only news of what was happening outside Kukes were the hourly BBC broadcasts from London I received on my little short-wave radio and occasional e-mails from the office. With a modem speed of 9600 kbs, the satellite phone hooked up to my laptop allowed me to receive e-mail, but not to surf the Web."

Being able to send and receive e-mails of text and photographs and communicate by voice instantaneously is a recent technological change that affects the coverage of humanitarian stories. There are still journalists alive, albeit very old, who worked under conditions that seem prehistoric now.

Not that long ago, it took literally weeks for reporters to file stories from the Third World. The famed World War II journalist, William Shirer, recalls in *The Nightmare Years,* that it took him three weeks to reach the *Chicago Tribune* with his exclusive account of the 1933 coronation of the king of Afghanistan. In his wickedly hilarious book, *Remote Peoples,* Evelyn Waugh describes how reporters covering Ethiopian Emperor Haile Selassie's 1930 coronation could communicate from Addis Ababa to the outside world only once a week. They had to file their stories describing the coronation before it actually took place.

In the early 1980s, when I started covering news overseas, the preferred way to send back a story was by punching a telex tape—either from a central cable office or from a hotel, if they had a telex. The story would clack and clatter out on a telex machine back at the paper.

In 1983, I started filing stories with my primitive RadioShack TR-80, an early laptop computer that journalists used at the time. I had to tip hotel switchboard operators in war-torn Beirut and Nairobi $50 each time I needed a rare direct overseas telephone line over which I could send my story. Almost all calls still went through a central exchange. It took hours to send a photograph. I had to go to the local Associated Press office with my film, wait until they developed it, select which photos to send back to the office, which, in turn, took many hours more until the photos were transmitted through London over the AP wire.

In rural areas, there was no communication at all. The only way I could learn what was going on in the outside world was to listen to BBC over my portable short-wave radio. Telephone communication did not exist.

All this is now ancient history. There is literally no spot in the world from which I cannot be instantly in touch with anyone in the United States. Hotels in even the most remote areas frequently receive twenty-four-hour access to CNN via satellite dish. The laptop-size satellite telephone I carry can be powered by batteries or through a vehicle's cigarette lighter receptacle. I can send and receive e-mail, and even send publication-quality photographs I've taken with my little point-and-shoot digital camera. Television reporters recently gained the ability to send grainy versions of their stories from literally anywhere in the world over modified and portable satellite telephones called videophones.

These new communications developments also open opportunities for humanitarian groups to make more information available to journalists.

My strategy for covering the Kukes story anticipated several stages. In the first few days, it was just a question of recording what I saw and sending it back. While I was doing this, I was busy developing sources among the organizations working there, trying to figure out who had the most accurate information. The more I learned, the more I began to perceive several larger stories. The first of these was the scope of the refugee flight and how well they were being cared for once they arrived in Albania. The second was what was happening back in Kosovo. After all, I had thousands of potential sources flooding across the border every day. The third was to tell the big, geopolitical picture behind this disaster. This I would try to weave into the more immediate stories to give the reader a sense of perspective.

Good journalists try to write stories that are interesting and offer perspective. You can't just keep describing the superficial scene you see everyday. You should start explaining it. But the explanation has to be interesting.

To do this, journalists look for anecdotal material to tell an engaging little story that serves as a vehicle for the larger story. Broadcasters have an even greater need for this interesting material. It could be what happened to one particular person, or family, or community. It could be how one humanitarian worker is struggling to cope. Or the visit of a high-ranking official, a visit to a hospital, a temporary children's center—you get the idea.

So this is what happened in Kukes.

When I first got out there, I encountered just a few over-whelmed humanitarian workers trying to create some sense of order. Within a few weeks, two full-blown communities had been established—humanitarians and journalists. This explosive growth is typical of major humanitarian disasters. Each community generally develops its own gathering places. In this case, they were the same—the Bar America, a sidewalk cafe/restaurant where exhausted workers and journalists could sit in the sun and enjoy a beer and an omelet. Local fixers gravitated to the Bar America, as well as disaster groupies who had made their way from Western Europe.

Fixers are very important to journalists covering a humanitarian disaster. I'm not sure what NGOs or PVOs call them, but I'm sure they have a term, because these people are essential. The name sounds sinister, but good fixers are prized and recommended by one journalist to another. A fixer is someone who is familiar with the local scene and players, but also understands the journalist's needs and speaks his language. A fixer sets up interviews with hard-to-get officials, translates or finds a translator, drives or finds a driver and a car, and, most importantly, knows when the situation has become too dangerous and how to get out of it quickly.

In this case, I didn't have a fixer because I had Fron, a respected figure in Albania, and Artan, a respected young historian. This was very important. A *New York Times* reporter showed up with no one at all and had to make do with a semi-literate taxi driver who seemed to misunderstand the situation. I teach my students that this is an area where they can turn to the humanitarian community for help. Expatriate humanitarians have the same needs for reliable local contacts.

Fron, himself, was writing stories for a Web site that published stories about the Balkan conflict. He gave me tremendous entree. We were able to go places where the Kosovo Liberation Army was hidden from the rest of the press. He and Artan kept me supplied with historical insights. In turn, I brought them a sense of perspective about the humanitarian story. I knew from previous experience that a couple of key people were submerged in the growing army of do-gooders, and I had to find them. They were the ones who knew what was really happening. This would make the difference between superficial and nuanced reporting.

How to find them? I teach my students techniques I learned doing rural community development in the Peace Corps, and then adapted to journalism. In the Peace Corps, we learned that to introduce change in a community, one had to learn who the truly influential people were and to gain their trust. These people were not necessarily those with big titles and, to find them, one had to understand the culture and how local communities made decisions. A quick way to gain people's confidence is to be introduced by a Sherpa, or mentor, who understands and is trusted by local people, but is a bit removed from the local scene. In a disaster situation, this means getting people back at the headquarters of humanitarian groups to vouch for you to their local representatives. Again, I teach my students to get in touch with these groups before they leave for the scene. After covering a few disasters, you and your work become known to many organizations. Of course, all this depends on having produced accurate coverage in previous stories—and having understood the sensitivities of humanitarian groups.

I was lucky in this case since we were among the first journalists to arrive. This is why it's important to move so fast to get to the scene. Again, this is an area where humanitarian organizations can be helpful to journalists.

It turned out that the key people in the quickly-growing humanitarian community were a young Swedish woman working for a tiny German NGO, one of the only ones there before the refugee flight started; an Albanian UNHCR employee, who had been assigned to Kukes earlier; and a former Belgian policeman, who had worked in the area for the Organization for Security and Cooperation in Europe. Later on, investigators for Human Rights Watch and the UN Tribunal for International War Crimes helped in interpreting what was happening inside Kosovo from interviews with scores of refugees.

It was important to find these people, since those nominally in charge were no help. In recent years, unremitting disasters and fickle, seesawing international funding have eroded the cadre of skilled personnel who can jump quickly into crises. UNHCR was the lead international agency for the Kukes crisis, convening a daily meeting of the growing group of humanitarians on the scene. The UNHCR chief for Albania had been out of the country when the crisis started, so his recently-arrived legal deputy, a Cambodian national, was in charge. He seemed incapable of decision-making, and the daily meetings never got past gripes sessions. Meanwhile, at the border a few miles away, thousands of people were wallowing in their own filth. It seemed as if UNHCR was reinventing the wheel. Sometimes the only people on the border greeting refugees were journalists and people from smaller humanitarian groups that had happened on the scene. No one seemed to be telling the refugees where to go or what to do. The situation was infuriating. A few months later in Kosovo, UNHCR again seemed unprepared for the returning refugees. This was a case beyond redemption by public relations. I discuss these problems later in the chapter.

It took weeks for UNICEF's technical staff to show up—but their publicists arrived much quicker. One day I sat on the terrace of the Bar America with a UNICEF press person from Rome. She had urged me to meet with an advance team that would help me with a story on refugee children. After several hours, an SUV pulled up with the team, which turned out to consist of a camera crew and a UNICEF press person from New York. They had been filming refugee children, drawing pictures of their traumatic flight from Kosovo for a promotional documentary. Only weeks later did professionals show up to work with the children.

In one of the early days of the crisis, I was gathering material for my daily story back to *Newsday*, wandering among exhausted and dehydrated refugees who had flopped on the nearest patch of ground just a few meters into Albania. Amid the crowd, a small team from Doctors of the World huddled over a man lying on a stretcher.

"Is it bad?" I asked one white-coated team member.

"Compound fracture of the ankle. He'll be OK," he replied professionally.

"Are you a physician?" I asked.

"No. I'm the press information officer."

Given a decade of endless complex humanitarian emergencies, why is the quality of humanitarian work so uneven? This is a question that bothers journalists covering disasters. Should they write about the defects in hopes that reform will follow? Would stories about humanitarian foul-ups overwhelm the more important, but less sexy, stories illustrating the underlying causes of humanitarian disasters? Should they ignore potentially scandalous situations because such stories endanger political and financial support for humanitarian organizations?

When covering humanitarian disasters, I frequently wonder if I am being fair. It's tough to be a humanitarian these days. Both humanitarians and journalists risk injury, death, or burnout every time they go to a disaster site. People begin to lose their perspective and their tempers. Back home, both humanitarian officials and editors face the inexorable pressures of costs, compassion fatigue, and growing isolationism. For private humanitarian organizations, this takes the form of lower individual donations. For UN humanitarian organizations, it takes the form of decreased economic and political support, especially from the United States. And for the media, it takes the form of risking advertising revenue by alienating readers and viewers with serious news about foreign humanitarian disasters.

SHARED DANGERS

In dealing with disaster, both press and humanitarian workers face many of the same dangers, challenges, and logistical needs. They have the same problems communicating and staying healthy, especially in poor, undeveloped countries. They both risk attack from armed gangs of young boys, some of them not even teenagers, working for corrupt warlords with no respect for human rights.

Between 1994 and 2001, 294 journalists were killed and 1,026 were jailed—most of them in developing countries, and the preponderance of them local journalists, according to the New York-based Committee to Protect Journalists. The annual rate seemed to be slowing down toward the end of the decade but there was a sharp spike in 2001—37 journalists killed and 118 imprisoned.

From 1992 through most of 2001, 204 civilians working for the United Nations were killed by ways other than natural causes or vehicular accidents. By far the largest group was working on humanitarian assistance—nearly 100.

From 1994 through the middle of 2001, some 255 UN personnel, seventy-two locally recruited, had been taken hostage, according to the United Nations. As of the fall of 2001, some forty were still arrested, detained, abducted, or "disappeared," according to the UN staff union. The International Committee of the Red Cross, whose workers rush into danger spots and face mounting risk in the field, reports it has averaged 130 security incidents annually since 1997. Nine ICRC workers were killed in 1996. Six were shot and hacked to death in the Democratic Republic of the Congo in April 2001.

Both journalists and humanitarian workers increasingly face "burnout," as comprehensively described in *Sharing the Front Line and the Back Hills. International Protectors and Providers: Peacekeepers, Humanitarian Aid Workers and the Media in the Midst of Crisis,* published in 2002 by trauma specialist and therapist, Yael Danieli.

I contributed a small article describing how I have learned to bounce back after covering humanitarian disasters. I had always been a little embarrassed about not recovering from these disasters like a tough guy. So I was both shocked and relieved to read in the Danieli book that journalists I admire had undergone the same, or even more severe, post-trauma problems—and that humanitarian workers often suffered worse.

COMPLEX HUMANITARIAN EMERGENCIES

The explosion of complex humanitarian emergencies after the collapse of the Soviet Union is the immediate reason for the increased risk of physical and emotional danger that journalists and humanitarian workers face. I had been covering disasters for years before I learned that humanitarian term of art. I heard it first in a 1996 conversation with now-U.S. Agency for International Development Director Andrew Natsios, who was then the head of World Vision.

These complex humanitarian emergencies are chaotic, even anarchic, situations where health, sanitary, economic, and communications systems have collapsed, while heavily armed, paramilitary groups from different ethnic and religious backgrounds try to destroy each other—with little regard for the Geneva Conventions of War. The struggles are epitomized by what happened in Bosnia, Rwanda, and the Democratic Republic of Congo. Military frontlines hardly exist. Disease, famine, and genocidal massacre ravage the civilian population.

Human rights violations are so rife that journalists and humanitarian workers are sometimes deliberately targeted to keep them from reporting back what they have seen—hence the increase in hostage taking, jailings, and killings.

During the Cold War, both superpowers had such control over the rest of the world that there were only a handful of such disasters at any one time. But when the Soviet Union disappeared, the number soared to more than thirty a year, severely taxing the international humanitarian community.

The CIA started putting out an annual report projecting global humanitarian emergencies for the coming year. According to the current report, the total number of humanitarian emergencies in August 2001 was twenty, down from twenty-five in January 2000.

The CIA's National Intelligence Council, which compiles the report, describes humanitarian emergencies as situations in which at least 300,000 civilians require international humanitarian assistance to avoid serious malnutrition or death.

The increased demand for international humanitarian aid pits one disaster against another in a struggle over scarce relief resources. Since 1992, wealthy countries have furnished little more than two-thirds of the emergency assistance asked for in UN Consolidated Appeals, the international mechanism that raises money to cope with complex humanitarian emergencies, according to the CIA report.

"Funding by donors of specific humanitarian emergencies tends to be heavily influenced by strategic concerns, *media attention* (my italics), and geographic proximity," the report says.

ETHIOPIA

The hunger for press coverage leaped during the Ethiopian famine of 1984, perhaps the first fully televised complex humanitarian emergency. For the first time, viewers actually watched people dying of hunger on television. Galvanized by this morbid sight, the U.S. public poured many millions of dollars on NGOs they associated with aiding the starving Ethiopian people. Some NGOs took in huge amounts and set a new standard for using the press to raise money.

The first American TV network to air the dying people was NBC. Kenyan photographer Mohammed Amin had shot the pictures of widespread dying among thousands of starving people who had fled to an ad hoc refugee camp on a desolate plain in Korem, Ethiopia.

Amin had been hired by World Vision, a California-based, evangelically-oriented private humanitarian group that was working in Ethiopia. World Vision's preferred method of fundraising was to purchase half-hour blocks of late-night or very early-morning time on local television stations, where they showed films of their staff working with starving people. What Amin brought back far exceeded their normal fare. They made the film accessible to the press. After it appeared on BBC, NBC happened to be the first network to discover it.

Scooped by NBC, the rest of the American press rushed toward Ethiopia. It just happened that *Newsday* was already working in Africa on a famine story. We had applied months before for Ethiopian visas. As a result, we were the first American newspaper on the ground, just a day or two after Amin's film was for seen in the U.S. As leader of the *Newsday* team, I had a unique opportunity to watch the feeding frenzy of press and humanitarian organizations. It was gruesome.

I came away from that experience with the disheartening feeling that fundraising and performance were not necessarily correlated. I'm sure I'm not the only journalist who had that feeling. It left me with a healthy skepticism about the claims of some humanitarian organizations, and admiration for others.

World Vision was the most effective group at fundraising and getting press attention. They had the system down to a science. On my return from Ethiopia in 1985, I visited their headquarters in Monrovia, California, and encountered a huge room—bigger than a basketball arena—where hundreds of people wearing telephone headsets were soliciting donations and following up on responses to the late-night television programs.

Their public relations staff was huge. Having heard months before I departed for Africa that I planned to write about humanitarian problems, a World Vision press representative had begun to call me with offers of help. I realized that she had actually been assigned to me, a sort of case officer. Her attention increased as my departure date approached. A few days before I left, she sent me a Federal Express package containing a pith helmet. I still haven't used it, although I think that, soaked beforehand, it will keep me cool some summer day in upstate New York.

Once in Ethiopia, I continued to be approached by World Vision press representatives, who obviously had been alerted to my presence and role by my case officer. They offered all kinds of help, including trips to Korem in one of the two airplanes they had, each emblazoned with the huge World Vision logo. At this time, thousands of unfortunates in Korem were sick and starving to death. They desperately needed food and medicine, which should have filled the planes instead of reporters.

I managed to get to Korem without them. But as literally hundreds of journalists from around the world poured into Addis Ababa, some others did take them up. When I got home, I saw that the World Vision plane, with its large logo, was in the background in many TV stories.

I don't want to single out World Vision for criticism. People I respect say it has raised its standards and effectiveness dramatically. But at that time, World Vision was by no means the most active or efficient humanitarian group in Korem. That category belonged to Doctors Without Borders, then an exclusively French group; British chapters of Oxfam and Save the Children; and, if I recall correctly, Irish Concern.

And while World Vision was the single largest beneficiary of voluntary contributions to private American humanitarian organizations during the Ethiopian famine, it was by no means the most effective throughout the rest of the country. Its fundraising seemed to be the tail wagging the dog. Its programs lagged far behind.

Another group that surprised me was Save the Children U.S.A., one of several national branches of a loosely affiliated organization also located in Great Britain and in Scandinavian countries. Few people outside of the humanitarian community realize that these are different organizations. Moved by TV pictures of Save the Children Fund U.K. workers helping starving people, many concerned Americans sent money to Save the Children U.S.A.

Millions of dollars rained on its Westport, Connecticut, headquarters. One would think that they would have passed the money along to their British counterparts in Ethiopia. But no, Save the Children U.S.A. kept the money and started up a small program in Ethiopia to justify their action. In contrast, Oxfam America, a very principled organization in my view, forwarded the contributions it received to Oxfam U.K., which was working in Ethiopia.

RISE OF NGOs

The proliferation of NGOs seeking media attention is due not only to the burst of complex humanitarian emergencies. Starting in the early 1990s, the UN began to allow increased participation by NGOs at large, decennial global meetings on such issues as environment, women's rights, and population control. The first example of this was the 1992 Rio Earth Summit, which produced Agenda 21 and the idea that rich countries of the north should compensate poorer countries in the south for the extra cost of developing industrially in a more environmentally sensitive way.

Traditionally, these global UN meetings were exclusively for member nations and official representatives. But Western environmental NGOs had become strong enough politically, especially with the rise of Green Parties in the parliaments of Europe, that they were given access to the proceedings—and a role in influencing the outcome. These groups, in turn, sponsored the participation of fledgling environmental groups from the Third World. Political reformers and revolutionaries throughout the Third World took the opportunity to get involved. The NGO Forum at Rio became a sounding board for all sorts of other grievances. This process continued to grow with the world population summit held later in Cairo and a worldwide meeting on women's rights in Beijing. At each gathering, the NGOs from the rich countries showed NGOs from poorer countries how to attract the press.

FOLLOW THE MONEY

To understand the culture of humanitarian organizations with which he or she is dealing, journalists should apply the old adage of investigative reporters—follow the money. Understanding where a group's support comes from explains its publicity needs. By no means am I arguing that a journalist should deliberately help groups raise money through publicity. But I am saying that

it is important to understand their needs to avoid being manipulated and to work harmoniously with them. The journalist's obligation is to convey a true picture of what is happening in a
disaster situation. If a humanitarian group can help, so much the
better. And if the story brings attention to their legitimately good
works, even better. But generally, they should be viewed as facilitator rather than the point of the story. The story should focus
on people in trouble, their needs, and how well they are being
met.

There's a great difference between the publicity needs of nongovernmental humanitarian groups in the United States and in
Western Europe—and, within Europe, between those in predominantly Catholic countries and those in Protestant countries.

This stems from who controls the dispensation and destination
of humanitarian aid. In Europe, the bulk of humanitarian aid is
provided by either governments or the church. In Europe's parliamentary systems, a large permanent bureaucracy develops and
implements humanitarian policy, which survives political
changes of government. In the United States, the public has a
greater role in influencing humanitarian aid—either through
Congress or through direct giving.

Traditionally, as pointed out by Alexis de Toqueville, Americans love to set up privately-funded voluntary organizations for
many purposes, not only humanitarian activities. These organizations are often called nonprofit groups in the U.S. If they do
humanitarian work, they are called private voluntary organizations, or PVOs. In Europe, the same types of groups are called
nongovernmental organizations, or NGOs, a reflection of the
greater role government funding plays in supporting them.

The upshot is that European NGO publicity needs pale in comparison to PVO needs in the United States, where the connection
between publicity and fundraising is intimate and insatiable. In
fact, the opportunity for private fundraising is so great that Euro-
pean-based humanitarian organizations—Amnesty International,
Doctors Without Borders, and Reporters Without Borders, for

example—are setting up U.S. counterparts with the same names to raise funds.

It was during a press freedom mission to Turkey that I saw vividly how European parliamentary funding of NGOs affects their behavior. The mission consisted of delegations from New York-based Committee to Protect Journalists and Reporters Without Borders, a French-based NGO, at that time financed primarily by the European Union. In contrast, CPJ refuses to accept government money, depending mainly on large American journalism companies and foundations for its support.

At the time, Turkey was the world champion of jailing and punishing journalists. The Turkish government had just changed and its new prime minister, apparently under orders from the military, was, at least temporarily, adopting a much more conciliatory approach to journalists. Many were being released from jail and the government was talking about easing its notorious anti-press laws. It was clearly a time to try negotiation and discussion rather than our usual stance of confrontation with Turkish government leaders.

We had far greater access to the country's top officials than I had experienced on previous CPJ missions to Turkey. When we sat down with Turkish President Suleyman Demeril, CPJ delegation leader Terry Anderson presented our position matter-of-factly but politely. Then the leader of Reporters Without Borders had his turn. In a strident voice, he waggled his finger at President Demeril, self righteously lecturing him on human rights. It was very counterproductive. I left the meeting angry at him. But, in retrospect, I realized what he was up to.

In Europe, Turkey's application for membership in the European Union is a controversial issue that arouses passionate arguments over its human rights policies, on one hand, and its allegations of European intolerance toward Muslims, on the other. Large Moslem Turkish immigrant communities in Western Europe, especially in Germany, rub up uncomfortably against the Christian majority. Demonstrating Kurdish immigrants frequently dramatize Turkish human rights violations. Complaining about Turkish human rights standards is a high priority for many members of the European Parliament, chief patron of Reporters Without Borders. In the United States, on the other hand, the Turkey issue is far less familiar and arouses little of the same emotion. Any conciliatory approach we made to President Demirel would have little effect on our private funders.

In Catholic countries of Europe, there is a greater tradition of giving humanitarian aid through the church, which buffers nongovernmental humanitarian agencies like Caritas from having to mount publicity campaigns to affect parochial political attitudes in each country. Their client is the more compassionate, less fickle Vatican in Rome. The Lutheran countries of Scandinavia have a very strong tradition of compassionate religious humanitarian agencies. In Great Britain, there are more secular NGOs, thus making them more dependent on popular opinion. But the five largest secular agencies, such as Oxfam, Save the Children, and the Red Cross, have a joint annual appeal that has developed a strong constituency, reducing the need to shock the public with pictures of starving children.

Pressures Mount for U.S. Publicity

Since the 1980s, several coincidental developments have added to the mania for U.S. press coverage of humanitarian activities: diminishing American government support for multilateral humanitarian aid (and the United Nations in general), and a growing emphasis on private humanitarian activity, starting with the Reagan and the first Bush administrations; the rise in humanitarian disasters as mentioned above; and the fantastic fundraising successes of groups like World Vision.

During the cold war, the U.S. system for dealing with overseas hunger emergencies was to distribute food aid multilaterally through the UN World Food Program or distribute it bilaterally through one of a handful of large, established American humanitarian PVOs like CARE. This was done under Public Law 480, which tapped into the enormous stock of surplus food the government maintained.

What I saw in Ethiopia was this system in transition. In Ethiopia, the lead agency hired by the U.S. to distribute the bulk of this food was Catholic Relief Services. CRS, the American equivalent of Caritas, didn't really have to worry about publicity since its funds came from the church and it had a long history of distributing aid for the U.S. government. Its publicity apparatus during the 1984 Ethiopian famine was minimal.

But some in the Reagan administration felt that traditional agencies like CRS or CARE were too liberal. They attempted, not too successfully, to funnel PL480 food aid through more politically conservative, evangelical Christian groups like World Vision. This was especially true in Central America.

At the same time, the United Nations system came under pressure. The Reagan administration had begun to cut back on financial support to force the UN to reform itself. Its humanitarian institutions could no longer automatically count on the United States for support.

Then the food surpluses in rich countries began to evaporate. First in the United States, in the Reagan administration, and more recently in Western Europe, agricultural subsidies became dirty words. The huge grain surplus in the U.S. and the "butter mountain" in Western Europe began to shrink. Wealthy countries would have to dip into taxpayer money to buy food to be given out to poor countries.

The impact of this became very clear at the decennial World Food Summit in Rome in November 1996, put on by the UN Food and Agriculture Organization. It introduced the international equivalent of the U.S. Welfare Reform Act that the Clinton administration and a newly Republican Congress had just enacted for the poor of the United States.

U.S. welfare reform gave American welfare recipients five years to get jobs and get off the government dole. The formal declaration endorsed at the Rome Summit pledged to cut the world's then 840 million hungry in half by 2010, a far more modest goal than the pledge to feed all the world's hungry enunciated at the previous World Food Summit in 1974. Lobbied for by the United States, this reduced goal reflected a decision to avoid large food aid commitments in the future.

The result of the declaration was that poor countries would have to either grow enough food for their own people or trade some other commodity—such as timber or minerals—to raise money to buy food. Even for starving people in poor countries, food was becoming a commodity. Ironically, even attempts to subsidize agricultural production in poor countries were being discouraged by market economy reforms that the Reagan administration had started pushing as a condition of International Monetary Fund loans.

Officials of food-producing countries made no attempt to disguise their dilemma in news conferences, speeches, and background papers: government farm subsidies were on the way out (although now partially revived by the second Bush administration and a Democratic Senate); food surpluses in rich countries were shrinking; and taxpayers in the U.S. and Western Europe were no longer willing to buy food for poor countries. At the same time the world demand for imported food, especially in poor countries, was soaring.

U.S. food aid told the story. It had dropped from 17.3 million tons in 1992 to 14 million tons in 1999 while needs grew. And looming over all this, another 2.6 billion people would need to be fed by 2025, experts predicted.

The upshot of this has been a growing appetite for public relations activities by UN humanitarian organizations. Large semi-autonomous agencies in the United Nations system—such as UNICEF, the WFP, and UNHCR—are hoping public relations will increase American public pressure on Congress and the White House to fund their particular mandates.

THE PRESS CUTS BACK

But this desire for more coverage of humanitarian issues comes at a time when the American press is spending less to cover the rest of the world. Whether or not they are reporting fully on humanitarian problems is least on the minds of beleaguered media executives. The daily newspaper industry is stymied by plummeting readership. The three major television networks are losing market share to cable television. Cable News Network's recent monopoly over twenty-four-hour news is being eroded by Rupert Murdoch's Fox Network. The entire media industry is cutting back spending because of a drop in advertising.

The first victim of all these factors has been expensive foreign news coverage. The general consensus in the media industry is that American readers and viewers are not interested in news about the rest of the world—unless there is a threat to the lives of American soldiers or to viewers and their families themselves. This would account for the temporary spike of interest in foreign news since the September 11 terrorist attacks.

Studies several years ago showed that as soon as a foreign news story came on the screen during the CBS Evening News with Dan Rather, viewers would start switching to other channels, according to Tom Bettag, then Rather's executive producer and now executive producer of ABC's Nightline.

Because the level of viewer market share determines advertising rates, TV executives pay close attention to these types of studies. Until September 11, spending and time budgeted for foreign news had been dropping for several years. The three big networks had closed most of their foreign bureaus and diverted resources to covering celebrity and personality news. The concept of important foreign news became a story like the death of Princess Diana.

Television cable news industry went through the same changes. CNN, which had formerly covered humanitarian issues quite extensively, changed format dramatically, cutting back on foreign coverage and introducing talk show formats and celebrity profiles.

Large regional newspapers, which had considered it an obligation to cover important foreign news with their own personnel, began to pull back. With the exception of a few large newspapers like *The New York Times, Wall Street Journal, Los Angeles Times* and the *Washington Post,* there was little original reporting overseas prior to September 11. The reason was not only financial, although ads were dropping because of the national economic slowdown. There was also the feeling that since newspaper readership was aging and shrinking, something drastic had to be done to attract younger readers. Sifting through demographic studies like tea leaves, many newspaper executives began to eliminate the longer, in-depth stories they felt alienated readers, and began to increase "news you can use" features about lifestyles, shopping, and entertainment.

Accelerating these changes has been the growing concentration of ownership of print and electronic media into the hands of a few large public corporations and a reduction in family-owned media.

Family-owned companies are accountable only to themselves. If they have a strong tradition of social responsibility, they can ignore ups and downs in the economy and continue to spend money on important stories that may not attract many readers. But even if they wanted to cover poor people in other countries, large publicly-owned newspaper companies must pay attention to Wall Street pressure to boost circulation and, thus, ad revenue. This means, for example, stories on Princess Diana rather than floods in Bangladesh.

Because most of the nation's large newspaper companies are publicly owned, they compete on the stock market with other companies for investors. Newspapers belong to the consumer cyclical sector, which they share with radio and television stations that can earn 30 percent to 40 percent in annual operating revenue. Thus, newspaper companies feel they must earn well over 20 percent in annual operating revenue to satisfy Wall Street analysts. Average daily newspaper operating revenues in the economically depressed year of 2001, for example, averaged about 18 percent and were considered disastrous.

The impact of this concentration of public ownership is dramatic. CNN, for example, used to be controlled by Ted Turner, who wanted to make money but was also devoted to using his network to promote world peace and prosperity. Turner sold control of CNN to Time Warner, more subject to pressures of its stockholders, but still a media company. Time Warner cut back some of Turner's emphasis on foreign news coverage. But the pace quickened when the company was gobbled up by AOL, a product of the tech stock bubble.

In the newspaper business, a few giant media companies—Knight Ridder, Gannett, and Tribune—have been gobbling up their competitors. Foreign news is suffering. Knight Ridder's *Philadelphia Inquirer*, for example, has gone from being a perennial Pulitzer Prize winner, known for its in-depth foreign coverage, to an aggressively local newspaper. Tribune, which recently bought the Times Mirror Company, is expected to start consolidating the extensive foreign reporting resources of the individual newspapers it has just bought, like the *Los Angeles Times*, the *Baltimore Sun*, and *Newsday*, which had won three Pulitzer Prizes in International Reporting in the last decade and a half. These three are among the few American newspapers that have been devoting time and space to covering humanitarian issues.

Even before Tribune starts homogenizing its company's foreign coverage, I doubt very much whether *Newsday* would now make available to any of its reporters the time and money that was at my disposal when I covered in the 1984 African famine.

9

The Sinews of Humanitarian Assistance: Funding Policies, Practices, and Pitfalls

Joelle Tanguy

"MONEY AND NOT MORALITY is the principle of commerce and commercial nations," wrote Thomas Jefferson to John Langdon. In humanitarian assistance, our readers should easily agree that morality, not money, ought to be the backing principle. Today's reality lies somewhere in between. Humanitarian operations provide life-saving assistance to millions, but are mostly funded through mechanisms of limited congruence to humanitarian objectives, tainted by political and economic influences, prejudiced by public perceptions driven by commercialized media, and interfering with effective accountability—itself a concept yet to be clearly defined.

Will humanitarian organizations successfully maneuver the complexity of their financial environment? Will we see the "politics of compassion" further deviate from the principles of humanitarian action? What redesign of the system is looming ahead? What is at stake for the hundreds of millions of people facing conflict and disaster and the more than 35 million displaced from their home?

To contemplate the questions that will define humanitarian assistance in the next decade, we must start by exploring the policies, practices, and pitfalls of today's system, as illustrated in the most recent developments.

Our starting point ought to be a definition of humanitarian action: the alleviation of human suffering through care and assistance by independent and impartial agents. Admittedly, nowadays, "humanitarian assistance" lines in the budgets of donor countries and NGOs have swollen progressively to include a larger scope of activities involving transitional development, even peace-building and conflict resolution work, carried out by various institutions and networks—even the military—in the latest phenomenon of "humanitarian interventions."

If the sinews of war are "men, money, materials, maintenance, and morale,"[1] those are, too, the sinews of humanitarian assistance, money bearing no small part in the equation. We will explore here how humanitarian action is funded today, the trends affecting these financial matters, and how they translate into operational and ethical issues. We will review the fundraising mechanism of nongovernmental organizations and international agencies involved in emergency operations, consider the evolving role of the media in the process of mobilizing public support, and explore the debates over the accountability of humanitarian organizations.

GOVERNMENTS LEAD GLOBAL HUMANITARIAN FUNDING

Overview

The bulk of emergency assistance funds come from governments and were greatly expanded in the last decades. To describe the trajectory in broad terms, let us say that annual humanitarian funding remained below U.S.$500 million in the 1970s, springing up in the mid-1980s with the Ethiopian and Sudanese crises, remaining around $1 billion until the end of the cold war, rising abruptly to between $4 billion and $5.5 billion with the Kurdistan, Somalia, Bosnia, and Rwanda crises of the early 1990s, and leveling off for a few years to between $3.5 billion and $4.5 billion annually before rising again with the Kosovo and, more recently, the Afghanistan crises. (See Figure 9.1.)

While this increase sounds like a positive development for the millions of people affected by instability since the end of the cold

Figure 9.1 Total Humanitarian Assistance 1989–1998 (in millions of U.S. dollars)

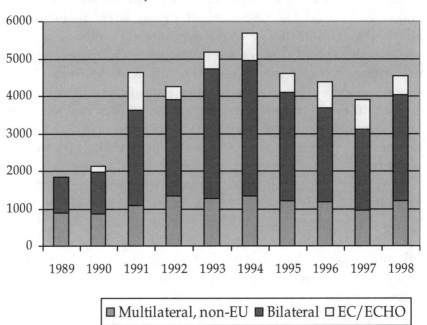

□ Multilateral, non-EU ■ Bilateral □ EC/ECHO

Source: OECD DAC statistics table 1 and 2a; WFP Annexes to Annual Report and IASC Global Humanitarian Assistance 2000 report table A1.

war, it should be put in perspective with the increase in per-capita wealth in donor countries, which rose from U.S.$21,000 to $28,000 per year in the 1990s. Within that same period, only some U.S.$5 per capita per year was allocated by donor countries to humanitarian assistance. (See Figure 9.2.)

Governments' funding for humanitarian assistance is both multilateral and bilateral. Multilateral assistance is channeled by the United Nations and the European Commission, while bilateral assistance may be allocated government to government or through NGOs. While in the late 1980s, the UN enjoyed a 40 percent to 50 percent share of humanitarian assistance, it had dropped by the late 1990s to 25 percent, while bilateral aid and EC shares expanded respectively to up to 60 percent and 20 percent.[2]

Figure 9.2 Humanitarian Assistance Per Capita

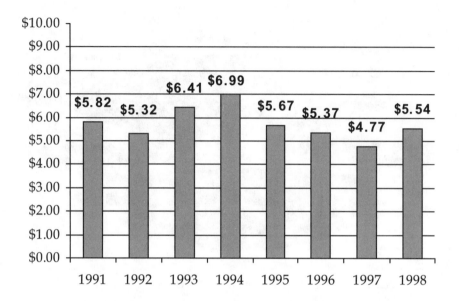

Source: OECD DAC statistics.

Throughout the 1990s, the United States was the leading donor to UN Consolidated Appeals in aggregate terms, providing, on average, a third of emergency assistance funds while four donors, including Japan and the European Commission, provided the next third. (See figure 9.3.) A large part of the U.S. contribution has been in food aid, which actually dominates the sectors of emergency assistance, capturing 60 percent of government donors' contributions to UN emergency appeals in 2001. (See Figure 9.4.)

In addition to funding from the thirty states that are members of the Organization for Economic Cooperation and Development (OECD), contributions from non-OECD countries have also risen over the years. While still a small portion of the total, these illustrate the "burden sharing" emphasized by parallel efforts to strengthen regional organizations such as the Organiza-

Figure 9.3   Top Ten Donors to UN Humanitarian Consolidated Appeals, 2001

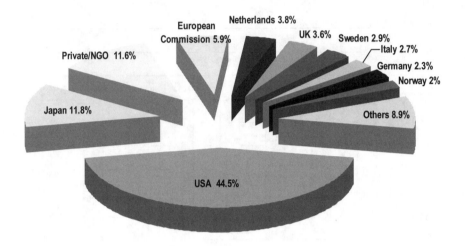

Source: ReliefWeb, consolidated appeal financial tracking system, 2001.

tion of African Unity (OAU). A rarely visible part of the humanitarian assistance equation has been the tremendous support of host countries neighboring the countries in crisis. They bear the largest burden in proportion to their resources, especially in Sub-Saharan Africa where the GNP is the lowest and the burden of refugees the highest. The increasingly restrictive asylum policies of OECD countries have further compounded the situation.

Nongovernmental organizations (NGOs) are also backing humanitarian assistance with private funds collected from their own civil societies: general public contributions as well as foundations and corporate gifts. The United Nations financial tracking shows them ranging 10 to 15 percent of total donations to Consolidated Appeals in recent years,[3] but this figure pertains only to UN appeals, and the overall impact of private support may be thus underestimated. Many in the NGO community, and even in UN agencies[4], are now working hard at their emancipation from gov-

Figure 9.4   Donor Contributions to UN Appeals by Sector, 2001

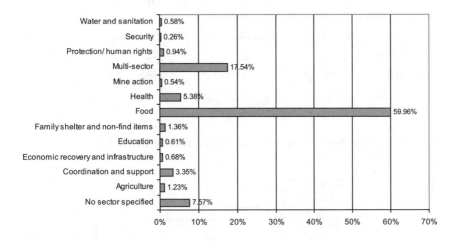

Source: OCHA, ReliefWeb financial tracking.

ernment foreign aid policies and at the cultivation of private, that is to say, nongovernmental, support.

Private backing of aid still lags significantly behind the volumes of government funding and the bulk of NGOs' relief operations remain dependent on government funds for emergency assistance. In fact, the channeling of government funds through NGOs expanded dramatically in the 1990s, with many governments expensing more than a quarter of their budgets in this manner. This dependency is a key feature of the relief community today.

Complex Funding Mechanisms and Resource Flows

While the flowchart in Figure 9.5 appears complex enough to illustrate the resource flows in the humanitarian aid system, it is only a two dimensional design of a multidimensional system. In each category of actors such as "donor agencies" or "international nongovernmental agencies," there are scores of independent institutions coordinating their funding and operational decisions rather poorly.

For example, in a single emergency situation, half a dozen independent UN agencies may be operating and competitively raising funds, including UNHCR, WFP, UNICEF, even WHO and

Figure 9.5   Resource Flows in the International Relief System

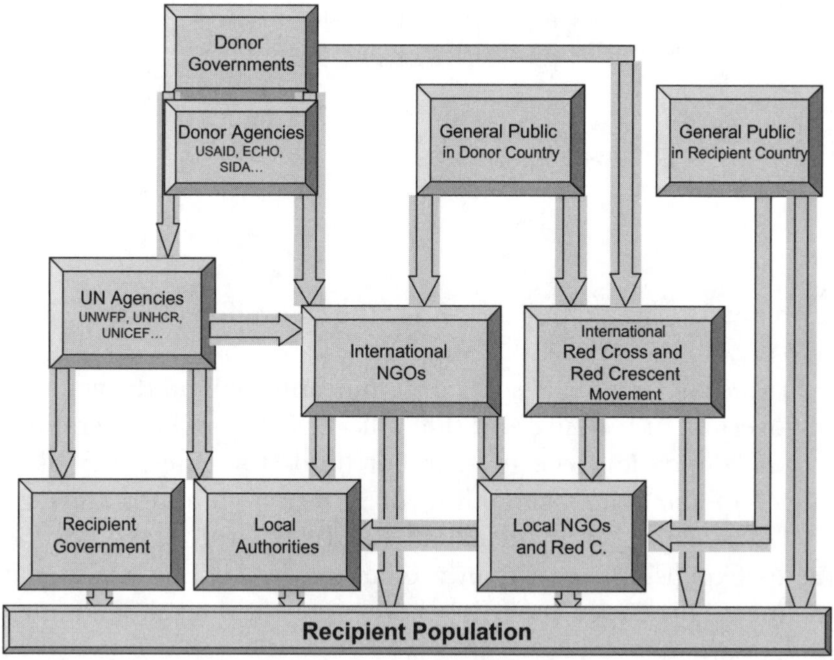

Source: J. Tanguy, 2001, adapted from OECD DAC working paper, "Guidance for Evaluating Humanitarian Assistance in Complex Emergencies," 1999, page 8, figure 1.

UNDP. As UN agencies are rarely delivering services directly to the population, they will grant funds to NGOs for relevant projects. Yet the same NGOs compete for the same government funds granted directly. These NGOs, which may number in the tens or even hundreds, are meanwhile competing with each other for both government donors' attention and media interest.

The "relief circus"[5] of Mogadishu, Goma, and Sarajevo, where hundreds of new NGOs appeared within a single month—often unprepared and untrained, and sometimes confused on their mission and role—while major NGOs competed aggressively for media and donor attention, are the most flagrant illustrations of how the complex system can go awry.

The picture ends up radically simplified in humanitarian crises enjoying little media coverage.[6] There, fewer players are at play, since budgetary constraints are forbidding, except for the rare few who have access to un-earmarked funds that can be deployed on the basis of humanitarian needs alone. When budgets are tight and players few, cooperation is often simplified and amplified in front of dire need—sometimes only a few hundred miles away from a "relief circus."

How does the system fare? As Shepard Forman concludes, "without systematic and transparent needs and impact assessments, it is difficult to determine whether existing levels of aggregate expenditure are, in fact, adequate. Unfortunately, government funding tends to arrive following the onslaught of a crisis, when political support has peaked, rather than in its incipient stages when comprehensive need assessments should be carried out. Moreover, national interest criteria usually guide donor government decisions and seriously compromise the equitable distribution of humanitarian assistance across crises, rendering it insufficient in many cases. In any event, there is a strong sense of resource constraint among the community of aid providers."[7]

The complexity of the funding mechanisms for humanitarian missions is daunting and impacts not only resources but also coordination and accountability practices.

MAJOR RECENT TRENDS

In the last decades, several developments dramatically altered the financial and operational environment of humanitarian assistance, in particular: the dwindling of development assistance budgets and their partial redirection toward emergency assistance; the proliferation of NGOs involved in humanitarian assistance along with the rapid growth of a few large international NGO networks; and the dependence on governments funding that still characterizes most relief agencies.

Dwindling Foreign and Development Aid

Official Development Assistance (ODA) budgets include both development and emergency assistance (and a number of other instruments), and are often managed by the same governmental institutions. ODA has dropped to its lowest levels in half a century. In 1999, only four of the twenty-two countries in the Development Assistance Committee of the OECD[8] actually met or exceeded the target of 0.7 percent of GNP for their level of foreign aid (Denmark, Norway, the Netherlands, and Sweden). The *last* of these twenty-two donor countries was the United States, which, although a leading donor and second only to Japan in total dollar value, is only contributing a mere 0.10 percent of GNP (ten times less than the Danes). Overall, ODA has also dropped as a percentage of donor government expenditures from an average of 0.8 percent in the early 1990s to 0.6 percent in the late 1990s.

Donors budgets were characterized in the 1990s by simultaneous drops in military and foreign aid spending, but while the military costs declined by 6 percent, foreign aid declined at the accelerated pace of 23 percent between 1992 and 1997.[9]

From Multilateral Development to Bilateral Humanitarian Assistance

During the same period, donor countries each allocated anywhere between 1 percent and 25 percent of their foreign aid bud-

Figure 9.6   Aid From All OECD-DAC Donors as a Percentage of GNP

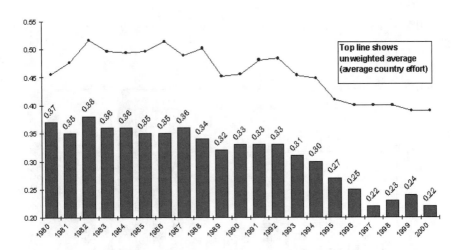

Source: OECD, 2001.

get to humanitarian assistance, but, on average, bilateral humanitarian assistance rose progressively to an average of 12 percent of bilateral ODA in 1999. Meanwhile, as we noted earlier, the share of humanitarian assistance channeled through the United Nations dropped by half within ten years while the shares of bilateral aid and European Community (EC) support expanded. By the late 1990s, bilateral donors controlled over 60 percent of humanitarian assistance.[10]

In each OECD capital, even when foreign aid budget discussions become intense, they rarely appear to threaten the bulk of humanitarian assistance that enjoys steady bi-partisan support. In *Foreign Affairs,* David Rieff cites a bitter U.S. State Department Official in Rwanda: "There's money for weapons, and money for starving refugees, and that's about it."[11]

The immediate consequence of the converging trends—

Figure 9.7   Bilateral Humanitarian Assistance as a Share of Bilateral ODA

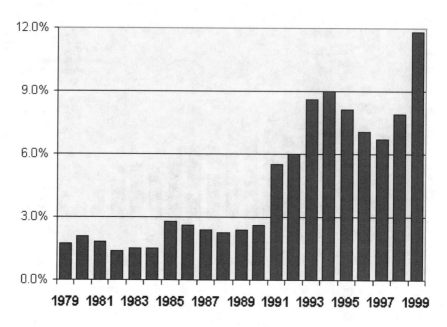

Source: OECD.

decreased ODA, decreased development aid, increased humanitarian assistance budgets—have been a re-composition of the field of humanitarian assistance with new actors, often originally development agencies who bring the development perspective to emergency assistance. At Oxfam, the share of emergency-related programs rose steadily to 40 percent of its U.K.£115 million in 2001. Save the Children and World Vision now operate more often in crises situations. Even human-rights organizations, such as Human Rights Watch and Amnesty, became more operational in the field and started tackling matters of refugee rights.

While this phenomenon enriched the debates and enabled new approaches to old humanitarian problems, it also brought tremendous confusion in the exercise of coordination and in the definition of humanitarian assistance itself.

With new players and new pressures came new concepts—some helpful, some not—such as "complex emergencies," "relief to development continuum," "nation building," "conflict prevention," even "humanitarian military intervention." The pressure of the human rights movement on the new and conceptually fragile community of relief workers led to heated debates often started without a solid grounding in humanitarian law, resulting in interesting yet often-dangerous turns in the positioning of "humanitarian actors" vis-à-vis their governments, military, local authorities, communities, etc. . . .

The shift in the field of humanitarian assistance may be as significant as that of the 1970s that brought a whole new generation of "sans-frontiers" organizations alongside—and in tension with—the Red Cross movement. This new shift is one whose final trajectory is not known yet: will the new "community of humanitarian actors" find its bearings in the post 9/11 world? The recent debates demonstrate the healthy space for soul-searching—yet the pressures may mount in the anti-terrorism war and "humanitarian" NGOs will need more than ever to know what humanitarianism stands for in order to stand for it.

A Breeding Ground of New NGOs

The 1990s were marked not only by the encounter and transformation of development aid and humanitarian assistance, but also by the proliferation of NGOs and the transformation of their collective power through civil society.

Even the United Nations acknowledged and institutionalized the phenomenon by the mid-1990s. In his 1998 report, the Secretary-General highlighted that from the forty-one NGOs granted consultative status by the Economic and Social Council (ECOSOC) in 1948, and 377 in 1968, the number of NGOs in consultative status had expanded to over 1,350. While 200 NGOs were associated with the Department of Public Information in 1968; there were now 1,550.

Back in OECD capitals, the same phenomenon can be observed. The number of aid agencies registered with USAID, the U.S. development agency, has tripled in twelve years since 1982. InterAction, an alliance of U.S.-based "international and humanitarian NGOs," both secular and religious, counts more than 160 members operating in over 100 countries. Ministry Watch, an online database serving potential donors to Christian ministries, lists forty-eight U.S. Christian organizations registered as carrying out relief and development work, including World Vision, Mercy Corps, and Samaritan's Purse. The situation is mirrored in Brussels, London, Paris, etc. . . .

Meanwhile, local NGOs in recipient countries have multiplied as well. The pace of their development varies tremendously from country to country, given the variety of political and economic contexts. Yet, many such groups are now partnering with international NGOs and UN agencies.

New Titans of Emergency Assistance

A July 2000 study commissioned by DFID, the British Department for Foreign International Development, on the role of NGOs and other charity flows concludes that some of the world's largest NGOs now have incomes larger than several bilateral donors, are active in more countries, and are certainly as influential in their ability to command public and political attention.[12]

While the study referred to development assistance, the same could be inferred of relief work of certain NGOs, whose budgets have risen over the last two decades. The lines between the two categories—humanitarian and development—have become rather blurred anyway. Initially a development organization, religious in its organizing principle, U.S.-born World Vision ventured into emergency assistance aggressively in the 1990s, and became a major player with an annual budget around the half-billion U.S. dollar mark! The large post-World Wars agencies such CARE, Oxfam, Save the Children U.K., and Catholic Relief Services similarly increased their emergency assistance activities in the 1990s and became small giants, with budgets of U.S.$200 million to U.S.$300 million. The *Médecins sans frontières* network, the largest of the 1970s generation of humanitarian NGOs, reached $320 million in 2000.

Compared to the titans of the U.S. nonprofit world, these organizations may not seem all that mighty. After all, CARE is ranking only eightieth among the top 400 U.S. charities, and Catholic Relief Services is ninety-fifth. Even World Vision, in its seventeenth position, is dwarfed by the likes of the Salvation Army and American Red Cross[13] whose budgets, $2.7 billion and $2.4 billion respectively in 2000, are more than five times World Vision's.[14]

Of course, all are dwarfed by corporate entities operating in many of the countries in crisis, such as those in the oil and extraction businesses. ExxonMobil, for example, is a U.S.$232 billion company. Yet its corporate philanthropy remains limited: its 1997 worldwide contributions were about $55 million, some $42 million in the United States and $13 million in other countries.

Let us not forget, however, that when compared with government donors, World Vision, with its half-billion dollar budget, is tailing Belgium's annual ODA budget of $753 million in 1999, and is ahead of Austria, Finland, and five other OECD countries. And the pack of other international NGOs challenged or passed Portugal, Greece, Ireland, New Zealand, and Luxembourg, whose annual ODA budgets range from $275 to $115 million.

While this ought to help foster the further development of civil society, it also encounters some serious limiting factors in emergency and especially conflict situations. Given the time pressure, sustainable capacity building is rarely engaged, and the relationship ends up often being a contractual arrangement in the delivery of goods and services. Furthermore, security and political issues come into play, and may compromise many local actors—the pressures on local NGO leaders being tremendous in times of crisis. The conflict also rarely affords them the luxury of neutrality and impartiality required of humanitarian operators, as was epitomized in Rwanda during the genocide, and even in the refugee camps. Somalia also witnessed the manipulation of humanitarian resources by a mushrooming army of warlord-owned local NGOs. . . .

A trend "from service delivery to leverage" may be in motion with the rise of civil society organizations worldwide. It will be slower at the heart of conflicts since, unsurprisingly, there is little "civil society" left at the heart of uncivil civil wars. But the emergence of many new NGOs on the frontlines is a new trend to reckon with—and build upon—while new "titans" emerge from the rapid expansion of major international NGO networks. (See box above.)

Independent NGOs?

The true limiting factor of these international NGOs' ability to actually command public and political attention for the exclusive benefit of their beneficiaries is the reality of their dependence to their institutional donors. A rare few are exceptions to the rule, but overall relief operators have been held hostage, willing or unwilling, to government funding.

Figure 9.8   A Measure of Independence? U.S. Nonprofit Agencies Private Funding Ratios

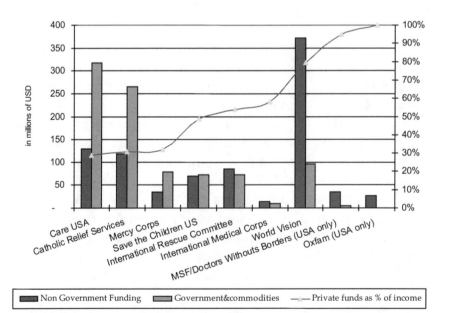

International networks have varying policies and practices. Save the Children Fund U.K. (SCF U.K.) has been faring slightly better than its U.S. partner, with 41 percent of its U.K.£115 million budget funded by governmental and multilateral agencies[15] whereas 49 percent of SCF U.S.A. budget is contributed by private donors. The Oxfam network is well supported by private donors, but Oxfam America's choice of 100 percent private funds is not shared by Oxfam U.K., whose cash and commodities support from government and multilateral agencies amounted to 30 percent of its income in 2001.

The political culture and history of U.S. and European organizations differ widely, especially in the relationship between civil society and government foreign policies. To describe it in very broad terms, while European NGOs often inherited from the decolonization era their suspicion of governments, traditional U.S. development agencies have never been in confrontation with the U.S. government which, even in the cold war, was seen as pushing forth a certain human rights ideal.

There is no line in the sand defining the ratio of private funds that would ensure operational and political independence of organizations. Some even argue that such heavy reliance on institutional funding is an asset—inexpensive fundraising and independence from the short attention span of the general public—with side effects requiring only to be properly managed.

It is therefore empirical evidence rather than scientific data that helps NGO executive teams and boards maneuver in this environment. That is, assuming there is maneuvering space for the humanitarian action: as humanitarian assistance becomes central to the foreign policy agenda, and with the rise of military interventions, this maneuvering space is shrinking.

In this context, one of the troublesome features of the disaster relief NGO community in the U.S. has been its general tendency to ignore the tension that lies between humanitarian, political, and military. Even as the Kosovo intervention unfolded, its own coordination team, the InterAction Disaster Response Committee, was dependent on the U.S. government's Office of Foreign

Disaster Assistance (OFDA) for the funding of its core activities, and had granted it the right to vet the appointment of its chief staff member.[16] In addition, InterAction senior staff has often been appointed from or to positions in the U.S. government, and in recent years, a number of its activities involved close collaboration with the military without a clear sense of mission. It worked extensively on the security of humanitarian workers, a preoccupation of many agencies, without ever decisively recognizing the threat emerging from humanitarian NGOs being seen in the field as the foot soldiers of military intervention. Set up in the mid-1980s as facilitator for NGOs to coordinate and help influence U.S. policy and debate on international issues, InterAction is now sometimes seen as the NGO liaison tool for the U.S. administration to orchestrate the support of NGOs.

Also of concern is the increased conditionality of some donor contributions: tying funds to purchases from an identified source—such as OFDA's insistence on U.S. sourcing of pharmaceuticals—or to political objectives—such as the German's government insistence on Bosnian repatriation in the late 1990s, despite NGO concerns for security conditions.[17]

All these developments are concurrent to tremendous changes in the environment of humanitarian assistance, especially in its relationship to peacekeeping, peace-enforcement, human rights and conflict prevention agendas. In the field, the fragmentation of armed movements, and the increasingly blurred distinctions between state and non-state, private and public, political and business initiatives, are leading to a confusion of roles and increased manipulation and misuse of aid. Yet aid organizations, although lamenting the "humanitarian alibi," are lined up to receive more government funding.[18]

A Contrasted View of Independence

Two "titans" of emergency assistance, World Vision and MSF, both have high private funding ratios, yet exercise their independence in rather contrasted ways:

Médecins sans frontières (MSF) was no exception to the trend of government dependence of humanitarian operators a decade ago: in the early 1990s, as many multilateral funds shifted under bilateral control, it was faced with the abrupt consolidation of its UN and European Union funding into Brussels's hands. The organization reacted immediately, and in 1992 went on to explore institutional donor diversification—new relationships with DIFID, USAID, SIDA, and AUSAID, for example—and to expand national and international private donor bases, with a focus on smaller donors rather than large philanthropic organizations. The institutional funding diversification was achieved within a year by its Paris-based organization, and the focus on building private donor bases paid off over time with the international network now enjoying a private funding ratio of 80 percent, raising some $260 million from 2.5 million private and individual donors worldwide.[19] This conscious effort to remain fiercely independent of political powers is a logical consequence of the exclusively humanitarian focus and the culture of the organization, as well as the cultural cradle of the May 1968 generation of French intellectuals who influenced its development.

World Vision, on the other hand, defines itself as the world's largest Christian international relief and development agency and was founded in the 1950s. It enjoys a rare position among U.S. relief and development organization: not only is it the largest of the U.S. relief operators, but 79 percent of its income comes from private sources, a significant difference with organizations such as CARE (29 percent) and Catholic Relief Services (31 percent).[20] Yet, rather than taking distances from political powers, World Vision has developed close ties with Washington, D.C., as demonstrated by the staffing shuffle over the years between the two institutions. For example, USAID's current Administrator is a former vice president of World Vision U.S., and had previously led the U.S. Office of Foreign Disaster Assistance (OFDA).

The International Red Cross: Growing Pains and Renewal

The Geneva-based International Committee of the Red Cross is the very institution legally entrusted since the late nineteenth century with the humanitarian responsibility to protect and assist the victims of armed conflicts and internal disturbances on a strictly neutral and impartial basis.

The National Societies of the Red Cross and Red Crescent Movement contribute to the ICRC budget and may, in some instances, also intervene with their own operations, with the support of the Red Cross and Red Crescent Federation, also based in Geneva. In crises situations, the ICRC becomes responsible for coordinating all external aid from Movement members to victims inside the country in crisis, whereas the Federation may coordinate the Movement's response to relief needs of refugees in neighboring countries.

The ICRC budget in 2001 was barely a billion dollars, including some $850 million to cover the costs of field operations. For its financing, the ICRC mostly relies on voluntary contributions from the governments representing States Party to the Geneva Conventions and multilateral institutions such as ECHO, from the National Red Cross and Red Crescent Societies, and from private sources, the Swiss public in particular. While the Red

Figure 9.9   ICRC Contributions Received in 2000

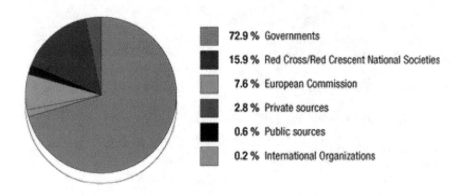

72.9 % Governments

15.9 % Red Cross/Red Crescent National Societies

7.6 % European Commission

2.8 % Private sources

0.6 % Public sources

0.2 % International Organizations

Source: ICRC.

Cross and Red Crescent Societies and a few other private sources provide almost 20 percent of the budget, the mainstay is backed by public sources, primarily governments.

The Federation is a separate institution, and its budget, independent of both ICRC and national societies, was CHF323 million in 2000, or some U.S.$200 million, half of it dependent on government funding.

The bulk (80 percent) of cash financing for the ICRC's field operations comes from some twenty governments and supranational donors such as the European Commission (ECHO). Governments' tendency toward earmarking their contribution for specific crises or services is a constraint of much concern to the ICRC.

The ICRC has been appealing to donors for more flexibility, as was the case in 2000 when it publicly announced a record funding shortfall, and again in late 2001 when Afghan operations ended up largely more funded than the 79 percent average in ICRC emergency appeals worldwide. It called for "donor flexibility on two levels. Firstly, should it become necessary, so as to allow earmarked contributions for Afghanistan to be brought forward to the 2002 budget for the Afghan conflict. This would secure a smooth continuation of operations and financial coverage of this operation for the first few weeks of 2002. Secondly, so that donor funding for Afghanistan is not detrimental to the important funding needs for humanitarian operations elsewhere in the world."

This recent development illustrates again how national interests and other factors unrelated to humanitarian needs play into the funding of assistance. The ICRC is legally bound to respond to all humanitarian crises, yet none of its government donors have the same obligation to provide adequate funding on an impartial basis to its operations, and, again, a major knot in the relief system finds itself at the mercy of public perceptions and political bias.

Fortunately, the strong humanitarian culture and independent management of the organization have so far helped preserve at least the perception of—and possibly the reality of—the ICRC independence from political agendas. Rather than funding problems, security incidents, brought about in part by its obligation to operate whatever the situation, appear to have been the main handicapping factors in the agency's performance in recent crises.

United Nations: Gaining Momentum or Loosing Ground?

The 1990s also saw the UN budget significantly expanded—by 30 percent in the decade—but with the concurrent move from multilateral to bilateral funding, discussed above, the United Nations no longer enjoys the same financial leadership role, and the UN appeals went irregularly funded, from 75 percent to 80 percent in the Rwanda and Kosovo crises years to below 60 percent in leaner years. See figure 9.10.

Among the challenges is the voluntary nature of the member states contributions that fund international emergencies operations—as opposed to the regular contributions to the UN, which are assessed on a scale approved by the General Assembly. Overall, funding remains crisis-driven, compelled by media pressure on the donor government through its general public, and frequently not allocated in proportion to the needs: some media-featured crises are heavily funded while others linger on underfunded.

In the early 1990s, the United Nations sought to improve its fundraising coordination mechanisms and put in place the Consolidated Appeal Process (CAP), a new tool for joint resources mobilization, under the oversight of what is now known as the UN Office for the Coordination of Humanitarian Assistance (OCHA), with a view to address the inefficiencies and pitfalls of UN agencies competing for funds.

Criticism that the effort yielded nothing else than a consolidated "shopping list" of independently designed and poorly coordinated projects of UN agencies and partners, led to further pressure for the CAP to develop into a strategic planning instrument, a tool to develop a common humanitarian strategy in a

Figure 9.10   Funding Rates for UN Consolidated Appeals (CAP) Between 1993 and 1999

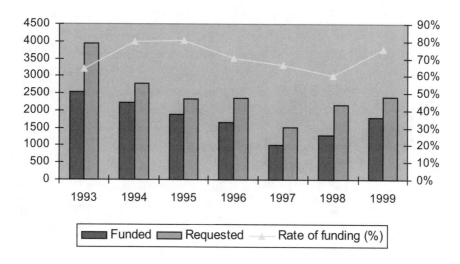

Source: OCHA CAP financial tracking data.

given country or region in response to a complex emergency. The CAP supposedly "enables the United Nations system and its partners to set clear goals and define priorities in a humanitarian operation."

The resources collected by the Consolidated Appeal are allocated to the various agencies of the United Nations System, with the World Food Program (WFP) and the High Commissioner for Refugees (UNHCR) getting the lion's share, with a respective 50 percent and 30 percent on average in the late 1990s. (See Figure 9.11.) It is also important to note that while, in 1988, almost three-fourths of WFP expenditures were for developmental activities, by 1998, the ratio had been inversed and more than 78 percent of its expenditures went to relief activities.

The CAP was one of several initiatives in the 1990s demonstrating a tendency toward integrated global responses under UN coordination. Much stress has been placed on the necessity of

Figure 9.11   Consolidated Appeals Distribution by Agency, 1994–1998 Average

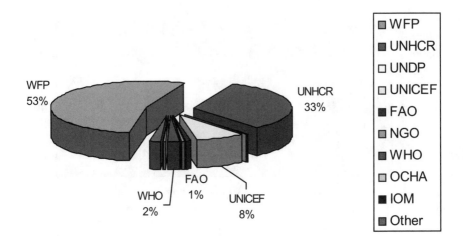

Source: OCHA-ReliefWeb CAPs financial tracking. "Other" includes UNRWA, for example.

better coordination between humanitarian agencies, but also on the design of integrated frameworks for humanitarian "diplomacy" linking humanitarian, political, and military (peacekeeping) strategies.

However, these beg the question of what befalls to the core principles of impartiality and independence of humanitarian operators enshrined in the Geneva Conventions, when these operators happen to be funded by political entities juggling political and military priorities along with, and sometimes ahead of, humanitarian ones. The matter gets worse when these agencies are further tightly directed by strategic plans of "humanitarian diplomacy," whose bottom line may not be exclusively humanitarian.

The response to UN Coordinated Appeals has been irregular. While the central role of the United Nations was reaffirmed and expanded in the last decade, budgets have not always followed or monies pledges been delivered, and UN agencies' senior officials have often found themselves begging for support, juggling unforeseen budgetary swings, and attempting to explore alternate resource mobilization paths: reaching out to corporations and the general public.[21]

The Case of UNHCR, the UN Refugee Agency

UNHCR heavily depends on voluntary contributions by governments. Only about 2 percent of the agency's annual budget is covered by regular contributions from the UN system. More than 90 percent of the UNHCR funds come from ten countries, with the United States accounting for 35 percent of donations.

With the 1990s proliferation of emergencies and its increased involvement inside conflict-torn states, the UNHCR expanded dramatically. Its staff doubled and its budget expanded from half a billion U.S. dollars in 1990 to $1.3 billion in 1996. Confronted with budget shortfalls, it has shrunk in recent years with cutbacks imposed by donor nations. Because the budget is approved each year by the fifty-seven UN members that make up its executive committee but many governments are failing to deliver the pledged funds, it experienced a $100 million funding shortfall in 2000. And despite further cuts, it was still facing a $126 million shortfall in late 2001, before the Afghanistan appeal for which, within a month, the international community pledged $400 million to the United Nations.

Control of humanitarian aid shifted from the UN system to bilateral and EC by the late 1980s with significant consequences in the field. One of the many outcomes was the weakened protection for refugees. UNHCR holds a double mandate of assistance and protection for refugees. As many governments ceased to channel their assistance through the UN and directly contracted their national or international NGOs to provide it, the UNHCR found itself with little ammunition to negotiate protection matters with reluctant host governments. Assistance was acquired through bilateral means, and the protection agenda spearheaded by the multilateral organization was often ignored, as the threat of removing assistance was no longer present.

Contributions to UNHCR from nongovernment sources have risen threefold over the past few years, from about $10 million in 1997 to $35 million in 1999. The Italian, American, and Japanese public heavily supported UNHCR in the Kosovo and other crises, featuring respectively at the twelfth, seventeenth, and nineteenth rank among the top twenty sources of funds of the agency worldwide.

In this fiftieth anniversary year of the Refugee Convention, as the Afghanistan situation unraveled, the refugee agency remained greatly dependant on government support for the fulfillment of its protection and assistance mandate toward 15 million refugees worldwide and millions of internally displaced.

Shared Concerns of Professionalism, Strategy, and Accountability

Along with the rise in budgets and political influence have come obligations for emergency operators who are now also being asked to be more professional, more strategic, and more accountable.

The call for more professionalism came, in particular, after the formal evaluation of the Rwanda refugee crisis, where performance of many relief operators turned out to be appalling: "NGOs played a vital role in the response, undertaking most of the delivery of assistance to beneficiaries. While many NGOs performed impressively, providing a high quality of care and services, a number performed in an unprofessional and irresponsible manner that resulted not only in duplication and wasted resources, but may also have contributed to an unnecessary loss of life. The need for NGOs to improve their performance is now widely recognized."[22]

When mortality and morbidity rates can escalate within days, the results of individual agencies have been linked to their access to rapid response funds, facilities, and human resources. With the wide swings in funding, developing—and sustaining over the years—an adequate infrastructure and the necessary competence for effective rapid deployment have been pressing issues for UN agencies as well as NGOs.

Yet governments have long been reluctant to pay for the required indirect headquarters costs. They have tended to fund operations where and when media and public pressure have mounted, rather than in the early stages when and where humanitarian assistance ought to be prepared and planned.[23] And for many NGOs, the funding of their headquarters and emergency preparedness infrastructure have been left to depend on private funds from the general public, de-facto affecting the true ratio of funds raised allocated to programs in the field and/or minimizing the effort.

Will the call for increased professionalism lead to the further development of a cadre of international civil servants to deliver aid? This would imply breaking away from the original traditions of voluntarism and solidarity. How would this affect humanitarian action at large?

The calls for more sophisticated analysis and strategic vision in assessing humanitarian space and deploying assistance are mounting with each crisis and failure. As aid can be taxed, hijacked, looted, or racketeered and humanitarian assistance can fuel war economies, relief workers are also being asked to avoid "doing harm while doing good." More and more, they need to carefully strategize their positioning and consider the local partners to join, the type of program to design, the control to exercise, and the level of aid to channel.

Finally, the call for accountability has led to numerous initiatives in recent years, as reviewed below, and will be a critical issue in the coming years for the relief agencies to develop a broader base of support.

THE GENERAL PUBLIC AND HUMANITARIAN CRISES

Public opinion is central to policy—at least when it is properly engaged. Since most "humanitarian crises" are fundamentally political crises with humanitarian consequences, the true potential impact on the situation often lies in foreign policy decisions by governments and multilateral institutions, far beyond the funding of humanitarian assistance. Humanitarian agencies are often caught between governments seeking an alibi for their political inaction (Bosnia, Rwanda) or linking humanitarian assistance to political or military aims (Afghanistan).

The increased global connectivity, through satellite news-feeds and the Internet, has not yet paid off in increased awareness and involvement by the general public, which would benefit both foreign policy decisions and the popular financial backing of humanitarian assistance. Even the much-debated CNN effect, the media pressure to which policy decisions may be applicable,[24] is fundamentally more about short term humanitarian response than effective awareness and engagement. Today, this awareness is dependent on media entities tending to focus on human tragedy rather than its political roots, and limiting coverage because of shortsighted commercial pressures.

Yet it is not impossible to think that a dramatic change is at hand that may enroll effectively many more private and individual donors to support humanitarian assistance, strengthen the backbone of private relief work anchored in civil society, loosen the straightjacket of government funding, and thus radically transform the field within less than a decade.

A Formidable Potential for Humanitarian Funding

A third of households in Britain donate to charities; 70 percent of Americans do; and nearly 22 million Canadians, or 91 percent of the population over age fifteen, made donations in 2000.

However, out of the $203.45 billion collected by nonprofit organizations in 2000 in the United States, for example, only 1.3 percent went to organizations involved in international affairs, less than half to environmental causes, ten times less than to education causes, while religion collected the lion's share with over a third of all donations.[25] One can read these statistics either with a sense of despair or as the demonstration that much potential remains untapped by humanitarian causes were they to reach the hearts and minds of donors more effectively.

Should another decade-long philanthropic expansion materialize, as in the 1990s, with a rise in annual and planned giving as well as corporate giving and an increases use of foundations as vehicles for personal giving, it would hold the promise of emancipation for relief and emergency assistance.

Even in a weak economy the trend for more international funding is in motion: each major disaster with a high media profile brings new private donors to the relief and development community, especially NGOs geared up for fundraising. Many of these donors will continue giving for overseas assistance: as the crises subside, NGO income settles back at much higher levels than before.

What will this emancipation take and where will it take us? While coordination issues skyrocket, both the emancipation of humanitarian assistance from political influence and its expanded potential to respond exclusively on the basis of need—and need alone—would yield tremendous beneficial outcomes. The final destination will depend on what ethics will be the backbone of humanitarian action as it flexes its financial muscle, and what model of accountability ends up being adopted by the community.

To be worthy of extended support from civil society donors, relief operators will have to build further credibility and help clean up what is sometimes coined "the business of foreign aid." It will require them not only to clarify their role in relation to interfering political and other agendas but also to reflect on the ethics of their work most congruent with their mission. Among the challenges, of course, feature the ethics of fundraising.

Hunger-Porn, Drug-Dumping, and the Ethics of Fundraising

In most OECD countries, numerous instruments are in place for charities' fundraising that are often supported by fiscal rules awarding tax-deductibility. Charities receive donations from the public in the form straightforward or annual gifts, payroll giving or planned giving, including trusts and bequests. They also get funded through trusts and foundations gifts, through lottery funding (in several European countries such as the Netherlands and the U.K.), through contributions from civil society move-ments such as churches or trade unions, through municipalities funding, and through matching gifts and straight contributions, in cash or in-kind, from corporate entities.

Separate from the instruments are the marketing campaigns that underpin them and the techniques used (advertising and public service announcements, direct mail and telemarketing, Web marketing, capital campaigns, etc.).

For example, corporate gifts may involve a cause-related mar-keting campaign associating the private and charitable brands. Planned giving may be solicited as part of a capital campaign aiming to raise funds for a specific endowment. Annual giving may be solicited in the form of membership to an organization, membership to an exclusive donor group of the organization, child or program sponsorship, etc.

Much of the debates on fundraising practices and ethics do not concern exclusively humanitarian assistance, but apply to agencies involved in both relief and development. Both merge in the public's mind and all can be discredited by the practice of a few.

The 1980s brought a series of tensions and scandals, such as the Forbes investigation in 1986 of child-sponsorship fundraising for development programs. The debates on "hunger pornogra-phy" went to the heart of the relief community dealing with fam-ine, yet they were initially prompted by ads of organizations funding development projects. The "drug-dumping" and other scandals of dumping planeloads of highly questionable commod-ities at the heart of a crisis are more recent developments, inex-tricably tied to relief work in humanitarian crises.

Let's explore the issues and how relief organizations are ad-dressing them.

Child-sponsorship. Child-sponsorship is a major marketing tool for development agencies, including those involved in relief. The single biggest growth area for non-emergency activities by NGOs is child-sponsorship. From the early 1980s to the mid-1990s, the group of child support agencies that includes World Vision, Plan, and Christian Children Fund grew by almost 40 percent per year. In Australia, child-sponsorship accounts for at least 50 percent of all private Australian donations to NGOs. Save the Children U.S.A. estimates that if donations to church-based organizations are subtracted, 70 percent of all remaining private donations are based on child-sponsorship.[26]

Beyond the appeal of children, it is the personal responsibility and person-to-person solidarity aspect of the marketing technique that makes it so powerful: it fundamentally echoes the basic humanitarian impulse that is nothing else than a person-to-person gesture of solidarity and responsibility.

While the marketing concept seems to imply that assistance is provided on the basis of an individual child, the operational practice has not always matched this public expectation, and most of the contentious debates have been over child-sponsorship. Because it so powerful, some agencies were tempted to use it as a marketing tool divorced from the true reality of their field operations, and turned it into an abusive marketing scheme.

The InterAction PVO standards[27] carefully lay out fifteen points to guide the use of child-sponsorship marketing tools and operational plans, from the obvious yet historically problematic "members shall be truthful in marketing and advertising" to more specific recommendations on policies, resource allocation, and accountability matters.

In-Kind Material Assistance. Less known to the general public, but tremendously contentious in the relief community, is the practice of material assistance through gifts-in-kind obtained from tax-deductible corporate contributions of stock and inventory of various commodities.

AmeriCares, often called (and self-described as) "the humanitarian arm of corporate America," argues that "by donating products to AmeriCares, companies save massive destruction costs, warehousing expenses, and headaches associated with returns, while they gain tax benefits, good public relations, and brand-name recognition in emerging markets"[28] and the *Wall Street Journal,* for example, has been very supportive of the organization's initiatives in its columns.

Again, while the concept sounds attractive, the practice has led to donor-driven and gifts-driven operational practices with tremendous downsides for the populations served. Shipping by AmeriCares of 10,000 cases of Gatorade to the Rwanda-Zaire border for cholera patients, seventeen tons of Pop Tarts to Bosnia, and 12,000 Maidenform bras to the Japanese earthquake victims[29] may not have met the consensual objective of ensuring that donations are "appropriate, based on assessment of local needs, and sensitive to the local culture or situation." Several agencies involved in non-cash donations from corporate inventories have been extensively criticized by UN, NGO, and local government authorities alike, for their inappropriate gifts leading to negative impacts, even toxic effects, as well as costly clean-ups, but also for

Table 9.1   U.S. Charities Raising the Bulk of their Resources from Gifts-in-Kind

U.S. charity	Total private support in 2000	Percentage of non-cash gifts	Rank among top 400 U.S. charities
Gifts In Kind International	$601,926,952	99.80%	7
Feed the Children	$395,581,981	82.40%	16
AmeriCares	$326,373,880	93.90%	20
Samaritan's Purse	$124,897,744	57.50%	88
MAP International	$98,328,312	96.40%	124
International Aid	$86,939,277	96.20%	149
Direct Relief International	$80,044,190	96.00%	165
Brother's Brother Foundation	$76,917,839	99.20%	172
Children's Hunger Fund	$71,405,010	99.00%	194
Operation Blessing	$66,267,401	79.70%	205
Catholic Medical Mission Board	$59,202,514	90.10%	231
Surgical Eye Expeditions International	$59,112,665	97.50%	232

Source: Chronicle of Philanthropy.

the development of dependencies and the undermining of local, sustainable solutions, as witnessed by this author.

The New England Journal of Medicine found that 50 percent to 60 percent of some 30,000 metric tons of drugs and medical materials donated to Bosnia and Herzegovina between 1992 and 1996 were inappropriate or otherwise unusable. It noted that most donations were pharmaceuticals with little remaining shelf-life, leading the investigators to suggest that the donors may have been "dumping" the medications to avoid disposal costs of approximately U.S.$2,000 per ton. Among items donated were supplies from World War II, plaster tapes from 1961, and medication for leprosy, a disease not found in the former Yugoslavia.[30] Medical teams in Kosovo found hair re-growth lotion shipped from the U.S. among the relief items distributed to medical clinics. *The Lancet* reported in January 1998 a request by two congressmen to the Internal Revenue Service to investigate whether pharmaceutical companies should be able to claim tax deductions for "humanitarian" donations to war-torn Bosnia and Herzegovina of medications that turned out to be useless.[31] Many such inappropriate donations in the Balkans, Central Africa, and other crisis locations, were traced back to donations in-kind by unscrupulous agencies.

Interestingly, organizations working on this model—tapping the tax-deduction potential of corporate charitable gestures— are seen as novel and creative alternatives to government-funded humanitarian action and appear to be very efficient thanks to low fundraising costs and overhead. Their public relation efforts underline this point: "Receiving virtually no government funds, AmeriCares has managed to deliver more than $1.2 billion in donated medicines around the world in its thirteen years of operation. Because aid is in the form of donated medicines, a dollar donation is leveraged into $44 of aid. AmeriCares, like the best-run companies, is lean and mean with an overhead of only 0.74 percent, a fact that led *Money* magazine to call it the number one best charity in America in December of 1993."[32]

To avoid further scandals about planeloads of highly question-able supplies and diversion of tax dollars to such activities, the community of relief actors attempted to self-regulate and articu-lated guidelines. Among them feature prominently the Inter-agency Gifts-in-Kinds Standards, the WHO guidelines on the Use of Essential Drugs, and InterAction's PVO guidelines on material assistance.

It is indeed important to support new initiatives from civil soci-ety that provide alternatives to the government-controlled system of the past decades. But they must also be scrutinized to ensure that such initiatives ultimately serve people in crises according to their needs and in respect of their dignity.

The Portrayal of Need. Much of the reporting of humanitarian cri-ses has been focused on emotion and short on analysis, and many relief agencies have played along happily. With their help rather than their resistance, much of the field reports sound the same because each is nothing but another version of the same fully-scripted morality play[33]—with plain and helpless victims, true he-roes (foreign humanitarian workers), and plenty of human trag-edy, but no analysis to go. As long as we fail to ground each crisis in its own history, and to depict accurately the combined human, political, economic, and other dimensions of the conflict, we will fail to go beyond short-term public sympathy at the most or, worse, compassion fatigue. Susan Moeller points out that "the public is given short shrift. They never really learn enough about a crisis to care about it." The habit of relief agencies to trade only in emotional fundraising appeals is also fueling problem.

Further damaging is the resulting distortion of perceptions of Africa and the developing world. To the Western World, Africa is portrayed as a continent of passive victims and barbaric fighters involved in constant "tribal warfare." (The Balkans, on the other hand, did not have "tribal warfare" but "ethnic strife," a distinc-tion Peter Shiras astutely points out.[34])

In 1992, the Somalia crisis provided another example of such bias and shortcuts, as reports Susan Moeller: "The stories depicted the victims of the famine as bereft of family, alone in their struggle for survival," and, "as a result, the impression was created of a man-and-God-forsaken people."[35]

The graphic images of starving, hollow-eyed children, helpless and feeble, menaced by vultures, have been used and abused repeatedly by several agencies, in a phenomenon coined angrily by relief workers as "hunger porn."[36] In an awkward effort to self-regulate this creeping phenomenon, relief agencies tried to explicitly define standards that have been blatantly ignored: "An organization's communications shall respect the dignity, values, history, religion, and culture of the people served by the programs. . . . They shall neither minimize nor overstate the human and material needs of those whom it assists. . . . There shall be no material missions, or exaggeration of facts, no use of misleading photographs, nor any other communication which would tend to create a false impression or misunderstanding."[37]

Much of the difficulty with the portrayal of need is as much the byproduct of the ethnocentricity of the "translators" as that of the sound-bite culture of modern media that requires crises to be summarized for public consumption in just a few seconds between two commercials.

Symbiotic but Chaotic Relationship to the Media. Toward a New Era?

Historically, the media has had a critical role in mobilizing public response to humanitarian crises. Since satellite news-feeds started to bring distant realities into everyone's living room in (almost) real time, relief work has repeatedly captured the public imagination, demonstrating the link between awareness and funding.

Journalists have relied on relief groups for access to and logistics in remote crisis sites, they have used Western relief workers to provide the emotional link to their home audience, they have relied extensively on the analysis and data of these groups—occasionally with some disenchantment. As the pressures of real-time coverage increased, the media came more and more to rely on sound bites from humanitarian workers.

Often described as a symbiotic relationship, it is also a chaotic one. "News media have all too often come to assume that humanitarian organizations are either partisan adversaries or commercial opportunists or both."[38] Meanwhile, relief workers have occasionally lost respect for the bulk of the journalist crowds' showing in the humanitarian circus for their lack of anticipatory coverage, brief attention span, and focus on human tragedy rather than political analysis. Yet these criticisms could just as well apply to many relief organizations themselves.

Dearth of In-depth and Critical Reporting. To capture public interest over the long term, both media outlets and relief groups will require some adjustments to their approach. Recent events might have brought international issues more to the forefront, but the qualitative transformation needed has yet to happen: ethnocentricity, scripted morality plays, short attention span, and lack of confidence or creativity still constrain foreign news coverage before it even rears its head to be chopped by commercially-driven editorial decisions shifting the focus to soft news.

Paradoxically, despite technological progress in this last "decade of the dish,"[39] media coverage of international issues had been spotty and even more fickle than government assistance. The American media in particular, but not exclusively, have grown increasingly narrow in their approach to the rest of the world. Garrick Utley points out that the passing of the cold war left American network television in a quandary over how to report international news. "Without stories from abroad that could be presented as part of an overall threat to American security," he argues, "newscasts suffered a severe loss in an increasingly competitive medium that thrives—perhaps depends—on drama and conflict to attract and hold an audience's attention."[40]

For example, little attention was given in the 1990s to Afghanistan, despite it being the number one source of refugees worldwide and the scene of a protracted civil war and repeated famines. Within a three-week period in the fall of 2001, Afghanistan coverage time on U.S. TV networks matched the entire extent of coverage of the previous decade.

Similarly, a few months before the Kosovo intervention, as Kosovar villages were pounded by Serbian artillery and people started to hide in the forests, a major American magazine argued there was "no longer a U.S. angle" to the story and canceled its reporter and photographer's visit to Kosovo when the American relief worker they had planned to feature went back home to the U.S. before the magazine could finalize the logistics of the trip. How could there be "no U.S. angle" to a story that would be a major theater of operations involving the U.S. and world militaries barely a few months later?

With the same short-sightedness, in May 1993, when the handover from the U.S. to the UN was carried out, most of the journalists in Somalia failed to listen to the rare few relief workers who were telling a different story from the one scripted in Washington and New York. The writing was on the wall; the upcoming violent confrontation was foreseen; they were preparing for it. Yet only sanitized news would make the cut, blindfolding us from a reality that would ultimately lead to utter failure in Somalia and paralysis in Rwanda. The fault was not the media's only: many relief agencies and government representatives acted as mouthpieces of the dominant discourse. The lack of political analysis was a shared and disastrous handicap.

With the pace of reporting imposed by new technology, journalists no longer enjoy the necessary time for careful analysis of the information submitted to them. This is placing a tremendous burden on relief organizations—a challenge that must be picked up even if it means that relief agencies must be more careful and professional in their approach. Their credibility is at stake.[41]

Collective Irresponsibility? One of the side effects of the dearth of in-depth and critical reporting is that little critical feedback reaches humanitarian workers and agencies who are almost always positively portrayed. Is it guilt about the little chance the crisis has to make front page that leads journalists to absolve the mistakes and failures of relief teams "who at least do try hard"? Even the manipulation of media—and humanitarian workers—by belligerents has been forgiven—or forgotten—on the Rwanda-Zaire border, most likely because the pressures of reporting were so tight that they required complicity with those who facilitated access to the scene.

In the coming years, as the media digests its Rwanda, Kosovo, and Afghanistan experiences, we ought to see a radical change occur. Information technology, broadcast media, and the Internet have a key role to play in both the portrayal of and even the actual humanitarian reality on the ground. For example, information needs of refugees are now being analyzed, and the role of broadcast, the Internet and local media in orchestrating violence is being highlighted in the Rwandan and Bosnian war crimes courts. In the future, media may well have a different role to play in the implementation of humanitarian assistance, and being more central on the ground may come to change attitude and culture.

Media outlets and reporters will in any case remain the key links between relief workers and their potential supporters in donor countries. Both must change their approach and reflect on their responsibilities to tackle the "disaster fatigue" of their editors and the general public. Should it happen, we might see a tidal-wave of public support for humanitarian work whose mission would be more scrutinized, yet all the more strong and worthy of financial contributions from individuals and civil society groups.

Big Problems, Small Print[42]

As many minutes of U.S. media coverage were devoted to Afghanistan in the entire decade of the 1990s as in a period of three weeks in the fall of 2001— Andrew Tyndall/ Harper's.[43]

Newspapers and TV news executives reduced the space and time devoted to foreign coverage by 70 percent to 80 percent during the past twenty years—David Shaw,[44] and 50 percent over the past decade according—Andrew Tyndall.[45]

Time devoted to foreign news on network TV dropped from 45 percent in the 1970s to 13.5 percent by 1995. Evening news broadcasts at ABC, CBS, and NBC devoted 35 percent of their time to international news in the 1970s but dropped it to 23 percent in 1995, and went on dropping further—Claude Moisy.[46]

U.S. TV networks have dropped international news coverage from 2,000 minutes in 1998 to 1,100 to 1,200 minutes in 2000—Andrew Tyndall.[47]

In all of 1991, when events unfolded and the country collapsed, coverage of Somalia events got three minutes of evening TV network news. In the first half of 1992, when the famine exploded, Somalia got eleven minutes in six months—Tyndall.[48] By the summertime, when media started to pay attention, the famine was well under way and had taken the lives of tens of thousands already. The peak of the coverage appeared in 1993, accompanying (or instigating?) American military disengagement from Somalia.

"The much touted globalization of news is more myth than reality," and U.S. media are not the only culprits: "West European TV stations and quality papers remain more internationally minded than U.S. media but pay scant attention to developments in Asia and Latin America"—London-based International Institute of Communications.

Conclusion: Accountability and the "Business of Foreign Aid"

In 1996, a scathing criticism of relief and development agencies in the *Times* read as follows:

"In the last century, merchant adventurers stirred the media to badger politicians over national pride. Gunboats and troop carriers were duly sent. The merchant adventurers of modern Africa are the aid agencies. . . . They are the biggest power brokers on the continent. They can move large quantities of money and supplies. They influence the outcome of wars. They occupy territory, wreck fragile market economies, encourage rural depopulation, and are obsessed with self publicity."[49]

If this becomes the public image of humanitarian assistance operators, the potential for relief work of expanded awareness and support by civil society at large, rather than government institutions, may never be tapped.

Yet much of what has led to the fiercest criticism lie in ambiguous political positioning, fragile ethics, and complex accountability lines—all issues that are now being widely debated in the relief community thanks to the outrage and warnings of a few of its members and observers. The community is now actively involved in soul-searching, exploring self-regulation and models of accountability. This augurs well for its potential to transform and mature gracefully.

Explorations with Self-regulation

A code of Conduct for the International Red Cross and Red Crescent Movement and NGOs in Disaster Relief was launched in 1994 and signed by more than 120 agencies. Some think that accreditation and/or legislation may be the next steps. But most of the discussions have been focused since on self-regulations initiatives.

After disenchanted assessments of the 1994 million-dollar-a-day assistance operation on the Rwanda-Zaire border, the impulse was given for a Humanitarian Charter and Minimum Standards in Disaster Response, a quantitative benchmarking system known as the Sphere Project developed by—and in intensive consultations with—relief agencies. Peer-review processes and social audits could use these benchmarks.

A further development, the Humanitarian Accountability Project, began by suggesting the establishment of a Humanitarian Ombudsman to deal with complaints regarding the adequacy of aid provided.

In tension with—and in response to—the above initiatives, a French-led initiative called the NGO Platform for a Different Quality Approach to Humanitarian Action—in short the Quality Platform—argued that technical standards cannot be dissociated from context and policy, and suggested instead an approach emphasizing political and context analysis, local participation, careful program design, learning from evaluations, and the use of proxy indicators to measure commitment to evaluation, learning, and public scrutiny.

Issues of quality and accountability have clearly occupied the relief community in the last few years, and the debates have also helped surface the questions of what constitutes humanitarian responsibility and where it ends.

An Elusive Model of Accountability

Given the multiplicity of stakeholders, there are still gaping holes in the accountability models discussed by humanitarian agencies who are struggling with such issues as:

How can solidarity, the key impulse of humanitarian assistance, be measured and benchmarked? Is quality a negotiated process? A generic benchmarkable concept? A fundamentally diverse and context-dependant notion? Who are relief agencies ultimately accountable to? Their board of directors? Their donors who provide the means? The principles? Of course, but overseen by whom? The recipients of their aid? Of course, but represented by whom? Is what's needed what's valued and valuable? Who ought to make such decisions? How? Can there be quantifiable service delivery indicators or should we develop principle compliance indicators? Should we use a social science model and focus on outcome and attribution? Or a program integrity model that focuses on the process and demonstrates the resources were allocated as planned? Are standards prone to abuse?

The chart in figure 9.5, illustrating the complex flows of resources in the system, also hints at the complexity of accountability in this field, when the true constituents have little power (even when one accepts the legitimacy of the local authorities and governments involved) compared to the donors, who, as major governments, not only fund assistance but influence the political environment of the crisis with their diplomatic and sometimes military strategies.

Given the recent efforts to improve quality and accountability, we may be witnessing at least the development of an accountability culture, if not yet an accountability structure or system. Should the next step involve more transparency, more willingness to expose the failures and facilitate collective learning, we may be already far ahead on the path of better matching the credibility of these relief organization to the size of their financial might and moral responsibility.

Political Responsibility of Relief Actors

Each crisis brings its learning curve—however imperfect. Bosnia challenged the political and human rights underpinnings of relief work and questioned its willingness to act as a fig leaf for political apathy. The Somalia experience sent a chill through the spine of the most eager interventionists and questioned the relationship between media, military, and relief teams. The learning curve from the Rwandan genocide was questionable but for the obvious fact that humanitarian assistance does not stop a genocide. With the Rwandan refugee debacle on the Zaire border, came questions about aid fueling wars, but also a call for minimum standards of accountability. The Kosovo chaotic response fundamentally questioned the relationship between relief agencies and their sponsors when those are belligerents, and the systemic failure of the system to protect internally displaced persons.

Truly, the toughest nut to crack may be that of the political responsibility of humanitarian actors. While relief groups might be able to learn to "do well while doing good" by steering accountability discussions in the proper direction, they will still have to learn to "be wise while doing good." Indeed, the responsibility of humanitarian operators is separate from political responsibility; the emancipation from government funding that we see possible in the decades to come is not insignificant, to say the least, in helping relief teams define those boundaries and the best way to leverage humanitarian action for the people it means to serve.

10

From the Other Side of the Fence: The Problems Behind the Solution

Abdulrahim Abby Farah

Introduction

THIS CHAPTER will identify some of the reasons that compelled African states to seek international assistance to meet the humanitarian needs of their populations that may have fallen victim to natural or man-made disasters. It will try to present the impressions of those who have been forced by circumstances to seek assistance—impressions not always brought to the attention of humanitarian missions. The chapter takes as its starting point the early 1960s, when dramatic political changes on the African continent ended the presence of the colonial powers and installed in their place an assembly of fifty-two sovereign independent states. It will attempt to show that some of the emergency situations that the newly independent states have had to deal with were not entirely of their own making, particularly situations whose roots go back into colonial times. However, since the 1960s, few African leaders can escape responsibility for any man-made types of disaster that occurred during their stewardship and that derived directly from their official policies, decisions, or acts. The roles played by the donor community and international humanitarian agencies will be briefly discussed, within the framework of their responses to appeals and their operations in the field.

Toward the latter part of the chapter, I have summarized a discussion, in a way a postmortem, that took place recently with a group of friends and acquaintances in Berbera (Somaliland) on the impact of war on their lives, and general remarks that they made on emergency relief operations that have been carried out in their region, and on the current role of relief agencies in their country. I believe that their experiences will facilitate an understanding of the reactions of the ordinary citizen to events not of their making and against which they have no defense. Moreover, the range of humanitarian problems that the country has experienced is a microcosm of the political ills that have afflicted the rest of the continent: interstate war, civil conflict, the mass internal displacement of entire communities, the flight of over half a million of the country's inhabitants to neighboring countries for asylum, the inflow of a similar number from neighboring areas, incompetent governance, the destruction of the national economy, the impoverishment of the population, and, finally, conflict between tribes for territorial supremacy and control.

In my lifetime I have been involved in several roles associated with disaster, in particular situations created by war and drought. Although my personal experience as a refugee was relatively short and much less distressing than the unfortunate victims we come across in camps, it was nonetheless an experience that has enabled me to better understand the despair and feelings of abandonment that they suffer. War caused my displacement within my country, it rendered me homeless, and it forced me to flee and seek asylum in a neighboring country as a war refugee.

Thankfully, there has been a positive side to my experiences. Early in my career, I was entrusted with the management and administration of a camp of several thousand drought and famine victims, as well as with relief and "back to work" projects in the rural areas of my country. As a United Nations Under-Secretary General, a major part of my responsibilities concerned Africa. I have seen the devastating consequences of drought, civil war, and floods in various African countries as well as my own, and have participated in discussions with donor countries and agencies for an appropriate response. I left the United Nations twelve years ago, but it seems that the humanitarian problems in Africa have not only worsened, but have spread.

FIRST OAU SUMMIT CONFERENCE

The Charter establishing the Organization of African Unity (OAU) was signed in Addis Ababa on May 25, 1963, by thirty-two heads of state and government. It was a historic occasion, bringing together, for the first time, the independent states of Africa.

I was a member of the Somali delegation that took part in that meeting. It was unforgettable in many ways: it succeeded in forging a bond that would strengthen and consolidate Africa's new-found unity; it reversed a trend that would have divided the continent into political groupings; it provided states with the legal instrumentalities to break down social, economic, and political barriers that had formerly kept them apart from neighboring states; it enabled African states to act collectively in other international forums on matters of common interest; and it allowed all African problems to be resolved within an African environment. The leaders did not forget the remaining African territories under colonialism. They pledged their help unconditionally. The leaders were confident about the course of future events, although some urged continued vigilance against possible attempts by others to undermine their newly-won independence. As one leader reportedly declared, "give me the political kingdom and all else will follow." Such was the confidence and the euphoria in those heady days.

I have seen few conferences comparable to that of the Addis Ababa conference: in the various conference rooms where the delegates debated, the atmosphere was filled with hope, optimism, and resolve about the future. Several states recognized the intractability of some of the problems that they had inherited from the colonial powers—problems that concerned their security, the living standards of their peoples, the weak and underdeveloped state of their economies—but, as some explained, they had come to Addis Ababa for one over-riding purpose: to establish a continental organization for all of Africa. The impression that I gained from various leaders that met with our delegation was that the problems facing each country, although complex, were not beyond resolution and needed time. New horizons, new opportunities, and new challenges had been opened for Africans! No African could have imagined that lurking in the future there could be a downside to independence!

As the ceremonies and celebrations marking independence receded into the background, the new governments began turning their attention not only to the domestic front but also to the outside world, where they hoped to find solutions to many of their major economic and social problems. African states recognized that their economies lagged far behind others, and that they would need the involvement and support of the developed states and financial institutions. Accordingly, they joined the United Nations and other allied organizations and agencies, cultivated contacts and subsequently entered into agreements with various states and financial organizations, and opened their doors to the outside world to allow others to gain a better understanding of African realities and aspirations.

SOCIAL AND ECONOMIC UNDERDEVELOPMENT

In the course of their official discussions abroad, it became readily apparent to the African states that the weak and underdeveloped economies they had inherited from the colonial powers placed them at considerable disadvantage with others in the highly competitive global market. Official delegations spent much of their time seeking grants, loans, investments, and development assistance. From the start, African states found themselves in a struggle with the social and economic problems that plagued their countries.

During the heyday of their campaigns for independence, they had set their sights on the political crown, thinking that with independence all else would follow. They were sadly mistaken. As the states subsequently found, many of their post-independence problems stemmed from the underdeveloped state of their economies—neither able to respond to the expectations of their peoples, nor incapable of serving as a launching pad for their economic development, and too weak to sustain any exceptional strains placed on the economy by disaster or external economic forces. In reality, the economy became the Achilles heel of Africa.

In the scramble for external development aid, African governments found that if their countries possessed economic resources or the potential, they had little difficulty in attracting foreign investments; on the other hand, states with few exploitable resources or marginal potential were left to their own devices. Unfortunately, the latter group were largely composed of states that were the poorest of the poor, unable to meet the basic needs of their own populations, politically precarious, and vulnerable to any kind of destabilizing force—natural or man-made.

As one African leader later observed, the African continent had the sad privilege of holding a whole array of negative records—the greatest concentration of refugees and displaced persons; one-half of the land-locked countries of the world; two-thirds of the least developed nations; the lowest literacy rate; the lowest level of development, with 70 percent of the population near or below the threshold of poverty; the highest rate of infant and child mortality; the highest incidence of HIV/AIDS; and a continent with endemic and unremitting drought and desertification.

In recent years there has been a change of attitude toward Africa. Because of the frequency of appeals for aid coming from the continent, some developed nations, together with international financial institutions, have begun taking a closer look at the continent's development needs and, on a bilateral basis, have taken steps to lighten its burden. Some of the poorer states have been released from the debts they have incurred, others have been granted an extended time for repayment, and there has been an encouraging trend toward strengthening the economic capacity of many developing states through capital investment and facilitating the access of their products to world markets.

Non-Intervention in Internal Affairs

In the course of a visit to Geneva some years ago, I was sitting in a hotel lounge waiting for a bus to take me to the airport en route to Africa, when I was greeted by a friend whom I had not seen for years. We sat together for a while, exchanging news about each other's activities, and while discussing recent events that had taken place in Africa, he asked, "What really is happening in Africa? All we hear about is fighting, refugees, and constant appeals for help—surely there must be a better alternative? If a government cannot govern a country properly, why cannot some organization, say the United Nations or the Organization of African Unity, simply go there and put things right? After all, we have an humanitarian obligation toward the poor civilians whose lives are constantly threatened."

I explained briefly that relations between international entities simply do not work that way, and went to on to describe the scope and limitations of each organization. We ended up on two conflicting concerns—the principle of non-interference in the internal affairs of a state and the humanitarian obligation to assist people in conditions of extreme distress and suffering. However, his questions occupied my mind for the greater part of my flight to Africa. I could not agree more with him that an acceptable alternative must be found that would bring a permanent halt to the insane violence that has virtually destroyed several countries in east, central, and west Africa, and left a few, like Somalia, as "failed states."

It was true, as my friend had said, that the scope and intensity of suffering, as well as the appeals for help, had increased in recent years to the point where people had begun to ask what prevented the international community from addressing the roots of these problems rather than responding to their consequences. International law does not allow any kind of intervention in the internal affairs of a state unless by invitation. The legal basis is contained in Article 2 (7) of the United Nations Charter, which stipulates: "nothing in the present Charter shall authorize the

United Nations to intervene in matters which are essentially within the domestic jurisdiction of any state."

Newly independent Africa was even more blunt about safeguarding sovereignty over its internal affairs. In the Charter establishing the Organization of African Unity, among the principles that bound all members to respect was one that affirmed "non-interference in the internal affairs of states." Another principle called for "respect for the sovereignty and territorial integrity of each state and for its inalienable right to independent existence."

Compare these legal provisions with what a former Secretary-General of the United Nations had to say on the matter in relation to our humanitarian obligations: "The time of absolute and exclusive sovereignty, however, has passed; its theory was never matched by reality. It is the task of leaders of states to understand this and to find a balance between the needs of good internal governance and the requirements of an ever more interdependent world."

This is a sobering statement. Disasters that originate from the folly of man are known for the violence and brutality they produce, the host of refugees and internally displaced people they create, the devastation and chaos they cause, and the simmering fires of hate and mistrust they leave behind. Some causes have their roots deep into history, others can be traced to the colonial period, but the majority is the product of modern times.

Today's revolutionary advances in the field of communications have prompted someone to describe the world as a global village—so small that it is no longer possible to be unaware of developments and happenings in other parts of the world, however distant, and not be affected in some way or other by their consequences. Modern communication has made it possible for the plight of disaster-stricken victims to be brought to the attention of people everywhere.

Despite such advances, some governments at war with their own people have made attempts to shield some disasters from international view, as a form of political punishment against the stricken areas. A famine situation occurred in Ethiopia in 1973–1974 where, if it were not for the initiative and daring of a foreign television team, the world would not have known anything about the terrible human disaster that was unfolding there, nor would the world have had the time to rush aid to save the lives of the remaining victims of the drought.

Unfortunately, there have been occasions when, despite the publicity given by the media, the slow response of the donor community allowed disaster situations to take thousands of lives that could have been saved, and destroy the livelihood of entire communities when such tragedies might have been prevented. Practically all of the disasters that have occurred in Africa in recent times have required resources beyond the capacities of the countries concerned, leaving them no alternative but to appeal for help to the international community.

POLITICAL INSTABILITY AND DISASTER

The bane of African states has been their inability to provide their people with stable, competent, just, and democratic governance. These inadequacies were reflected in the increasingly adverse reactions of the population to official policies and measures, which they felt to be unfair or unacceptable. Expectations began to give way to disillusionment and disaffection. The promises of better living conditions did not materialize. Economies remained as they were when the colonial power departed, infrastructure and social services were still at an embryonic stage, urban populations increased as people left the rural areas in search of work. Added to these woes, although publicly concealed, was a growing rift between the civilian leaders and those of the military. While it was acknowledged that the "old" guard politicians had led their countries to independence, the military were convinced that they were better educated and equipped to carry on the challenge for nationhood.

Paradoxically, the new national army in each country was the creation of the newly elected government. To many governments, military power was a symbol of strength and also the means by which the laws of the land could be enforced, internal order maintained, and borders protected. More money was spent on equipping and maintaining the military force then than on most of the other services. It was truly a case of governments creating monsters they could not control.

The first indication of possible problems from this source came toward the end of 1960 with the attempted coup against the Emperor of Ethiopia by a unit from his own palace guards. In the following years, many civilian regimes fell to the military as the power struggle intensified and spread throughout all regions of the continent, for example, in Ghana, Nigeria, Ethiopia, Uganda, Libya, and Algeria. In justification of their actions, the military invariably leveled charges of mismanagement, corruption, misappropriation, inefficiency, nepotism, and tribalism against the ousted civilian government.

The military regimes fared no better. Many of the same charges that they had leveled against the politicians were hurled back at them, not only by civilians, but also by ambitious or disgruntled groups within the military! Africa has had nearly forty years of such internal struggles and, apart from a few states, has very little to show for it except that rulers no longer label themselves "Life President," although few are prepared to abide by the results of the ballot box or the constitutions that curbed their power and limited their terms. In keeping with the times, some military rulers have exchanged their military uniforms for civilian dress to increase their political acceptability.

MAN-MADE DISASTERS

The more sinister type of disasters are those that are the makings of man himself—the man-made disasters: interstate conflict, as between Tanzania and Uganda, Ethiopia and Somalia; civil war, as in Angola, Sierra Leone, Nigeria, and Mozambique; intertribal or interethnic strife, as in Burundi and Rwanda; and similar situations where communities within a state are ruthlessly oppressed and forced to flee for their safety. All have become an acute source of concern for the international community. Not only have they increased in frequency, but the brutality and utter disregard for human life exhibited in many of these unfortunate situations has been appalling.

The Problem of Border Disputes

Another source that has produced the potential for conflict is the legacy of unresolved border or territorial disputes within Africa that were created and left behind by the colonial powers. Although more than twenty five border disputes remained unresolved in 1964—like an explosive device that might detonate without warning—the Organization of African Unity, meeting in Cairo that year, felt it would be in the interests of all if such disputes were shelved temporarily to allow adequate time for the process of mediation or bilateral negotiations to take place. Accordingly, the OAU declared that until such time as a peaceful resolution of a problem was reached, all the concerned states should respect the colonial-drawn borders they inherited on independence. In spite of the OAU declaration, several of these disputes have developed into open warfare, the latest being the Ethiopia/Eritrea border conflict of 1998. Now, some are asking when and where will the next border explosion take place.

The struggle for power has also taken on another, more ominous dimension—a struggle between the regime in power and sections of the civilian population, as in Sudan, Somalia, and Angola. Contemporary Africa is replete with situations where the leader has lost the support of his people, yet refuses to step down graciously. The rest of the scenario is easy to imagine. The leader defies the constitution, assumes dictatorial powers, and leaves his people with no option but to resist. In most situations, the outcome is a long, drawn-out civil war, entailing widespread casualties among the unarmed civilian population, the displacement of masses of people, and unimaginable misery and suffering. Some leaders have even gone to the extent of promoting or encouraging conflict within tribes for their own ends.

The refugee situation has also its tremendous downside. It has been known that a few states, at odds with their neighbors, have recruited the services of, or allowed, refugees to carry out hostile activities against their country of origin despite international rules prohibiting such conduct. Quite obviously, such practices will certainly perpetuate problems between the states concerned.

NATURAL DISASTERS

In addition to these types of man-made disasters, independent Africa has had to contend with the vagaries of nature. Prolonged drought, large-scale famine, and disastrous floods have been the most persistent causes of natural disaster to afflict the continent. The states concerned have been sometimes helpless to do anything about them—possessing neither the resources, nor the technical knowledge to handle them when they occur.

Paradoxically, natural disasters seem to happen more frequently in countries that are already impoverished, and whose fragile economies can collapse easily under intense pressure from such sources. The pastoral people of the Sahara in West Africa, the nomads of the Horn of Africa, the Bushmen and others of southern Africa, are constantly on the move in search of pasturage and water for their flocks of sheep and goats or herds of cattle and camels. Should the rains fail, and the animals die, the means for their existence is lost—causing suffering and death. Then, there are the subsistence farmers and their families inhabiting the same regions, whose livelihood is as precarious as that of the pastoral people, having no alternative but to eke an existence from the few crops that their over-farmed land can grow, relying entirely on their labor and the hospitality of nature. And, when the drought occurs, the specter of disaster spreads its deadly mantle over the land, destroying crops and farm animals, and depriving the farmer and his family of their only source of sustenance.

Drought has been described as a creeping form of disaster—it takes time for signs of its approach to manifest themselves. As has been demonstrated in the past, the success in minimizing its destructive consequences is often determined by the measures taken before or during its onslaught. Was the government aware of its approach? Had early warning systems been set in place? Were the warning signs heeded, or were they simply ignored? Was the aid response adequate and in time? These are but a few of the questions that will occupy the minds of those who care and want to help.

Africans have also had to contend with other forms of natural disaster, primarily the sudden type such as earthquakes, hurricanes, and heavy storms that have led to devastating floods in low lying regions, such as in Mozambique, giving little or no time for people to escape to safety. In the disaster-prone countries of Africa, the question is not whether the affected state has the capacity in terms of resources and experience to manage the situation alone, but whether international aid can be delivered there in time and in sufficient amounts to contain and respond effectively to the tragedy that threatens.

THREE TYPICAL CASE HISTORIES AND THE LESSONS LEARNED

The Sahelian Drought of 1973

Since the great Sahelian drought of 1973, an expansive network of early warning systems has been set up by the international community to monitor any unusual changes in weather patterns that could alert states, as well as other interested agencies, of the makings of a possible disaster situation. Fortunately, in some situations the early warning systems have produced the desired effect: the affected states concerned, as well as the international community, were able to initiate preventative measures and set in motion their relief operations. Unfortunately, this has not been the experience of a number of states where, despite repeated warnings, the international community was slow to respond, and when they did respond, the aid arrived too late or was too little. Even more tragic have been situations in which distressed populations have appealed for food and have had their appeals ignored by their own governments as a political punishment.

What lessons can be learned from these situations? Let us examine briefly the Sahelian disaster mentioned above because it happened to be Africa's first major natural disaster since the continent achieved independence. It took the form of a relentless pervasive drought that gnawed for five years at the heart and body of six West African states bordering the southern edge of the Sahara desert. When it ended in 1973, the drought had caused an appalling loss of life, and the displacement of more than two million pastoral people who, because of the destruction of their livestock, were forced by circumstance to seek shelter in hastily improvised refugee camps so that they might survive. In one of the major studies conducted on the causes and consequences of the disaster, it was concluded that relief for the affected countries was due to "failure to heed early warnings, to plan in advance, and to monitor and coordinate rescue efforts." (1)

The Ethiopian Droughts of 1973–1974 and 1984–1985

On the heels of the Sahelian disaster came the Ethiopian famine of 1973–1974 that devastated two of its provinces, causing unnecessary loss of life and resulting in grave charges being leveled at the government for having denied aid and concealed information on the intensity of the famine, and yet allowing the export of large quantities of wheat so that proceeds could be used for other purposes. Fortunately, a foreign television team visited the provinces and, through the release of its film, brought international attention to the disaster. This case demonstrates the important role played by the media in breaking the pattern of silence, thus enabling aid to reach the stricken population.

Eleven years later, an even greater tragedy struck Ethiopia, arising again from drought and famine in its northern regions. On that occasion, the government, as well as representatives of various agencies of the United Nations, maintained that early warning reports and appeals had been sent to all potential donors, but that they were either ignored or accorded insufficient credence. Cold war considerations were claimed by some to be the reason for the poor response. Others charged that the government had been guilty of using food aid as a political weapon against rebellious communities. Instead of giving food to the stricken areas, it was alleged, the authorities had sold the country's grain reserves to procure arms. A complicating dimension to the situation was added when the government decided to transport and resettle thousands of famine victims to other areas far from their traditional habitat—a policy, many charged, reminiscent of Soviet deportations to Siberia!

The Somalia Drought of 1974–1975

Somalia was also confronted with a similar problem concerning the future of tens of thousands of pastoral people, living in the northern regions of the country, who had become displaced after drought had decimated their livestock and left them helpless. Faced with the problem of maintaining and feeding such large numbers in camps for an indefinite period, the Somalia government decided to establish settlements for them in the southern regions, some seven hundred miles distance from their normal habitat. Huge Soviet transport planes were employed to help in the transfer, and for what they could not carry, road transport was used.

It was a hurriedly organized operation, but by the time it was over, large numbers had been relocated in camps in various agricultural areas and along the coast. The plan was to provide the pastoralists with an alternative type of livelihood by employing them on large collective farms and fishing cooperatives, and train them to become eventually either agriculturalists or fishermen.

It is said that one can take a horse to water, but that it cannot be forced to drink. In a way this is what happened in the case of the displaced pastoralists. Above all, they could not accept that they should abandon their lives as pastoralists, and in a matter of months they became restless by having to work in a highly controlled environment, in an occupation that they detested, and live in surroundings to which they could not adjust.

It did not take long before the pastoralists began making plans to return to the familiar environment of the arid plains and pastures, and to the only way of life that they had known. Many of them sought work as laborers in nearby countries to earn enough money to replace the livestock they had lost, but the majority made their way back home as soon as they heard that the drought had ended, the weather had normalized, and life was again full of hope and opportunities for those who returned. Today, a few families remain in the settlement areas, the only living evidence of a plan that just could not work, and even that evidence is being steadily erased by time.

African Refugees: Sharing the Burden

In Africa, natural calamities such as drought and man-made disasters have been responsible not only for the displacement of entire communities within the borders of their own country, but also for the movement across international borders.

While there are many things that the rest of the world can teach Africa, in one area Africa has few peers—the compassion it shows to war or famine-stricken people seeking the safety of their territories. It is not a shipload, trainload, or even busload of refugees that I have in mind. At times, it has not been unusual to see a poor African state accept the inflow of tens of thousands of people fleeing the perils of war and of hunger. Even though their economies could hardly cope with the basic needs of their own populations, I have yet to hear that an African state has closed its borders to prevent the inflow. Instead they have generously shared the little that they have with the less fortunate.

Naturally, in the case of large numbers of refugees, their presence imposes a considerable burden on the fragile economies of recipient states. In recent years, African states appealed to the international community to help in sharing the burden, stating frankly that the impact on their economies, services, and infrastructures is far too great for them to handle alone. There has been a growing acknowledgement that allowance for the refugee presence should be made by donors when preparing their bilateral aid programs, or included in their contributions to agencies like the UN High Commission for Refugees.

HUMANITARIAN ASSISTANCE: IMPROVING ITS EFFECTIVENESS

In addition to its chronic economic problems, all of Africa's regions have had to contend with a series of disasters—natural as well as man-made. Each situation has caused widespread misery, heavy loss of life, displacement of populations, and the destruction of a way of life for thousands of its inhabitants. The tragic truth about disaster in developing countries, particularly in the least developed areas, is that the affected states seldom possess sufficient resources or capacity to initiate preventative action during the early stages to contain or mitigate its consequences.

Coordination in Diversity

Humanitarian emergencies, as the term implies, means, in essence, a situation that accords priority above all else to the saving of lives and the alleviation of suffering. However, relief operations do not proceed always as smoothly as the parties involved had hoped, not only for reasons of commitment, but often from varying standards of operational experience and readiness. It is inherent in the nature of an international emergency operation that relief teams will be composed of teams of diverse cultural origins, training, and experiences. In takes considerable leadership and patience to bring together a large international team, coordinate their contributions, and meld their activities with the various branches of the host country. It would be prudent, too, for international relief workers, who are sent to work in a least developed state for the first time, to acquire beforehand an understanding of the social and economic problems that beset such states, and the fragility of their infrastructure and governance. International teams arriving to help in a disaster seem to have no knowledge of the country's fragile infrastructures and governance, and the burden that is placed on the government's capacity to handle the large shipments of relief supplies that accompany them. Equally irritating is the "we know best" attitude some display whenever suggestions are made.

Inadequate Response to Appeals

Many African states believe that international donors could improve the effectiveness of their humanitarian assistance if they would be more appreciative and more responsive to their appeals for disaster relief in times of emergency. They cannot help feeling anxious when carefully drafted appeals, often prepared with the assistance of an impartial international agency, receive an inadequate and sometimes tardy response. The impression is often given that the international community is not convinced about the true situation behind the appeal, or has little confidence in the appeal itself. Worse still, some donors show no interest in helping particular countries for one reason or the other. There have been several major disasters where it would have been possible to save thousands of lives if humanitarian aid had arrived in time and in sufficient quantities.

Fundraising–Accountability and Transparency

Again there is the question of fundraising. The media has reported many cases where humanitarian organizations have raised funds for a major disaster situation, but instead of the funds going to the stricken country, they have been spent largely at the headquarters of the donor organizations or used on other field projects, with only a small percentage reaching the recipient country. In the African view such a practice is entirely unacceptable. It is only fair that the recipient state should know the amount of funds that have been raised in its name, and should be consulted on how the funds should be spent. Moreover, as in the case of the recipient state, there should also be accountability on the part of the donors, particularly in regard to funds that have been raised in the name of the recipient state.

Networking or Nepotism

Lastly, there is the question of strengthening local capacities. Local graduates and professionals strongly resent being passed over or even ignored by donor states and humanitarian organizations when recruiting staff for key posts in their field missions and filling them with recruits from overseas. The local people attribute this policy to international networking—an arrangement whereby an organization tended to recruit expatriate colleagues and acquaintances to fill positions in the field that could easily be performed by locally qualified persons. The usual justification is that the candidate is known to the organization and that his/her services are immediately available. Little or no thought is given to the important question of helping to build local capacities. It often happens that once an emergency has passed, the expatriate personnel return to their headquarters or move on to another theatre where disaster assistance is needed. When they go, the organization concerned should, at least, leave behind a cadre of experienced local personnel with the requisite training to carry out relief work in any future emergencies. Moreover, the experience gained by local personnel would constitute a permanent asset for the country.

The Recovery Phase

Of course, the end of the emergency does not necessarily mean an end to the problems that it has caused. Lives may have been saved, suffering minimized, and the humanitarian situation contained. Still, the affected state has to cope with the recovery phase of rehabilitating the affected communities, restoring services, providing alternative means of livelihood, strengthening infrastructure, and making life in the affected areas livable and capable of sustaining the population living there. The needs are overwhelming, offering relief and development-related organizations unlimited opportunities to help complete the humanitarian work they had started. As the World Bank has said, the recovery phase can take several years to complete, and instead of going one step further with their aid, donors rush to other regions once the drama of the emergency is over.

SOMALILAND—A MICROCOSM OF DISASTER SITUATIONS

The information that follows is my recollection of visits that I made to Somaliland in 1983, at a time when the military regime was in power, and again in 1993 and 2000, after its fall. The government and the people had begun the challenging process of restoring law and order, disarming the numerous tribal militia that were a leftover from the civil war, jump-starting the economy, and re-establishing the few social services that it could afford. The population, in turn, was occupied salvaging property, rebuilding homes, cultivating their farmlands, setting up small businesses, looking for work, and desperately seeking news about the whereabouts of missing family members.

It was during one of those intolerably hot steamy evenings for which Berbera is renowned that I decided to invite a few friends over at the hotel where I was staying for tea and talk. I deliberately mixed the group so that with their diverse backgrounds, I could get a fairly good perspective of what had happened, what was happening, what should happen to improve the lot of the people who had been uprooted by the civil war. I hoped that during our informal discussions on the ills that confronted our country, they would mention how the civil war had affected the lives of their communities, and any thoughts they may have on the delivery and the effectiveness of the international aid community.

It took place in the garden area of the house where I was staying. The group included two elders, a merchant, two officials, representatives of two local nongovernmental agencies, and a young Somali graduate.

I gave the floor to the young graduate, who had recently completed his studies in Britain, having gone there first as a fourteen-year-old refugee with his mother and other members of his family. From an earlier talk with him, I knew that he was all pepped up, critical of local conditions, and anxious to air his views on almost everything that had to do with Africa and, in particular, his own country. His name was Hassan, and he said something to this effect:

"Why is it that whenever I read anything about Africa in today's newspapers it invariably relates to some critical situation: an impending natural disaster, civil strife, tribal war, interstate conflict, undemocratic government, poverty and underdevelopment, refugees and internally displaced people, environmental degradation, and the alarming spread of HIV/AIDS? Why can't Africans do something about these problems? Aren't these problems of our own making, or can we reasonably place the blame somewhere else? And, if the problems are within our capacity to solve, why aren't we doing something instead of appealing constantly for international aid and expecting others to do what we should be doing ourselves? I feel that this problem has been created by your generation (indicating the two elders), and it is time that we younger people took charge of our own destiny."

As Hassan spoke, I looked in the direction of some older friends to gauge their reactions. It was not the first time that we had heard dissenting voices from the younger generation placing blame for all the woes that had befallen their communities on the elders for incompetent leadership, limited knowledge, tribal bias, poor judgment, and a refusal to move with the times.

Who Is to Blame?

One of the elders replied that it was easy for the young generation to place all blame on the shoulders of the older generation for the sins of the past and the wrongs of the present. An understanding of the past throws more light on the solutions to present problems. As a case in point, he mentioned Somaliland's longstanding territorial dispute with Ethiopia—a dispute that the former colonial power created when it arbitrarily negotiated a boundary agreement with Ethiopia without consulting or seeking the approval of the people or their representatives. The agreement robbed the population of their rightful ownership over large tracts of land, making Somali citizens living there aliens in their own land. Despite numerous appeals for redress to the colonial power and to the United Nations, Britain handed over the unresolved problem to the incoming Somali government. The dispute resulted in frequent border incidents and, in 1964 and 1978, to open war—wars that led to the tragic upheavals of tens of thousands of Somalis.

Fratricidal Strife: The Worst of all Wars

Another elder observed that perhaps the most tragic of all war situations was when clans or communities, in a fratricidal struggle, waged war against each other, at times for territorial supremacy or control over watering centers or in satisfaction of a blood feud. In such cases, hostilities could be brought to a halt, and sometimes resolved, particularly if the parties concerned respected the application of customary law and there was wise leadership. But wars that pitted the state against particular communities were the most difficult to resolve as civilian communities, in normal circumstances, are exceedingly vulnerable and not equipped to defend themselves against any onslaught by the state. Tragically, this scenario was played out in Somaliland when, in 1988, several major cities and nearby settlements were leveled by aerial and land bombardments of the ousted military regime, resulting in the machine gunning of civilians as they tried to escape by foot to the Ethiopian border, some sixty to eighty miles away.

The elder, seemingly affected by the graphic picture he had recalled, disclosed the fact that both he and his family were among those who made the long trek, and who were forced by circumstance to spend the next three years in one of the refugee camps. In all, he said, a quarter of a million inhabitants sought asylum in Ethiopia; more than 40,000 perished in the bombardment and while fleeing for safety. What added to the people's suffering, the elder concluded, was the feeling that the plight of the population had not only been ignored by the international community, but that no protests had been publicly lodged with the ousted regime for its indiscriminate use of arms against the defenseless population.

Underdevelopment

A heated discussion took place on the question of economic reliance and of the capacity of Somaliland to provide better living standards for its people. One of the officials said that it was a question of legacy—the legacy of underdevelopment left by the colonial power, Britain—and during the years of independence, the deliberate neglect of Somaliland's economy by the military regime. He felt that Somaliland's experience in this respect was also shared to some extent by African states elsewhere. To illustrate his point, he referred to conditions existing in Somaliland at the time of independence.

After eighty-five years under British colonial rule, the colonial power had trained only one doctor and two engineers. The higher echelons of the administration were still in the hands of expatriates, including the police and military forces and all technical departments. The national budget still required a substantial grant to enable the country to balance its books, and, apart from its livestock industry that had been the mainstay of the economy since time immemorial, the potential of its long coastline for fishing had not been touched, and the agricultural sector was left underdeveloped, necessitating reliance on imported foodstuff. Generally speaking, the condition of Somaliland's social and economic infrastructure at the time of independence could be described as rudimentary in nature and totally inadequate as a springboard for development. In ending his observations, he smilingly said that the economy that was handed over to the Somaliland government in 1960, although underdeveloped, was far stronger, and in a much better condition, than the economy that was left to the people by the military regime after forty years of independence!

The Impact of War and Politics

At this stage, one of the officials, an experienced administrative officer, spoke at length on some of the matters raised by the graduate. He said that he appreciated the concerns that had been expressed, but that those who lived outside the country seemed to lose touch with some of its realities. Often, in measuring and comparing Somaliland's failures and achievements, the expatriate Somali seemed to use as a yardstick conditions of life in their adopted country coupled with whatever information they may have gathered in their academic studies. Such comparisons were invalid because of contrasting differences in history, culture, and in development. Independence, he said, had brought hopes that the elected government would bring an end to all of their woes. The citizens had been led to expect increased opportunities for employment, creation of new industries, an expanded network of schools and hospitals, the end of tribalism, and, above all, peace. No longer, people thought, would they need to depend on the old traditional system where the clan was responsible for the welfare of its members. Unfortunately, and without knowing it, the country was not prepared for such a revolutionary change in the social and political systems, nor were the new leaders experienced or capable of dealing with the rising tide of expectations they themselves had stimulated.

What followed was a weakening of the traditional structure of society, a failure on the part of the elected representatives to govern efficiently, and a military dictatorship of twenty years that brought the entire country to its knees. Oppressed by their own government, robbed of their livelihood, and displaced by war, the condition of the population was such that had it not been for the intervention of the international community with offers of aid, medicines, and shelter, only God knows what would have been their ultimate fate. Somaliland today no longer resembles the Somaliland of pre-independence days, when the overwhelming majority had a stake in the pastoral economy capable of providing them with support in times of need.

Today, urban centers are crowded by refugees and former pastoralists displaced by war and by famine; the former urban dwellers, who included the merchants, the professionals, the technicians, and the educated classes, fled the country following the bombardment of their towns, creating a vacuum with the loss of their experience, training, and expertise. The present government does not have the resources to rehabilitate the economy or continue services that had been enjoyed in better days. It has directed its efforts mainly toward the restoration and maintenance of peace and security, to the disarming of tribal militia, to the establishment of adequate governance, including a parliament, a judiciary, and a countrywide administrative system. In the social field, its resources have allowed the reopening of schools and hospitals, although well below the level that it intends to provide when additional resources become available.

International NGOs—As They Are Sometimes Seen by Others

Throughout our discussions, the local NGO representatives, who were relatively young, listened carefully to what had been said and wanted us to know something about their work and the problems they were encountering. One of them disclosed that he previously worked for one of the international agencies before joining his present local organization. At the outset, he was very complimentary in remarks on the activities of some of the international agencies—governmental and nongovernmental—that were financially supporting several emergency relief programs and a few rehabilitation projects. However, he said, the needs of the country were so great that the aid being received from those international agencies, however welcome, was like a drop in the ocean. What has been the response to the many appeals for aid that have been launched? Was it true that more than 75 percent of funds collected by some agencies go to sustain luxury budgets at the headquarters of the agency, and that less than 20 percent actually reaches the field?

His impressions of some of his expatriate colleagues were mixed. He respected a few not only for the sincerity and commitment they brought to their work, but also for their overall knowledge and persistent interest in educating themselves on the customs and culture of the people. There were others, he said, who were inexperienced and displayed no enthusiasm for the work they were assigned; they treated relief work more as a job than as a vocation and seemed insecure when dealing with local officers of equal or better academic qualifications.

Blunt Criticism

Another former NGO worker was more blunt in his criticism. He said that since donor states and international governmental agencies had cut down on the provision of direct aid to African states and were channeling a substantial proportion through international nongovernmental organizations to handle, the importance of the latter had so grown that some of their representatives acted more like colonial governors rather than the representative of humanitarian agencies people had known. The speaker stated that while he was aware of the reasons why some donors had lost faith in the integrity and the ability of several governments to utilize their aid for the purposes agreed, by making the international nongovernmental organization a conduit for such aid, it had elevated the latter to a pseudo-colonialist position. The effect was that some organizations had become arrogant in their relations with host governments, and there was a trend for them to dictate their own agendas and establish their own priorities.

He then proceeded to address his remarks to staff matters and to the need for better coordination between the NGO community and the government, as well as between the NGOs themselves. He remarked that while the amount of aid was small relative to the needs of the country, he and others were shocked by the extravagant manner in which some field representatives of international agencies spent money on their own comfort while being stingy about the few dollars that were given to the local staff. He cited what he considered to be inordinate sums of money spent on air travel, on mission, or on vacation.

Related to the contribution of international nongovernmental agencies, he agreed with his colleague that the country needed the help that international agencies were giving, particularly health, education and training programs, and programs associated with the rehabilitation and development of the agricultural sector, water and marketing development, and the prevention of environmental degradation. He confirmed that local NGOs were assisting in the execution of these programs, however, the funding that was made available was in the form of seed money, and totally insufficient to have any real impact in the short and medium term.

Equally disconcerting was the frequency of changeover in expatriate staff, as if one or two tours was more than anyone could handle. If the changeover was motivated by a desire to fill the departing expatriate's post with a local professional, the situation would be acceptable, but often inexperienced expatriate staff fill the post vacated. Meanwhile, the local professional is kept in his or her national post regardless of experience or professional qualifications. Occasions do arise when the performance of local staff may merit promotion to an international position—but these are infrequent and few.

In concluding his statement, the former NGO worker said that the term "voluntary work" had lost its meaning during the military regime, and it has been difficult to rekindle that spirit. Previously, people in the rural areas would offer their services voluntarily for such small village projects as the construction of feeder roads, hospital improvements, the sinking of wells, and similar types of projects. The ousted military regime made such service compulsory—and volunteers were treated even worse than indentured labor, a sure way of alienating communities that wanted to help in their own time and on their terms. At that point, our tea and talk ended.

CONCLUDING REFLECTIONS

O living man! What revelations
Await you in this world?
The wretchedness that today is mine
May be your fate tomorrow.
(from a Somali poem composed by
an elder made destitute by famine)

A new trend has begun to manifest itself in places like Somaliland, as well as in other parts of Africa—a trend where the young, educated generation are questioning the performance of past and present leaders, and voicing their dissatisfaction with the current situation in their respective countries. In Somaliland, they are being spurred in their demand by the thousands of young men and women from their country who now live in the developed world where governance is stable, standards of living high, and where there is a scrupulous respect not only for the rule of law but for the human rights of all. They all want an end to corrupt and inefficient governance, to unjust policies that force populations to flee their land and pit brother against brother in a fratricidal war in which everyone is a loser. They want peace, justice, and the development of their country so that all can benefit from its blessings.

SELECTED WEB SITES

The United Nations Office for the Coordination of Humanitarian Affairs: *http://www.reliefweb.int/ocha_ol/index.html* or *http://www.un.org/ha*

Food and Agriculture Organization: *http://www.fao.org*

United Nations Development Programme: *http://www.undp.org*

United Nations High Commissioner for Human Rights: *http://www.unhchr.ch*

United Nations High Commissioner for Refugees: *http://www.unhcr.ch*

United Nations Children Fund: *http://www.unicef.org*

United Nations Relief and Works Agency for Palestine Refugees in the Near East: *http://www.unrwa.org* and *http://www.un.org/unrwa*

UNAIDS: *http://www.unaids.org*

World Food Programme: *http://www.wfp.org*

World Health Organization: *http://www.who.org*

International Organization for Migration: *http://www.iom.ch* and *http://www.iom.int*

International Monetary Fund: *http://www.imf.org*

World Bank: *http://www.worldbank.org*

REGIONAL ORGANIZATIONS

The European Community Humanitarian Office: *http://europa.eu.int/comm/echo/en/present/manda_en.html*

BILATERAL ORGANIZATIONS

The [British] Department for International Development: *http://www.dfid.gov.uk*

Canadian International Development Agency: *http://www.acdicida.gc.ca*

Center for Disease Control and Prevention: *http://www.cdc.gov*

Japan International Cooperation Agency: *http://www.jica.go.jp/Index.html*

United States Agency for International Development: *http://www.info.usaid.gov*

RED CROSS AND RED CRESCENT MOVEMENT

International Committee of the Red Cross (ICRC): *http://www.icrc.org*

International Federation of Red Cross and Red Crescent Societies: *http://www.ifrc.org*

NONGOVERNMENTAL ORGANIZATIONS (NGOs)

Amnesty International: *http://www.amnesty.org*

Catholic Relief Services: *http://www.catholicrelief.org*

Center for International Health and Cooperation: *http://www.cihc.org*

Doctors Without Borders: *http://www.dwb.org*

Human Rights Watch: *http://www.hrw.org*

InterAction: *http://www.interaction.org*

International Diploma in Humanitarian Assistance: *http://www.idha.ch*

International Rescue Committee (IRC): *http://www.reliefnet.org/rnet/irc.html*

Médecins sans frontières: http://www.msf.org

Oxfam: *http://www.oxfam.org*
World Vision: *http://www.worldvision.org*

INTERNATIONAL COURTS

The International Court of Justice: *http://www.icj-cij.org*
International Criminal Tribunal for the Former Yugoslavia: *http://www.un.org/icty*
International Criminal Tribunal for Rwanda: *http://www.ictr.org*

NOTES AND REFERENCES

Notes to Chapter One
Humanitarian Action in the Twenty-first Century:
The Danger of a Setback
Paul Grossrieder

1. Christianity is understood here to refer to the religion and the sociological reality, and not to the Christian faith as the transcending of religion.

2. As François Bugnion wrote in a 1991 ICRC memo: "The Cold War therefore weighed heavily on relations between the ICRC and the USSR, on the ICRC's possibility to act in the conflicts stemming from rivalry between the two blocs, in particular in Korea, Indochina, and Afghanistan. . . . It was not until January 1992, after the break-up of the USSR, that the ICRC was authorized to contact the newly independent governments and offer them its services" (original in French).

3. J. C. Rufin, *Mondes rebelles* (Paris: Michalon, 1996), p. xiii.

Notes to Chapter Two
Scope of International Humanitarian Crises
Ibrahim Osman

1. Time trend in the number of people affected by disasters is presented for the period from 1992 to 2000, as data for complex disasters for the year 2001 is not available at this point.

2. All figures are expressed in 1996 U.S.$, rounded to the nearest million.

3. See chapter 2 Appendix for a definition of natural and technological disasters.

4. The costs of disasters are notoriously difficult to estimate, and the figures should be used with caution.

5. Note that those two figures are not directly comparable.

6. Conflict in Haiti in 1994 was the only conflict in the Americas for which humanitarian assistance was recorded by OCHA during the period examined. If we excluded that conflict, the lowest level of average assistance per affected person would have been in Africa, U.S.$42.24—less than 25 percent of the average in Europe.

7. The definition of natural disasters is taken from CRED, while that for complex disasters, from ReliefWeb.

REFERENCES TO CHAPTER THREE
THE LANGUAGE OF DISASTERS: A BRIEF TERMINOLOGY OF
DISASTER MANAGEMENT AND HUMANITARIAN ACTION
S. W. A. Gunn, M.D.

Clarke, R., A. Ehrlick, S. W. A. Gunn, et al. *London under Attack: Report of the GLAWARS Commission.* Oxford and New York: Blackwell, 1986.

Gunn, S. W. A. *Civil Protection Multilingual Lexicon.* Commission of the European Communities (in data bank). EU: Brussels, 1992.

———. "The Language of Disasters." *Prehospital and Disaster Medicine,* 1990, no. 5:373–376.

———. *Multilingual Dictionary of Disaster Medicine and International Relief* (English, French, Spanish, Arabic). Dordrecht, London, Boston: Kluwer Academic Publisher, 1990. New edition 2002. (Translated into German, Japanese, Italian, Russian.)

———. "On man-conceived disasters." *J. Humanitarian Med.,* 2001, no. 1:7–8.

Gunn, S. W. A., C. Murcia, and F. Parakatil. *Dictionnaire des Secours d'Urgence en cas de Catastrophe.* Paris: Conseil International de la Langue Francaise, 1984.

Simmonds, S., P. Vaughan, and S. W. A. Gunn. *Refugee Community Care.* Oxford: Oxford University Press, 1983 and 1985.

UNESCO. "Disaster and Conflict." In *Encyclopaedia of Life Support Systems.* Paris, 2001.

REFERENCES TO CHAPTER FOUR
TRAINING FOR HUMANITARIAN ASSISTANCE
Kevin M. Cahill, M.D.

Cahill, K. M. *A Framework for Survival: Health, Human Rights, and Humanitarian Assistance in Conflicts and Disasters.* New York: Routledge, 1999.

———. *Preventive Diplomacy.* New York: Routledge, 2001.

Perrin, P. *Handbook on War and Public Health.* Geneva: ICRC, 1996.

NOTES TO CHAPTER FIVE
TEAMWORK IN HUMANITARIAN MISSIONS
Pamela Lupton-Bowers

1. The quotations included here were made in personal conversations over a period of several years. They are from humanitarian workers from many organizations.

2. Russel Dynes (1990).

3. ACORD (1992).

4. Hugo Slim (1995).

5. Kathleen Carely and Jack Harrald (1993).

6. Tony Vaux (2001).

7. Mintzberg (1989).

8. There are some fascinating texts on NLP, a very small number of which I have included in the References at the end of these Notes. But I must point out that it is impossible to gain a true understanding of NLP through simply reading. You have to experience it for yourself to understand the potential it can have in improving communication excellence.

9. Peter Russell's *The Brain Book* (New York: Penguin, 1979) gives an interesting and readable presentation of application of brain research on self-improvement; while Sally P. Springer and George Deutsch's *Left Brain, Right Brain: Perspectives from Cognitive Neuroscience* (New York: Freeman Worth, 1997) offer a more science-based review of recent discoveries.

10. Psychologist B. W. Tuckman identified these stages of team development in the 1970s.

11. Dorothy Leonard and Susaan Straus, "Putting Your Company's Whole Brain to Work," *Harvard Business Review* (July–August 1997).

12. This list is a composite of many lists created over several years.

13. Tony Vaux (2001).

14. P. Hersey, K. H. Blanchard, and D. E. Johnson, *Management of Organizational Behavior,* 8th ed. (originally published in 1977) (New Jersey: Prentice Hall, 2001). This eighth edition is an excellent text. I was very excited to get my copy. It is so full of the classical research and models that it makes many other texts redundant.

15. K. H. Blanchard, *Slotting in the right manager. Choosing a manager whose style suits the situation* (New York: Summit Books, 1991).

16. Carl Rogers and H. Jerome Frieberg (1994).

17. Hersey, Blanchard and Johnson, *Management of Organizational Behavior,* 8th ed., has one of the better coverages of theories of motivation and behavior that I have read.

18. An interesting perspective on dealing with stress is presented in Ian McDermott and Joseph O'Connor, *NLP and Health* (1996).

19. Janis, "Victims of Groupthink," cited by Post (1993).

20. A. George, "The Impact of Crisis Induced Stress on Decision-Making," in *The Medical Implications of Nuclear War,* ed. F. Soloman (Washington D.C.: National Academy Press, 1986), p. 33.

21. Military psychologists say that soldiers and sailors in their first battle suffer immense stress before and during the fighting, and may confuse perceptions with reality. Soldiers often shoot at shadows and at each other in their first night in a combat zone. Extract from "Errors by a Tense U.S. Crew Led to Downing of an Iran Jet," *The New York Times,* 3 August 1988.

22. Harvey Robbins and Michael Finley, *Why Teams Don't Work* (1995) (San Francisco, CA: Bernett-Koehler Publishers, 2000). This is a great, readable book to take on mission.

23. Maddux (1990).

REFERENCES TO CHAPTER FIVE
TEAMWORK IN HUMANITARIAN MISSIONS
Pamela Lupton-Bowers

Blanchard, K. H. *Slotting In the Right Manager. Choosing a Manager Whose Style Suits the Situation.* New York: Summit Books, 1991.

Covey, R. Stephen. *Principle-Centered Leadership*. New York: Fireside, Simon Schuster, 1992.

Duffield, M. "Complex emergencies and the crisis of developmentalism." *IDS Bulletin* 25, no. 4 (1994): pp. 37–45.

George, Susan. "Food, famine, and service delivery in times of emergency." Chap. 3 in *Ill Fares the Land: Essays on Food, Hunger and Power*. London: Penguin, 1990.

Handy, C. *Understanding Voluntary Organizations*. London: Penguin Books, 1998.

Harvey Jones, John. *Making it Happen: Reflections on Leadership*. London: Collins, 1998.

Hersey, P., K. H. Blanchard, and D. E. Johnson. *Management of Organizational Behavior: Leading Human Resources*. New Jersey: Prentice Hall, 2001.

LeBoef, Michael. *How to Win Customers and Keep them For Life*. New York: Berkley, 1987.

Leonard, D., and S. Straus. "Putting Your Company's Whole Brain to Work." *Harvard Business Review* (July–August 1997).

Livingston, Sterling J. "Pygmalion in Management." *Harvard Business Review* (July-August 1969).

Maddux, Robert. *B Team Building*. London: Kogan Page, 1988.

Manzoni, Jean-François, and Jean-Louis Barsoux. "The Set-Up-To-Fail Syndrome." *Harvard Business Review* (March–April 1998).

McCann, Dr. Dick. *How to Influence Others at Work*. Butterworth: Heinemann, 1985.

McDermott, I., and I. Shircore. *NLP and the New Manager*. London: Thorsons Publishing, 1998.

O'Conner, J., and Ian McDermott. *An Introduction to Neuro-Linguistic Programming*. London: Thorsons Publishing, 2000.

Peters, Tom, and Nancy Austin. *A Passion for Excellence*. New York: Random House, 1985.

Post, Jerrold M. "The Impact of Crisis-Induced Stress on Policy Makers." Chap. 20 in *Avoiding War*, edited by Alexander L. George. Bolder, CO: Westview, 1991.

Robbins, H., and M. Finley. *Why Don't Teams Work? What Went Wrong and How to Make It Right*. Kuala Lumpur: Advantage Quest Publications, 1996.

Roberts, M. *Change Management Excellence*. Bancyfelin Carmarthen, U.K.: Crown House Publishing, 1999.

Spears, Larry C., and Michele Lawrence, eds. *Focus on Leadership: Servant-Leadership for the Twenty-first Century.* New York: J. Wiley, 2002.

Vaux, Tony. *The Selfish Altruist: A Profile of Relief Work in Famine and War.* United Kingdom: Earthscan, 2001.

Ward, M.. *50 Essential Management Techniques.* United Kingdom: Ashgate Publishing Company, 1995.

Waterman Jr., Robert H. *Frontiers of Excellence: Learning From Companies That Put People First.* London: Nicholas Brealey Publishing, 1994.

Further Reading

NLP

Andreas, S., and C. Faulkner. *NLP: The New Technology of Achievement.* London: Nicholas Brealey Publishing, 1994.

Bandler, R., and J. Grinder. *Frogs Into Princes.* Moab, Utah: Real People Press, 1979.

———. *The Structure of Magic. NLP.* 2 vols. Palo Alto, CA: Science & Behavior Books, 1975–1976.

Berne, E. *Games People Play.* New York: Grove Press, 1978.

Dilts, Robert. *Changing Belief Systems with NLP.* Capitola, CA: Meta Publications, 1990.

McDermott, Ian, and J. O'Connor. *NLP and Health.* London: Thorsens, 1996.

McDermott, Ian, and I. Shircore. *NLP and the New Manager.* London: Orion Business, 1999.

Cognitive Differences

Russell, Peter. *The Brain Book.* New York: Plume Books, Penguin, 1979.

Springer, Sally., and George Deutsch. *Left Brain, Right Brain.* 5th ed. New York: W. H. Freeman & Company, 1981.

The Learning Organization

Garratt, B. *The Learning Organisation: Developing Democracy at Work.* Reprint, London: Harper Collins Business, 2000.

Senge, P. M. *The Fifth Discipline: The Art and Practice of the Learning Organisation.* Reprint, London: Random House, 1990.

Notes to Chapter Six
Humanitarian Ethical and Legal Standards
Michel Veuthey

1. Yersu Kim, "Global Problems And Universal Values," available at *http://www.unesco.org/opi2/philosophyandethics/pronpro.htm* "The last decade of our century is witness to a rising demand for a universal ethics. Against the backdrop of the positivistic abstinence on questions of value and of the relativism of values of the preceding decades, there is an increasing search for universal values and principles that could serve as the basis for collective efforts toward peace and development, as well as for peaceful and productive interaction among nations and societies. . . . In 1993, representatives of more than 120 religions of the world, meeting for the first time in one hundred years in the Parliament of the World's Religions in Chicago, adopted a Declaration toward a Global Ethics. . . . In 1996, some thirty former heads of state and government who constitute the InterAction Council made an appeal for a set of "Global Ethical Standards" needed to deal with the global problems facing humanity in the twenty-first century." Yersu Kim, Director, Division of Philosophy and Ethics, UNESCO.

2. Michael Renner, "Breaking The Link Between Resources And Repression," chap. 7 in *World Watch Institute State Of The World 2002: Special World Summit Edition* (New York: W. W. Norton & Company, 2002).

3. *Ethics & International Affairs,* vol. 13 (New York: Carnegie Council on Ethics and International Affairs, 1999), contributions from Thomas G. Weiss, Cornelio Sommaruga, Joelle Tanguy, Fiona Terry, David Rieff, and others. *http://www.cceia.org/lib_volume13.html*

4. See H. E. J. Cowdrey, "The Peace and the Truce of God in the Eleventh Century," *Past and Present* (1970), pp. 42–67; Georges Duby, "The Laity and the Peace of God," *The Age of Chivalry,* trans. Cynthia Postan (London: Edward Arnold, 1977); *The Peace of God: Social Violence and Religious Response in France Around 1000 A.D.,* ed. Thomas Head and Richard Landes (Ithaca: Cornell U. Press, 1995). See also *http://www.mille.org/people/rlpages/paxdei.html*

5. See Semichon, *La paix et la trêve de Dieu* (Paris, 1869); Huberti, *Gottes und Landfrieden* (Ansbach, 1892), The Catholic Encyclopedia, vol. 10. *http://www.newadvent.org/cathen/*; See also *http://www.hillsdale.edu/*

dept/History/Documents/War/Med/1063-peace.htm and *http://www.bartleby*
.com/65/tr/truceGod.html

6. New Testament Matt. 7:7–12; but also Muhammad 13ᵉ Hadiths
de Nawawi; Mahavira: Yogashastra 2, 20; Bouddha Sutta Pitaka, Udana-
vagga 5, 18; Confucius; Analecta 15, 23; Mahabaharata 5: 15, 17; Tal-
mud bab, Shabbat 31a; Baha'u'llah: Kitab-i-aqdas 148; Isocrate:
Nicoclès 61. Calendrier inter religieux 2001–2002 (Geneva: Enbiro
Lausanne & Plate-Forme inter religieuse, 2000).

7. Platon, *La République,* trans. R. Baccon (Paris, 1966), pp. 224–
227. See also André Bernand, *Guerre et violence dans la Grèce antique*
(Paris: Hachette, 1999); Pierre Ducrey, *Le traitement des prisonniers de
guerre dans la Grèce antique* (Paris, 1978); and Jacqueline de Romilly, *La
Grèce antique contre la violence* (Paris: Ed. de Fallois, 2000).

8. Frank Keitsch, *Formen der Kriegführung in Melanesien* (Bamberg,
1967), p. 380.

9. Maurice R. Davie, *La guerre dans les sociétés primitives. Son rôle et son
évolution. Traduit de l'anglais par M. Guérin* (Paris: Payot, 1931). (The
Evolution of War: A Study of Its Role in Early Societies [New Haven:
Yale University Press, 1929]).

10. E. E. Evans-Pritchard. *The Nuer. A Description of the Modes of Livelihood and Political Institutions of a Nilotic People* (Oxford: Oxford University Press, 1940).

11. Buddhism contains two fundamental principles, maitri (friendli-
ness, benevolence) and karuna (mercy, compassion), closely related to
the principle of humanity.

12. For Hinduism, numerous rules on the kind treatment to be
granted to the vanquished are found in the Mahabharata (XII, 3487,
3488, 3489, 3782, 8235), which also prescribes loyalty in combat (XII,
3541, 3542, 3544–51, 57–60, 64, 3580, 3659, 3675, 3677). See also the
famous Laws of Manu, VII: 90–93 (*The Laws of Manu* [Oxford, 1886]).

13. On Taoism, see Gia-Fu Cheng, and Jane English, trans., *Lao Tse:
Tao Te Ching* (New York: Vintage, 1972), in particular no. 68 ("a good
winner is not vengeful") and no. 38.

14. See Barbara Aria and Russell Eng Gon, *The Spirit of the Chinese
Character* (San Francisco: Chronicle Books, 1992), p. 47.

15. On Bushido, see Sumio Adachi, "Traditional Asian Approaches:
A Japanese View," *Australian Yearbook of International Law* 9 (1985): pp.
158–167; and, by the same author, "The Asian Concept," *International*

Dimensions of Humanitarian Law (Paris: UNESCO, 1986): pp. 13–19, which also considers Buddhism.

16. On Judaism, see Erich Fromm, *You Shall Be As Gods* (New York: Holt, Rinehart and Winston, 1966).

17. On Christianity, Max Huber, *The Good Samaritan: Reflections on the Gospel and Work of the Red Cross* (London: Gollancz, 1945). See also Joseph Joblin, *L'Eglise et la Guerre. Conscience, violence, pouvoir* (Paris, 1988) and in particular, for *jus in bello,* page 193 and onwards; Alfred Vanderpol, *La doctrine scolastique du droit de la guerre* (Paris, 1919).

18. On Islam, see, among others, Hamed Sultan, "The Islamic Concept," *International Dimensions of Humanitarian Law* (Geneva/Paris: UNESCO/Nijhoff, 1988): pp. 29–39; Marcel Boisard, *L'Humanisme de l'Islam* (Paris, 1979); Jean-Paul Charney, *L'Islam et la guerre. De la guerre juste à la révolution sainte* (Paris, 1986). See also M. K. Ereksoussi, "The Koran and the Humanitarian Conventions," *International Review of the Red Cross* (May 1962); Ameur Zemmali, *Combattants et prisonniers de guerre en droit islamique et en droit international humanitaire* (Paris: Pedone, 1997).

19. On African customs, see Emmanuel Bello, *African Customary Humanitarian Law* (Geneva: ICRC, 1980); and Yolande Diallo, "Humanitarian Law and African Traditional Law," *International Review of the Red Cross* (February and August 1976).

20. See Geoffrey Best, *Humanity in Warfare. The Modern History of International Law of Armed Conflicts* (London: Weidenfels and Nicolson, 1980).

Michael Ignatieff, *The Warrior's Honour. Ethnic War and the Modern Conscience* (New York: Viking, 1998). A study compares this warrior's honor with today's ethnic conflicts.

21. See Eric Fromm, *The Anatomy of Human Destructiveness* (New York: Holt, Rinehart and Winston, 1973), p. 168.

22. The full text, available at *http://www.mtholyoke.edu/acad/intrel/kant/kant1.htm* is: "No State shall, during War, permit such Acts of Hostility which would make mutual Confidence in the subsequent Peace impossible: such are the employment of assassins ("percussores"), poisoners ("venefici"), breach of Capitulation, and Incitement to Treason ("perduellio") in the opposing State."

23. *http://35.1911encyclopedia.org/L/LA/LAS_CASAS_BARTOLOME_DE.htm*

24. See Giulio Basetti Sani, *L'Islam et St François d'Assise. La mission prophétique par le dialogue* (Paris: Publisud, 1987).

25. World Conference on Religion and Peace. Mission Statement available at *http://www.wcrp.org/RforP/MISSION_MAIN.html*

26. *http://www.millenniumpeacesummit.org*

27. United Nations Press Release SG/SM/7965, September 24, 2001.

28. A/56/523, November 2, 2001, available, as well as other documents on this Year, at *http://www.un.org/documents/dialogue.htm*

29. A/56/419.

30. A/54/60.

31. *Protocol for the Prohibition of the Use of Asphyxiating, Poisonous or Other Gases, and of Bacteriological Methods of Warfare,* Geneva, June 17, 1925.

32. *Declaration Renouncing the Use, in Time of War, of Certain Projectiles,* Saint Petersburg, November 29/December 11, 1868.

33. The Fourth Convention respecting the Laws and Customs of War on Land and its Annex: Regulations Concerning the Laws and Customs of War on Land, The Hague, October 18, 1907.

34. See Jean Pictet, *Humanitarian Law and the Protection of War Victims* (Leiden, 1975).

35. This was the term used by the Diplomatic Conference on the Reaffirmation and Development of International Humanitarian Law applicable in Armed Conflicts (CDDH), which met at Geneva from 1974 to 1977 to adopt the two Additional Protocols to the Conventions of 1949.

36. "Laws of war" is the expression still most widely used today in military circles. Cf Frederic de Mulinen, *Handbook on the Law of War for Armed Forces* (Geneva: ICRC, 1987); or Thomas B. Baines, "The Laws of War and the Rules of Peacekeeping," presented to the Joint Services Conference on Professional Ethics, January 30–31, 1997, at the National Defense University, Washington, D.C. Available at *http://www.usafa.af.mil/jscope/JSCOPE97/Baines97.htm*

37. Law of Geneva is sometimes used with the intention of stressing aspects relating to the protection of victims of war, as opposed to the regulation of conduct as regards methods and means of destruction between combatants, designated by the expression "Law of The Hague."

38. The Protocols of 1977 have to some extent merged the Law of Geneva and the Law of The Hague; this was merely the culmination of

a trend that began when the rules of The Hague relating to the treatment of prisoners of war were incorporated and expanded upon in the Second Geneva Convention of 1929, and later the Third Convention of 1949; similarly, the Fourth Convention of 1949 incorporated most of The Hague Regulations of 1907 on military occupation. All this is of considerable significance: apart from the historical memory, it is the customary nature of the rules of The Hague (and hence of the provisions incorporated in 1949 and 1977) which should be emphasized.

39. This was the term used by the United Nations for almost ten years after the International Conference on Human Rights held in Teheran (April 22–May 13, 1968). Numerous resolutions of the United Nations General Assembly, advocating further codification and describing how this was to be done, were adopted under the heading of Respect for Human Rights in Armed Conflicts," as well as reports by the Secretary-General of the United Nations (A/7720 in 1969, A/8052 in 1970, A/8370 in 1971, A/8781 in 1972, A/9123 in 1973, A/9669 in 1974, A/10195 in 1975).

40. See Georges Abi-Saab, "The Specificities of Humanitarian Law," in *Studies and Essays on International Humanitarian Law and Red Cross Principles in Honour of Jean Pictet*, ed. Christophe Swinarski (Geneva: ICRC, 1984), pp. 265–280.

41. See Henry Dunant, *A Memory of Solferino* (Geneva: ICRC, 1939).

42. Geneva Convention for the Amelioration of the Condition of the Wounded and Sick in Armed Forces in the Field, August 12, 1949; Geneva Convention for the Amelioration of the Condition of the Wounded, Sick, and Shipwrecked Members of the Armed Forces at Sea, August 12, 1949; Geneva Convention Relative to the Treatment of Prisoners of War, August 12, 1949; Geneva Convention Relative to the Protection of Civilian Persons in Time of War, August 12, 1949.

43. Protocol Additional to the Geneva Conventions of August 12, 1949, and relating to the Protection of Victims of International Armed Conflicts (Protocol 1); Protocol Additional to the Geneva Conventions of August 12, 1949, and relating to the Protection of Victims of Non-International Armed Conflicts (Protocol 2).

44. See *Commentary on the Additional Protocols of June 8, 1977, to the Geneva Conventions of August 12, 1949* (Geneva: ICRC, 1987), p. 381, ¶ 1364.

45. The International Tribunal for the Prosecution of Persons Responsible for Serious Violations of International Humanitarian Law

Committed in the Territory of the Former Yugoslavia since 1991 was established by the Security Council on May 25, 1993.

46. The International Criminal Tribunal for the Prosecution of Persons Responsible for Genocide and Other Serious Violations of International Humanitarian Law Committed in the Territory of Rwanda and Rwandan Citizens Responsible for Genocide and Other Such Violations Committed in the Territory of Neighboring States between January 1 and December 31, 1994, was established by the Security Council on November 8, 1994.

47. See the Tadic Case: International Criminal Tribunal for the Former Yugoslavia, *Prosecutor v. Dusko Tadic a/k/a "Dule"*: Decision on the defence motion for interlocutory appeal on jurisdiction. Decision of October 2, 1995, case no. IT-94-1-AR72. Two articles written on this case: John Dugard, "Bridging the Gap Between Human Rights and Humanitarian Law: The Punishment of Offenders," *International Review of the Red Cross*, no. 324 (September 1998): pp. 445–453; and Thomas Graditzky, "International Criminal Responsibility for Violations of International Humanitarian Law Committed in Non-international Armed Conflicts," *International Review of the Red Cross*, no 322 (March 1998): pp. 29–56.

48. See I. William Zartman, ed., *Collapsed States. The Disintegration and Restoration of Legitimate Authority* (Boulder: Lynne Rienner, 1995), p. 301; and the Preparatory Document Drafted by the ICRC for the First Periodical Meeting on International Humanitarian Law, "Armed Conflicts Linked to the Disintegration of State Structures," mentioning Resolution 814, ¶ 13 (Somalia), Res. 788, ¶ 5 (Liberia), Geneva, January 19–23, 1998.

49. See Robert Fox, "On the Age of Postmodern War. Beyond Clausewitz: the Long and Ragged Conflicts of the Coming Millennium," *The Times Literary Supplement*, 15 May 1998.

50. As Martin Van Crefeld puts it in *The Transformation of War* (New York: Free Press, 1991), "Once the legal monopoly of armed force, long claimed by the State, is wrestled out of its hands, existing distinctions between war and crime will break down."

51. ICRC Commentary III, Article 1. Available online at: *http://www .icrc.org/ihl.nsf/b466ed681ddfcfd241256739003e6368/49cfe5505d5912d 1c12563cd00424cdd?OpenDocument*

52. International Court of Justice, Case Concerning the Military and Paramilitary Activities in and Against Nicaragua *(Nicaragua v. United*

States of America), Judgement of June 27, 1986 (Merits), vol. 114, ¶ 218. On this case, see: Rosemary Abi-Saab, "The 'General Principles' of Humanitarian Law According to the International Court of Justice," *International Review of the Red Cross* (July–August 1987): pp. 367–375.

53. The United Nations Convention on the Prohibition of Military or Any Other Hostile Use of Environmental Modification Techniques (ENMOD), adopted on December 10, 1976.

54. Convention on the Rights of the Child, adopted by Resolution 44/25 of the United Nations General Assembly on November 20, 1989.

55. See Michael Ignatieff, "The Attack on Human Rights," *Foreign Affairs* (November/December 2001).

56. See the interesting article by Chih-yu Shih, "Opening the Dichotomy of Universalism and Relativism," *Human Rights and Human Welfare. International Review of Books and Other Publications* 2, no. 1 (January 2002), reviewing Linda S. Bell, Andrew J. Nathan, and Ilan Peleg, eds., *Negotiating Culture and Human Rights* (New York: Columbia University Press, 2001); and Daniel A. Bell, *East Meets West: Human Rights and Democracy in East Asia* (Princeton: Princeton University Press, 2000).

57. See Amartya Sen, *Development as Freedom* (New York: Random House, 2000).

58. Paragraph 2 of the Proclamation of 1968 Tehran reads as follows: "The Universal Declaration of Human Rights states a common understanding of the peoples of the world concerning the inalienable and inviolable rights of all members of the human family and constitutes an obligation for the members of the international community."

59. Paragraph 1 of the 1993 Vienna Declaration states that: "The World Conference on Human Rights reaffirms the solemn commitment of all States to fulfil their obligations to promote universal respect for, and observance and protection of, all human rights and fundamental freedoms for all in accordance with the Charter, other instruments relating to human rights, and international law. The universal nature of these rights and freedoms is beyond doubt. . . .

All human rights are universal, indivisible, and interdependent and interrelated. The international community must treat human rights globally in a fair and equal manner, on the same footing, and with the same emphasis. While the significance of national and regional particularities and various historical, cultural, and religious backgrounds must be borne in mind, it is the duty of States, regardless of their political, economic, and cultural systems, to promote and protect all human rights and fundamental freedoms."

60. I. C. J. Reports (1951), p. 12. See Christa Rottensteiner, "The Denial of Humanitarian Assistance as a Crime Under International Law," *International Review of the Red Cross,* no. 835 (1999): pp. 555–582.

61. See the Web site dedicated to the Charter: *http://www.europarl.eu-.int/charter/default_en.htm* The text was published in the Official Journal of the European Communities, C 364/1 (2000).

62. For this "third generation of human rights," see: Karel Vasak, "Pour une troisième génération des droits de l'homme," in *Studies and Essays on International Humanitarian Law and Red Cross Principles,* ed. Christophe Swinarski (Geneva: ICRC, 1984), pp. 837–845; Karel Crawford and Hans Kruuk, *The Rights of Peoples* (Oxford: Oxford University Press, 1992).

63. See: Edith Brown Weiss, ed., *Environmental change and international law: New challenges and dimensions* (Tokyo: The United Nations University, 1992). *http://www.unu.edu/unupress/unupbooks/uu25ee/uu25 ee0k.htm*; and especially: Alexandre Kiss, "An Introductory Note on a Human Right to Environment," *http://www.unu.edu/unupress/unup books/uu25ee/uu25ee0k.htm*; "The Fundamental Right to Life at the Basis of the Ratio Legis of International Human Rights Law and Environmental Law," *http://www.unu.edu/unupress/unupbooks/uu25ee/uu25ee0p .htm* See also the "Report of the Joint OHCHR-UNEP Seminar on Human Rights and the Environment," January 16, 2002, E/CN.4/ 2002/WP. 7 (March 22, 2002), submitted to the Fifty-eighth Session of the Commission on Human Rights. *http://www.unhchr.ch/huridocda/ huridoca.nsf/Documents?OpenFrameset*

64. Declaration on the Right to Development, G.A. res. 41/128, annex, 41 UN GAOR Supp. (no. 53) at 186, UN Doc. A/41/53 (1986). Available at the University of Minnesota Human Rights Library Web site: *http://www1.umn.edu/humanrts/instree/s3drd.htm*; and on the UN Web site: *http://www.un.org/documents/ga/res/41/a41r128.htm.* See also Arjun Sengupta "The Right to Development as a Human Right," on the François-Xavier Bagnoud Center for Health and Human Rights, Harvard University, Web site: *www.hsph.harvard.edu/fxbcenter/FXBC_ WP7—Sengupta.pdf*

65. See the Web site of the Office of the High Commissioner for Human Rights: *http://www.unhchr.ch/html/menu2/10/e/rtd_main.htm*; and the Report of the High Commissioner for Human Rights, submit-

ted in accordance with Commission on Human Rights resolution 1998/72.

E/CN.4/2002/27 (November 27, 2001) available at: *http://www.unhchr.ch/huridocda/huridoca.nsf/Documents?OpenFrameset*

66. Statement in January 1997. *http://www.unesco.org/general/eng/whatsnew/decl.eng.html*

67. See the WHO Web site "Health as a Human Right," *http://www.who.int/archives/who50/en/human.htm*; and the interdisciplinary discussion held at Harvard Law School in September 1993, *http://www.law.harvard.edu/programs/HRP/Publications/economic1.html*; and Henrik Karl Nielsen, *The World Health Organisation—Implementing the Right to Health,* as well as "Health and Human Rights. An International Journal" published by the François-Xavier Bagnoud Center for Health and Human Rights, Harvard University, since 1994. *http://www.hsph.harvard.edu/fxbcenter/journal.htm*

68. E/CN.4/2002/52 (January 21, 2002) and Add. 1 (February 26, 2002). *http://www.unhchr.ch/huridocda/huridoca.nsf/Documents?OpenFrameset*

69. See the FAO Web site: *http://www.fao.org/Legal/rtf/rtfood-e.htm*

70. See Resolution A/RES/56/155 ("The Right to Food"), adopted on December 19, 2001.

71. Jean Ziegler (Switzerland). See A/56/210 ("Preliminary Report"), July 21, 2001, and E/CN.4/2002/58 (January 10, 2002), "Report by the Special Rapporteur, Mr. Jean Ziegler, on the Right to Food Submitted in Accordance with Commission on Human Rights Resolution 2001/25," and Add. 1 ("Mission to Niger"), January 23, 2002.

72. See *The Fundamental Principles of the Red Cross and Red Crescent Movement,* 2nd ed. (Geneva: ICRC, 1996).

73. See Jean Pictet, *The Fundamental Principles of the Red Cross. Commentary,* (Geneva, 1979).

74. Text available at: *http://www.doctorswithoutborders.org/about/charter.shtml*

75. See: Hugo Slim, "Relief Agencies and Moral Standing in War: Principles of Humanity, Neutrality, Impartiality and Solidarity," *Development in Practice* 7, no. 4 (1997): pp. 342–352; Denise Plattner, "ICRC Neutrality and Neutrality in Humanitarian assistance," *International Review of the Red Cross,* no. 311 (1996): pp. 167–179; Rony Brauman, *Devant le Mal: Rwanda. Un Génocide en Direct* (Paris: Arléa, 1994). See also: Frances Smith, "Principles of Engagement for Emergency Humanitarian Assistance in the DRC:" *http://www.odihpn.org/report.asp?*

ReportID= 1071; and "Principles of Engagement for Emergency Humanitarian Assistance in the Democratic Republic of Congo," United Nations Session 8: Handout 8.4: *http://coe-dmha.org/unicef/ HPT_Session8Handout8_4.htm*

76. See Code of Conduct for Law Enforcement Officials, adopted by General Assembly resolution 34/169 of December 17, 1979: *http:// www.unhchr.ch/html/menu3/b/h_comp42.htm*

77. Code of Conduct for the International Red Cross and Red Crescent Movement and NGOs in Disaster Relief: *http://www.ifrc.org/ publicat/conduct/index.asp*

78. See *http://www.sphereproject.org*

79. A Universal Declaration of Human Responsibilities (Proposed by the InterAction Council), September 1, 1997: *http://www.asiawide.or.jp/ iac/UDHR/EngDecl1.htm*

80. See *http://www.tgwu.org.uk/voluntarysector/peopaid.htm*

81. See *http://www.hapgeneva.org*

82. See "Ethics of Humanitarian Aid: Consultation on Humanitarianism and Ethics," *APRODEV Bulletin* (Stony Point, New York), February 1997. *www.oneworld.org/aprodev/feb97_6.htm*

83. Caritas International's Guiding Values and Principles: (1) Dignity of the human person, (2) Preferential option for the poor and marginalized, (3) The Universal Destination of the Earth's Good, (4) Solidarity, and (5) Stewardship.

84. See the World Vision International Web site, *http://www.wvi .org/home.shtml,* which states that: "The World Vision Partnership shares a common understanding bound together by six core values. These core values are the fundamental and guiding principles that determine World Vision's actions. The core values are our aim, a challenge that we seek to live and work to. *We are Christian. We are committed to the poor. We value people. We are stewards. We are partners. We are responsive.*"

85. See the following Web sites: *http://www.tandf.co.uk/journals/tfs/ 15027570.html* (Journal of Military Ethics); *http://dir.yahoo.com/Government/Military/Ethics/, http://www.usna.edu/Ethics/* (Center for the Study of Professional Military Ethics); *http://plato.stanford.edu/entries/war/* (Stanford Encyclopedia of Philosophy); *http://www,iihl.org* (International Institute of Humanitarian Law).

86. See Cees de Rover, "Police and Security Forces. A New Interest for Human Rights and Humanitarian Law," *International Review of the Red Cross,* no. 835 (September 1999): pp. 637–647; and C. de Rover, *To*

Serve and to Protect. Human Rights and Humanitarian Law for Police and Security Forces (Geneva: ICRC, 1998).

87. The Hippocratic Oath (available at *http://classics.mit.edu/Hippo crates/hippooath.html*) and the following document of the World Medical Association: "World Medical Association Resolution on Human Rights" (adopted by the Forty-second World Medical Assembly, Rancho Mirage, California, U.S.A., October 1990, and amended by the Forty-fifth World Medical Assembly, Budapest, Hungary, October 1993, the Forty-sixth General Assembly, Stockholm, Sweden, September 1994, the Forty-seventh General Assembly, Bali, Indonesia, September 1995).

Having regard to the fact that:

1. The World Medical Association and its member associations have always sought to advance the cause of human rights for all people, and have frequently taken actions endeavoring to alleviate violations of human rights;
2. Members of the medical profession are often among the first to become aware of violations of human rights;
3. Medical Associations have an essential role to play in calling attention to such violations in their countries.

The World Medical Association again calls upon its member associations:

1. To review the situation in their own countries so as to ensure that violations are not concealed as a result of fear of reprisals from the responsible authorities, and to request strict observance of civil and human rights when violations are discovered;
2. To provide clear, ethical advice to doctors working in the prison system;
3. To provide effective machinery for investigating unethical practices by physicians in the field of human rights;
4. To use their best endeavors to ensure that adequate healthcare is available to all human beings without distinction;
5. To protest alleged human rights violations through communications that urge the humane treatment of prisoners, and that seek the immediate release of those who are imprisoned without just cause; and
6. To support individual physicians who call attention to human rights violations in their own countries." *http://www.wma.net/e/ policy/20-2-90_e.html*

88. See the Code accepted in 1954 by the World Congress of the International Federation of Journalists (IFJ), and amended in 1986: *http://www.ifj.org/ifj/codee.html*; and the Databank for European Codes of Journalism Ethics: *http://www.uta.fi/ethicnet/*

89. See *http://www.unglobalcompact.org/un/gc/unweb.nsf/content/the nine.htm*

90. Common Article 1 to the 1949 Geneva Conventions.

91. ICRC, *ICRC Commentary on the Additional Protocols* (Geneva: ICRC, 1987), p. 35, ¶ 39.

92. ICRC Commentary 3, p. 18 (Article 1). See: Luigi Condorelli and Laurence Boisson de Chazournes, "Quelques remarques à propos de l'obligation des Etats de 'respecter et faire respecter' le droit international humanitaire 'en toutes circonstances,'" in *Studies and Essays on International Humanitarian Law and Red Cross Principles*, Christophe Swinarski, ed. (Geneva: ICRC, 1984), pp. 17–35; and Umesh Palwankar, "Measures Available to States for Fulfilling Their Obligation to Ensure Respect for International Humanitarian Law," *IRRC*, no. 298 (1994): pp. 9–25.

93. The 1949 Geneva Conventions as well as Additional Protocol 1, for the States Party to this Protocol. See the *ICRC Commentary on the Protocols*, ad Article 1 of Protocol 1, pp. 35–38.

94. Article 7 ("Meetings"): "The depositary of this Protocol [Switzerland] shall convene a meeting of the High Contracting Parties, at the request of one or more of the said Parties and upon the approval of the majority of the said Parties, to consider general problems concerning the application of the Conventions and of the Protocol." Such a meeting was convened by Switzerland on December 5, 2001 in Geneva ("Conference of the High Contracting Parties to the Fourth Geneva Convention").

95. *ICRC Commentary on the Additional Protocols*, p. 36, ¶ 43. See also Michel Veuthey, "Pour une politique humanitaire," in *Studies and Essays on International Humanitarian Law and Red Cross Principles*, Christophe Swinarski, ed. (Geneva: ICRC, 1984), pp. 989–1009.

96. Training is an obligation according to the Four 1949 Geneva Conventions. Article 47 of the First Convention states the following: "The High Contracting Parties undertake, in time of peace as in time of war, to disseminate the text of the present Convention as widely as possible in their respective countries, and, in particular, to include the study thereof in their programs of military and, if possible, civil instruc-

tion, so that the principles thereof become known to the entire population, in particular to the armed fighting forces, the medical personnel and the chaplains." The Second Convention contains a similar provision (Article 48). Article 127 of the Third Convention adds the following paragraph: "Any military or other authorities, who in time of war assume responsibilities in respect of prisoners of war, must possess the text of the Convention and be specially instructed as to its provisions." Article 144, ¶ 2 of the Fourth Convention reads as follows: "Any civilian, military, police or other authorities, who in time of war assume responsibilities in respect of protected persons, must possess the text of the Convention and be specially instructed as to its provisions." Additional Protocol 1: (a) Reaffirms the duty to disseminate (Article 83—Dissemination); and (b) Adds the obligation to ensure that legal advisers are available (Article 82—Legal Advisers in armed forces).

Additional Protocol 2, applicable in non-international armed conflicts, simply states that "This Protocol shall be disseminated as widely as possible" (Article 19—Dissemination).

97. Article 36 ("New Weapons") of Protocol 1 reads as follows: "In the study, development, acquisition, or adoption of a new weapon, means, or method of warfare, a High Contracting Party is under an obligation to determine whether its employment would, in some or all circumstances, be prohibited by this Protocol or by any other rule of international law applicable to the High Contracting Party."

98. The Four 1949 Conventions contain common provisions on the "Repression of Abuses and Infractions:"

- —First Convention: Article 49–51
- —Second Convention: Article 50–52
- —Third Convention: Article 129–131
- —Fourth Convention: Article 146–148
- —Article 85 of Additional Protocol 1 reaffirms those provisions, adds a few acts to be considered as grave breaches (especially attacks against civilians and civilian objects), and classifies grave breaches of the 1949 Conventions and Protocol 1 as war crimes.

See also Maria Teresa Dutli and Cristina Pellandini, "The International Committee of the Red Cross and the Implementation of a System to Repress Breaches of International Humanitarian Law," *IRRC*, no. 300 (May 1994): pp. 240–254.

99. See George A. B. Peirce, "Humanitarian Protection for the Vic-

tims of War. The System of Protecting Powers and the Role of the ICRC," *Military Law Review* 90 (1980): pp. 89–162; and D. P. Forsythe, "Who Guards the Guardians? Third Parties and the Law of Armed Conflict," *American Journal of International Law* 70 (1976): pp. 41–61.

100. H. Coulibaly, "Le rôle des Puissances protectrices au regard du droit diplomatique, du droit de Genève et du droit de La Haye," in *Implementation of International Humanitarian Law,* F. Kalshoven and Y. Sandoz, eds. (Dordrecht: Martinus Nijhoff, 1989), pp. 69–78. C. Dominice and J. Patrnogic, "Les Protocoles additionnels aux Conventions de Genève et le système des Puissances protectrices," *Annales de droit international médical* 28 (1979): pp. 24–50. J.-P. Knellwolf, "Die Schutzmacht im Völkerrecht unter besonderer Brücksichtigung der schweizerischen Verhältnisse" (Dissertation Bern, Bern: Ackermanndruck, 1985). B. Laitenberger, "Die Schutzmacht," *German Yearbook of International Law* 21 (1978): pp. 180–206.

101. It was used in Suez in 1956, in Goa in 1961, and between India and Pakistan in 1971. For a more recent example, see the State Department Press Briefing, Thursday, April 1, 1998: "The United States Government is contacting authorities in Belgrade through our Protecting Power, Sweden, in regard to the illegal abduction of three American servicemen who were serving in non-combatant status in Macedonia. There is no basis for their continued detention by the Belgrade authorities. We insist that they be provided any necessary medical assistance and treated humanely and in accordance with all prevailing international agreements and standards. We will hold Belgrade authorities responsible for their safety and treatment." *http://www.aiipowmia.com/inter/in040299e.html*

102. Protocol 1, Article 2, Letter C.

103. Third Geneva Convention, Article 126.

104. Fourth Geneva Convention, Article 143.

105. Fourth Geneva Convention, Articles 59 and 61.

106. Third Geneva Convention, Article 123.

107. Fourth Geneva Convention, Article 140.

108. First Geneva Convention, Article 23.

109. Fourth Geneva Convention, Article 14.

110. Fourth Geneva Convention, Article 30.

111. Article 9 of Conventions 1, 2, and 3; Article 10 of the Fourth Convention.

112. Common Article 3 to the 1949 Conventions.

113. The Web site of the Commission: *http://www.ihffc.org*

114. See Patrick Healy and Kimberly Prost, "International Criminal Law" McGill University Faculty of Law: *http://www.law.mcgill.ca/academics/coursenotes/healy/intcrimlaw/* and the following links mentioned there: *Nuremberg Trials*, London, Agreement of August 8, 1945 (*http://www.yale.edu/lawweb/avalon/imt/imt.htm*); Charter of the International Military Tribunal (*http://www.yale.edu/lawweb/avalon/imt/imt.htm*); Judgment of the IMT for the Trial of German Major War Criminals (*http://www.yale.edu/lawweb/avalon/imt/imt.htm*).

115. See the following links, quoted by Patrick Healy and Kimberly Prost, *Jurisdiction of the Yugoslavian and Rwandan* Ad Hoc *Tribunals*, Security Council Resolution 827 (1993), May 25, 1993 (*http://www.un.org/Docs/sc.htm*); Security Council Resolution 955 (1994), November 8, 1994 (*http://www.un.org/Docs/sc.htm*); Statute of the International Criminal Tribunal for the Former Yugoslavia ("ICTY"), Articles 6, 8, 9 (*http://www.un.org/icty/basic.htm*); Statute of the International Criminal Tribunal for Rwanda ("ICTR"), Articles 5, 7, 8 (*http://www.ictr.org*); ICTY, Rules of Procedure and Evidence, Rules 7–13 (*http://www.un.org/icty/basic.htm*); ICTY, *Prosecutor v. Dusko Tadic a/k/a "Dule,"* Appeals Chamber Decision on the Jurisdictional Motion, October 2, 1995, ss. 9–48, 9–64 (*http://www.un.org/icty/cases-ae2.htm*); *Substantive Law and the* Ad Hoc *Tribunals*, Statute of the ICTY, Articles 2–5, 21 (*http://www.un.org/icty/basic.htm*); Statute of the ICTR, Articles 2–4, 20 (*http://www.ictr.org*); ICTY, *Prosecutor v. Drazen Erdemovic*, Appeals Chamber, Joint separate opinion of Judge McDonald and Judge Vohrah, ss. 32–58, 66, 73–91; Separate and dissenting opinion of Judge Cassese, ss. 11–12, 40–51 (*http://www.un.org/icty/cases-ae2.htm*); ICTR, *Prosecutor v. Jean-Paul Akayesu*, Trial Chamber, Summary of the Judgment (*http://www.ictr.org*); ICTR, *Prosecutor v. Jean-Paul Akayesu*, Trial Chamber, Judgment, ss. 5.5 and 7 (*http://www.ictr.org*); *Evidence, Procedure, and the* Ad Hoc *Tribunals*, ICTY, Rules of Procedure and Evidence, Rules 39–43, 54–61, 89–98 (*http://www.un.org/icty/basic.htm*); ICTY, *Prosecutor v. Dusko Tadic a/k/a "Dule,"* Judgment on evidentiary matters (*http://www.un.org/icty/cases-te.htm*); Judgment on Corroboration in section V(c), Judgment on Hearsay in section V(h), ICTY, *Prosecutor v. Blaskic*, Judgment on the request of The Republic of Croatia for review of the decision of Trial Chamber 2 of July 18, 1997, ss. 25–60 (*http://www.un.org/icty/blaskic/ace14.htm*).

116. See: *Jurisdiction of the ICC: Trigger Mechanisms and the Exercise of*

the Court's Jurisdiction (*http://www.un.org/icc/backinfo.htm*); Rome Statute of the International Criminal Court, Articles 11–15, 17–18 (*http://www.un.org/icc*); *Substantive Law and the ICC: Crimes within the Court's Jurisdiction* (*http://www.un.org/icc/backinfo.htm*); Rome Statute of the International Criminal Court, Articles 5–9, 21, 22–33, 55, 67, 69 (*http://www.un.org/icc*); Preparatory Commission for the International Criminal Court: Results of Working Groups on ICC Rules of Procedure and Evidence; Most recent laws (*http://www.un.org/law/icc/prepcomm/docs.htm*).

117. ICRC, *International Criminal Court: A Reality at Last* (Geneva: ICRC, April 11, 2002).

118. See the Web site of the CPT: *http://www.cpt.coe.fr*

119. Elisabeth Kardos-Kaponyi, "The Charter of Fundamental Human Rights in the European Union," p. 139, mentions the Office for Democratic Institutions and Human Rights (ODHIR), the High Commissioner of National Minorities and the Representative on Freedom of the Media. Document available online: *www.lib.bke.hu/gt/2001-1-2/kardos-kaponyi.pdf*

120. Ibid., pp. 140–170.

121. The ICRC can offer its good offices to facilitate the establishment of hospital zones (according to Article 23 of the First 1949 Convention) and safety zones (Article 14, First Convention). Other institutions or persons could offer their good offices. See B. G. Ramcharan, *Humanitarian Good Offices in International Law: The Good Offices of the United Nations Secretary-General in the Field of Human Rights* (The Hague: Martinus Nijhoff, 1983).

122. See Roy W. Gutman, "Spotlight on Violations of International Humanitarian Law. The Role of the Media," *IRRC*, no. 325 (December 1998): pp. 619–625; Urs Boegli, "A Few Thoughts on the Relationship Between Humanitarian Agencies and the Media," *IRRC*, no. 325 (December 1998): pp. 627–631, and, more generally, Danieli, Yael, ed., *Sharing the Front Line and the Back Hills. International Protectors and Providers: Peacekeepers, Humanitarian Aid Workers and the Media in the Midst of Crisis* (Amityville, NY: Baywood Publishing, 2002).

123. See the open letters sent to public officials in Washington, D.C., and in Europe after September 11, 2001, in order to promote the application of international humanitarian law and fundamental human rights guarantees. See also the open letter sent to the Revolutionary Armed Forces of Colombia-People's Army (FARC-EP) on May 8, 2002,

denouncing the use of indiscriminate weapons (gas cylinder bombs) as contrary to international humanitarian law. A copy of the letter sent to Commander Marulanda can be found at *http://www.hrw.org/press/2002/ 05/colombia0508.pdf*

124. See Rainer Hofmann, ed., and Nils Geissler, assist. ed., "Non-State Actors as New Subjects of International Law—From the Traditional State Order Toward the Law of the Global Community," *Proceedings of an International Symposium of the Kiel Walther-Schücking Institute of International Law, March 25 to 28, 1998* (Berlin: Duncker und Humblot, 1999). Daniel Byman, Peter Chalk, Bruce Hoffman, William Rosenau, David Brannan, *Trends in Outside Support for Insurgent Movements* (Washington, D.C.: Rand, 2001).

125. See the "Guidelines for Engaging Non-State Actors in a Land-mine-Ban," at *http://www.icbl.org/wg/nsa/library/draft%20guidelines .html*; and Claude Bruderlein, "The Role of Non-State Actors in Building Human Security: The Case of Armed Groups in Intra-State Wars," *Policy paper for the Centre for Humanitarian Dialogue,* Geneva, Switzerland (prepared for the Ministerial Meeting of the Human Security Network in Lucerne), May 2000. *www.hdcentre.org/NewsEvents/1999/Policy% 20paper.doc*

126. Safeguarding human rights is not only the concern of governments and international organizations. Representatives of other international and local players, like human rights defenders, drawn from civil society, have also felt committed to this issue for a long time. See "The 'Human Security Network' Commitments" at the Second Ministerial Meeting in Lucerne, Switzerland, May 11–12, 2000. *http://www .humansecuritynetwork.org/commit-e.asp*

127. See the following Human Rights Watch appeals: "Israel/Palestinian Authority: Protect Civilians, Allow Independent Reporting," HRW Press Release, April 3, 2002, at http://hrw.org/press/2002/04/ isr-pa040302.htm; "Jenin: War Crimes Investigation Needed: HRW Press Release, May 3, 2002, at *http://hrw.org/press/2002/05/jenin 0503.htm*

128. See Daniel L. Smith-Christopher, ed., *Subverting Hatred. The Challenge of Nonviolence in Religious Traditions* (New York: Orbis Books, 1998).

129. See *http://www.santegidio.org/* and Andrea Riccardi, *Sant'Egidio, Rome et le monde,* Beauchesne éditeur (Paris, 1996); and Philippe Leym-

arie, "Les bâtisseurs de paix de Sant'Egidio," *Le Monde Diplomatique* (Septembre 2000): pp. 16–17.

130. Zbigniew Brzezinski, "The Century of Megadeath," Chap. 1 in *Out of Control. Global Turmoil on the Eve of the Twenty-first Century* (New York: Charles Scribner's Sons, 1993).

131. See the most recent definition of "Genocide" in Article 6 of the Rome Statute of the International Criminal Court: "For the purpose of this Statute, 'genocide' means any of the following acts committed with intent to destroy, in whole or in part, a national, ethnical, racial, or religious group, as such: *(a)* Killing members of the group; *(b)* Causing serious bodily or mental harm to members of the group; *(c)* Deliberately inflicting on the group conditions of life calculated to bring about its physical destruction in whole or in part; *(d)* Imposing measures intended to prevent births within the group; *(e)* Forcibly transferring children of the group to another group."

132. Michael Cranna, ed., *The True Cost of Conflict* (London: Earthscan, 1994), p. 197.

133. "The Causes of Conflict and the Promotion of Durable Peace and Sustainable Development in Africa." Report of the Secretary-General, Paragraph 4, April 16, 1998.

134. Gérard Prunier, *The Rwanda Crisis 1959–1994. History of a Genocide* (New York: Columbia University Press, 1997), p. 354.

135. Ibid., p. 346.

136. See "Armed Conflicts Linked to the Desintegration of State Structures," Preparatory Document drafted by the ICRC for the First Periodical Meeting on International Humanitarian Law, Geneva, January 19–23, 1998.

137. Viktor E. Frankl, *Man's Search for Meaning* (New York: Pocket Books, 1985), p. 179.

138. Ilene R. Prusher, "For War-Crimes Tribunal, 'Justice' is a Relative Term," *The Christian Science Monitor,* 15 February 2002.

139. See John F. Murphy, "Civil Liability for the Commission of International Crimes as an Alternative to Criminal Prosecution," *Harvard HRJ* 12 (Spring 1999), pp. 1–56; and Human Rights Watch, "Business and Human Rights: Law Suits Under the Alien Torts Claims Act (ACTA)," available at: *http://www.hrw.org/wr2k2/business.html*

140. See *http://www.wordspy.com/words/ethicsdeficit.asp*

141. See Alex Boraine, *A Country Unmasked: Inside South Africa's Truth*

and Reconciliation Commission (New York: Oxford University Press, 2001).

142. See the official Web site of the South African TRC at: *http:// www.doj.gov.za/trc/*; The full report is available online at: *http://www .polity.org.za/govdocs/commissions/1998/trc/index.htm*; A printed version (five volumes and a CD-ROM) was published (London, U.K.: MacMillan, March 1999).

143. Apartheid has been declared a grave breach of international humanitarian law in Protocol 1 (Article 85, ¶ 4, *[c]*).

144. Michael Jesse Battle and Desmond Mpilo Tutu, *Reconciliation: The Ubuntu Theology of Desmond Tutu* (Cleveland, OH: The Pilgrim Press, 1997).

145. Marvin Frankel, *Out of the Shadows of the Night: The Struggle for International Human Rights* (New York: Delacorte Press, 1989).

146. Susan Slyomovics, "A Truth Commission for Morocco," *Middle East Report* 218 (Spring 2001). *http://www.merip.org/mer/mer218/218_ slymovics.html*

147. See the 2000 Report of the UN Office of the High Commissioner for Human Rights to the General Assembly (A/55/38, ¶ 37–45). *http://www.hri.ca/fortherecord2000/vol2/sierraleonega.htm.* "The report notes that the OHCHR provided technical assistance to the government in drafting the law on the Truth and Reconciliation Commission (TRC). The OHCHR also developed a project for the preparatory phase of the Commission. The resumption of hostilities in May 2000 caused the Security Council to reconsider the role of UNAMSIL as well as other justice issues, including the establishment of a court to try human rights and humanitarian law abuses related to the conflict. The High Commissioner stated that these issues are crucial for the proper functioning of the TRC. The ongoing armed conflict, however, has delayed the implementation of the preparatory phase of that Commission."

148. Priscilla B. Hayner, "Fifteen Truth Commissions," *Human Rights Quarterly* 16, no. 4 (November 1994): pp. 597–655; Mike Kaye, "The Role of the Truth Commissions in the Search for Justice, Reconciliation, and Democratisation: Salvadorean and Honduran Cases," *J. Lat Amer. Stud.* 29, pp. 695–716; Neil J. Kritz, ed., *Transitional Justice: How Emerging Democracies Reckon with Former Regimes,* 3 vols. (Washington, D.C.: USIP, 1995); José Zalaquett, "Moral Reconstruction in the Wake of Human Rights Violations and War Crimes," in *Hard Choices,* ed. Jonathan Moore (Lanham, MD: Rowman & Littlefield, 1998), pp.

211–227; and the Web site of the USIP: *http://www.usip.org/library/truth.-html*

149. See Priscilla B. Hayner, *Unspeakable Truths: Confronting State Terror and Atrocity* (New York: Routledge, 2001).

150. See this prayer by Archbishop Tutu: "We pray that wounds that may have been re-opened in this process have been cleansed so that they will not fester; that some balm has been poured on them and that they will now heal." *http://www.macmillan-reference.co.uk/PandH/TRC foreword.htm*

151. See the Executive Summary of the Global Report at: *http://www.icrc.org/icrceng.nsf/5cacfdf48ca698b6412562242003b3295/be5298c00 339e340c1256af4004efaf3?OpenDocument*

152. "Human rights is a complex idea with differing emphases even as between various Western societies. Only with appropriate humility and self-doubt can true dialogue be encouraged." Stephen J. Toope, "Cultural Diversity and Human Rights" (F. R. Scott Lecture). *http://collections.ic.gc.ca/tags/cultural.html*

153. Paul Grossrieder, "Humanitarian Standards and Cultural Differences," in ICRC, *Seminar for Nongovernmental Organizations on Humanitarian Standards and Cultural Differences.* Summary Report, ICRC & The Geneva Foundation to Protect Health in War, Geneva, December 14, 1998.

154. See Umesh Palwankar, "Measures Available to States for Fulfilling Their Obligation to Ensure Respect for International Humanitarian Law," *IRRC*, no. 298 (1994): pp. 9–25. *http://www.icrc.org/Web/Eng/siteeng0.nsf/iwpList113/35289C31F0187A41C1256B6600591427*

155. Such as the U.S. Foreign Assistance Act, which forbids security assistance to any government that "engages in a consistent pattern of gross violations of internationally recognized human rights" [22 U.S.C. Secs. 2034, 2151n].

156. Of special interest are: Resolution 764 (1992) of July 13, 1992, in which the Security Council reaffirmed that all parties are bound to comply with the obligations under international humanitarian law and, in particular, the Geneva Conventions of August 12, 1949, and that persons who commit or order the commission of grave breaches of the Conventions are individually responsible in respect of such breaches; Resolution 771 (1992) of August 13, 1992, in which it demanded that all parties immediately cease and desist from all breaches of international humanitarian law; Resolution 780 (1992) of October 6, 1992, in

which it requested the Secretary-General to establish, as a matter of urgency, an impartial Commission of Experts to examine and analyze the information submitted pursuant to resolutions 771 (1992) and 780 (1992), together with such further information as the Commission of Experts may obtain, with a view to providing the Secretary-General with its conclusions on the evidence of grave breaches of the Geneva Conventions and other violations of international humanitarian law committed in the territory of the former Yugoslavia.

157. Mary Griffin, "Ending the Impunity of Human Rights Atrocities: A Major Challenge for International Law in the Twenty-first Century," *International Review of the Red Cross*, no. 838 (2000): pp. 369–389.

158. Resolution 827.

159. Article 2 of the Statute.

160. Article 3.

161. Article 4.

162. Article 5.

163. See Iain Guest (Overseas Development Council) on National Public Radio ("All Things Considered"), Friday April 16, 1999. "The Hague Tribunal was established by the UN Security Council in May 1993, ostensibly to deter war crimes, but the [Security] Council squabbled over funding and even delayed appointing a prosecutor for a year" (on July 8, 1994, Resolution 936, appointing Richard J. Goldstone).

164. See Patricia Grossman, "Bring Warlords to Justice," *International Herald Tribune*, Saturday/Sunday, 9/10 March 2002, p. 10.

165. See the following recommendations by Amnesty International:

1. Ratify the Rome Statute of the International Criminal Court and enact effective implementing legislation to cooperate fully with the Court.

2. Enact and use universal jurisdiction legislation for the crimes of genocide, crimes against humanity, war crimes, torture, extrajudicial executions and "disappearances," in order that their national courts can investigate and, if there is sufficient admissible evidence, prosecute anyone who enters its territory suspected of these crimes, regardless of where the crime was committed or the nationality of the accused or the victim.

3. Enact legislation to ensure effective cooperation with the International Criminal Tribunals for the Former Yugoslavia and for Rwanda and any other international criminal court created in the future.

166. International humanitarian law is one of the many legal, political, ethical instruments, in today's global disorder, to deal with our "genocidal mentality" and to "become healers, not killers, of our species." Robert Jay Lifton and Eric Markusen, *The Genocidal Mentality. Nazi Holocaust and Nuclear Threat* (New York: Basic Books, 1990), p. 279.

167. See *http://www.guardian.co.uk/waronterror/story/0,1361,583 028,00.html*; Dr. Scilla Elworthy, "Conflict Resolution in the Twenty-first Century," Tuesday, October 30, 2001; and Michel Veuthey, "Remedies to Promote the Respect of Fundamental Human Values in Non-International Armed Conflicts," *The Israeli Yearbook on Human Rights* 30 (2001): pp. 37–77.

168. The March 2002 issue of *Democracy Issues,* an electronic journal published by the United States Department of State, is dedicated to human rights education. It includes some interesting contributions, including articles by Felisa Tibbitts ("Emerging Models for Human Rights Education") and Nanc Flowers ("Human Rights Education in U.S. Schools"); an interview with human rights educators from South Africa ("Human Rights Education in Diverse, Developing Nations: A Case in Point—South Africa"); and an article on training for judges, prosecutors, attorneys, and the police ("International Human Rights Training" by Michael Hartmann). The journal also features a short bibliography and related Web sites. The full text of the journal can be found at: *http://usinfo.state.gov/journals/itdhr/0302/ijde/ijde0302.htm*

169. Including by campaigns for a universal ratification of human rights and international humanitarian law treaties. See Hans-Peter Gasser, "Steps Taken to Encourage States to Accept the 1977 Protocols," *IRRC,* no. 258 (May 1987). Another example is the campaign conducted in February 2002 to recommend to the U.S. Senate that it ratify the Optional Protocol to the Convention on the Rights of the Child on the Involvement of Children in Armed Conflict. *http://world.pylduck .com/02/0212.html*

170. See the ICRC's "Woza Africa! Music Goes to War." This was the slogan adopted by six popular African musicians who, responding to the ICRC's call, led a campaign in 1997 to help curb the indiscriminate violence that has long plagued their continent. The musicians strove to reach people's hearts and minds through a series of original songs, which they performed live and recorded.

171. See "Commitment to Global Peace," The Millennium World

Peace Summit of Religious and Spiritual Leaders, New York, August 2000. *http://global-forum.org/research/globalpeace.html*

172. See the educational programs of the International Committee of the Red Cross (ICRC) (*www.icrc.org*), Red Cross and Red Crescent National Societies, as well as by UNESCO (*www.unesco.org*) and human rights NGOs such as Human Rights Watch, Human Rights Internet, and academic institutions such as the International Institute of Humanitarian Law in San Remo (Italy) with courses on laws of war for military personnel, on refugee law, and on international humanitarian law (*www.iihl.org*).

173. It is not only needed to stop the use of child soldiers (*http://www.hrw.org/campaigns/crp/index.htm*), but also to reintegrate them into society. See Mike Wessels, "Child Soldiers," *Bulletin of Atomic Scientists* (Chicago, Nov/Dec. 1997) (*http://pangaea.org/street_children/africa/armies.htm*); and the Web site of the Office of the SRSG for Children and Armed Conflict (*http://www.undp.org/erd/recovery/ddr/organizations/osrg.htm*); and UNICEF, "Children at both ends of the gun:" *http://www.unicef.org/graca/kidsoldi.htm*

174. See *Amnesty International Handbook,* 7th ed., available online, at: *http://www.amnesty-volunteer.org/aihandbook/,* especially chap. 4 ("Campaigning") and chap. 5 ("AI Action—Advice and Guidelines"); as well as the excellent *Human Rights Education Handbook* (University of Minnesota: Human Rights Resource Center, 2000), available online at: *http://www.hrusa.org/hrmaterials/hreduseries/hrhandbook1/toc.html*

175. See Morton Winston, "NGO Strategies for Promoting Corporate Social Responsibility," *Ethics & International Affairs* 16, no. 1 (spring 2002). According to Morton Winston, there is a basic divide between NGOs:

(a) Engagers try to draw corporations into dialogue in order to persuade them by means of ethical and prudential arguments to adopt voluntary codes of conduct, while confronters believe that corporations will act only when their financial interests are threatened, and therefore take a more adversarial stance toward them.

(b) Confrontational NGOs tend to employ moral stigmatization, or "naming and shaming," as their primary tactic, while NGOs that favor engagement offer dialogue and limited forms of cooperation with willing MNCs.

176. See William Hartung, "The New Business of War: Small Arms and the Business of Conflict," *Ethics & International Affairs Annual Jour-*

nal of the Carnegie Council on Ethics and International Affairs 15, no. 1 (2001). The author's argument is the following: The proliferation of internal conflicts fueled by small arms poses a grave threat to peace, democracy, and the rule of law. The weapons of choice in today's conflicts are not big-ticket items like long-range missiles, tanks, and fighter planes, but small and frighteningly accessible weapons ranging from handguns, carbines, and assault rifles on up to machine guns, rocket-propelled grenades, and shoulder-fired missiles. In conflict zones from Colombia to the Democratic Republic of the Congo, picking up a gun has become the preferred route for generating income, obtaining political power, and generating "employment" for young people, many no more than children, who have little prospect of securing a decent education or a steady job. Ending the cycle of violence fueled by small arms must become a top priority for the international community. No single treaty or set of actions, however, will "solve" the problem of light weapons proliferation. What is needed is a series of overlapping measures involving stricter laws and regulations, greater transparency, and innovative diplomatic and economic initiatives.

177. See Anna Segall, "Economic Sanctions: Legal and Policy Constraints," *IRRC* 81, no. 836 (December 1999): pp. 763–784; and Claude Bruderlein, "UN Sanctions Can Be More Humane and Better Targeted," *Public Affairs Report* (University of California, Berkeley) 41, no. 1 (January 2000) *http://www.igs.berkeley.edu/publications/par/Jan2000/ Bruderlein.html* ; Arthur C. Helton and Robert P. DeVecchi, "Human Rights, Humanitarian Intervention and Sanctions," *http://www.foreign policy2000.org/library/issuebriefs/IBHumanRights.html* ; and H. C. Graf Sponeck, "Sanctions and Humanitarian Exemptions: A Practitioner's Commentary," *European Journal of International Law* 13, no. 1 (2002): pp. 81–87. Full text available at: *http://www3.oup.co.uk/ejilaw/current/ 130081.sgm.abs.html*

178. See Michel Veuthey, "The Contribution of the 1949 Geneva Conventions to International Security," *Refugee Survey Quarterly* 18, no. 3 (1999): pp. 22–26.

179. See Oxfam, "Africa at the Crossroads," *Oxfam Policy Papers*, no. 19 (March 2002). *http://www.oxfam.org.uk/policy/papers/africacrossroads/ africacrossroads.h tml*

180. See Michael K. Addo, ed., *Human Rights Standards and the Responsibility of Transnational Corporations* (The Hague: Kluwer Law International, 1999).

181. See Antonio Cassese, "The Martens Clause: Half a Loaf or Simply Pie in the Sky?" *EJIL* 11, no. 1 (2000): pp. 187–216; Theodor Meron, "The Martens Clause, Principles of Humanity, and Dictates of Public Conscience," *AJIL* 94, no. 2 (2000): pp. 78–89; Shigeki Miyazaki, "The Martens Clause and International Humanitarian Law," in *Etudes et essais sur le droit internationl humanitaire et sur les principes de la Croix-Rouge en l'honneur de Jean Pictet,* ed. C. Swinarski (Geneva: ICRC, 1984), pp. 433–444.

REFERENCES TO CHAPTER SIX
HUMANITARIAN ETHICAL AND LEGAL STANDARDS
Michel Veuthey

Abi-Saab, Georges. "The Specificities of Humanitarian Law." In *Etudes et essais sur le droit internationl humanitaire et sur les principes de la Croix-Rouge en l'honneur de Jean Pictet,* edited by C. Swinarski. Geneva: ICRC, 1984, pp. 265–280.

———. "The Implementation of Humanitarian Law." In *The New Humanitarian Law of Armed Conflict,* edited by A. Cassese. Naples: Ed. Scientifica, 1979.

Abi-Saab, Rosemary. *Droit humanitaire et conflits internes. Origines et evolution de la réglementation internationale.* Paris: Pedone, 1986.

Abrams, Elliott, ed. *Honor Among Nations. Intangible Interests and Foreign Policy.* Washington, D.C.: Ethics and Public Policy Center, 1998.

Akhavan, Payam. "Beyond Impunity: Can International Criminal Justice Prevent Future Atrocities?" *AJIL* 95 (January 2001): pp. 7, 7–19, 22–31. (Available in PDF format at *www.asil.org/ajil/recon2.pdf*)

Aldrich, George. "Establishing Legal Norms through Multilateral Negotiations: The Laws of War." *Case W. Res. Journal of International Law* 9, no. 1 (1977).

Ali, Tariq. *The Clash of Fundamentalisms, Crusades, Jihads, and Modernity.* New York: Verso, 2002.

Anderson, Mary. *Do No Harm. How Aid Can Support Peace—Or War.* Boulder, Colorado: Lynne Rienner Publishers, 1999.

Anderson, Mary, and Peter J. Woodrow. *Rising From the Ashes. Development Strategies in Times of Disaster.* Boulder, Colorado: Lynne Rienner Publishers, 1998.

Australian Department of Foreign Affairs and Trade. *Human Rights Manual 1998. http://www.dfat.gov.au/hr/hr_manual/*

Barber, Ben. "Feeding Refugees, or War? The Dilemma of Humanitarian Aid." *Foreign Affairs* (July/August 1997).

Bello, Emmanuel. *African Customary Law.* Geneva: ICRC, 1980.

Benthall, Jonathan. *Disasters, Relief and the Media.* London: I. B. Tauris, 1993.

Berkeley, Bill. *The Graves Are Not Yet Full: Race, Tribe and Power in the Heart of Africa.* New York: Basic Books, 2001.

Best, Geoffrey. *Humanity in Warfare: The Modern History of the International Law of Armed Conflicts.* London: Weidenfels and Nicolson, 1980.

Bettelheim, Bruno. *The Informed Heart. A Study of the Psychological Consequences of Living Under Extreme Fear and Terror.* New York: The Free Press, 1960.

Beyani, Chaloka. "The Legal Framework for an International Humanitarian Ombudsman." Paper prepared for the Ombudsman Project Steering Committee, October 1999. (www.oneworld.org/ombudsman/articles/legalfin.html)

Blank, Laurie. *The Role of International Financial Institutions in International Humanitarian Law. Report from the International Law Working Group.* Washington: USIP, 2002.

Boisard, Marcel. *L'humanisme de l'Islam.* 3rd ed. Paris: Albin Michel, 1979.

Boisson de Chazournes, Laurence, and Luigi Condorelli. "Common Article 1 of the Geneva Conventions Revisited: Protecting Collective Interests." *IRRC* 82, no. 837 (March 2000): pp. 67–87.

Bonard, Paul. *Modes of Action Used by Humanitarian Players.* Geneva: ICRC 1999.

Bothe, Michael, Karl Josef Partsch, and Waldemar A Solf. *New Rules for Victims of Armed Conflicts. Commentary on the Two Protocols Additional to the Geneva Conventions of 1949.* The Hague: Martinus Nijhoff, 1982.

Bouchet-Saulnier, Françoise. *The Practical Guide to Humanitarian Law.* Lanham, MD: Rowan & Littlefield, 2002.

Bowen, John R. "The Myth of Global Ethnic Conflict." *Journal of Democracy* (1996): 3–14.

Brauman, Rony, ed. "L'humanitaire n'a pas vocation à être un Père Noël universel" ou *Le Dilemme Humnaitaire.* Paris: Textuel, 1996.

Broyles, William. *Brothers in Arms: A Journey from War to Peace.* New York: Knopf, 1986.

Bruderlein, Claude. "The Role of Non-State Actors in Building Human Security: The Case of Armed Groups in Intra-State Wars." Policy paper for the Centre for Humanitarian Dialogue, Geneva, Switzerland (prepared for the Ministerial Meeting of the Human Security Network in Lucerne), May 2000. *www.hdcentre.org/NewsEvents/1999/Policy%20paper.doc*

Brzezinski, Z. *Out of Control. Global Turmoil on the Eve of the Twenty-First Century.* New York: Charles Scribner's Son, 1993.

Bugnion, Francois. *Le Comité international de la Croix-Rouge et la protection des victimes de la guerre.* Geneva: CICR, 1994.

Cahill, Kevin M., ed. *A Framework for Survival. Health, Human Rights and Humanitarian Assistance in Conflicts and Disasters.* New York: Routledge, 1999.

———. *Preventive Diplomacy: Stopping Wars Before They Start.* New York: Routledge, 2000.

Campbell, Colm. "Peace and the Laws of War: The Role of International Humanitarian Law in the Post-Conflict Environment." *International Review of the Red Cross,* no. 839 (June 30, 2000): pp. 627–651. (Available at: *www.icrc.org*).

Carbonnier, Gilles. "Corporate Responsibility and Humanitarian Action" *IRRC* (December 2001): pp. 947–967.

Cassese, Antonio. *International Law.* Oxford: OUP, 2001.

———. "The Martens Clause: Half a Loaf or Simply Pie in the Sky?" *EJIL* 11, no. 1 (2000): pp. 187–216.

Chabal, Patrick, and Jean-Pascal Daloz. *Africa Works. Disorder as Political Instrument.* Oxford: James Currey, 1999.

Cochrane, James, John De Gruchy, and Stephen Martin, eds. *Facing the Truth: South African Faith Communities and the Truth and Reconciliation Commission.* Athens, OH: Ohio University Press, 1999.

Council for a Parliament of the World Religions. *Declaration of the Religions for a Global Ethic. http://astro.temple.edu/~dialogue/Antho/kung.htm*

Cranna, Michael, ed. *The True Cost of Conflict. Seven Recent Wars and Their Effects on Society.* New York: The New Press, 1994.

Crocker, Chester A., Fen Osler Hampson, and Pamela Aal, eds. *The Challenges of Managing International Conflict.* Washington, D.C.: USIP, 2001.

Cuerra-Lugo, Victor de. "Protecting the Health Sector in Colombia: A Step to Make the Conflict Less Cruel." *IRRC* (December 2001): pp. 1111–1126.

Cutts, Mark. "Practice and Principle in Humanitarian Responses to Complex Emergencies." Master's thesis, Cambridge: Queens' College, July 14, 1997 (International Relations).

———. "The Humanitarian Operation in Bosnia, 1992–95: The Dilemmas of Negotiating Humanitarian Access." *New Issues in Refugee Research*, Working paper no. 8, Geneva: UNHCR (May 1999): pp. 10–25. (Available in PDF format at *www.unhcr.ch*).

Dahmane, Farid. "Wahid.Les mesures prises par le Conseil de Sécurité contre les entités non étatiques. Une tentative de cerner l'application du Chapitre VII aux conflits internes." *African Journal of International and Comparative Law* 11, no. 2 (June 1999): pp. 227–244.

Danieli, Yael, ed. *Sharing the Front Line and the Back Hills. International Protectors and Providers: Peacekeepers, Humanitarian Aid Workers and the Media in the Midst of Crisis.* Amityville, NY: Baywood Publishing Company, 2002.

Destexhe, Alain. *L'humanitaire impossible.* Paris: A. Colin, 1994.

Destexhe, Alain, and others. *Rwanda and Genocide in the Twentieth Century.* New York: New York University Press, 1996.

Dherse, Jean-Loup, and Hugues Minguet, O.S.B. *L'éthique ou le chaos?* Paris: Presses de la Renaissance, 1998. *http://www.ndganagobie.com/ethique_fr.htm*

Doswald-Beck, Louise, and Sylvain Vité. "International Humanitarian Law and Human Rights." *International Review of the Red Cross*, no. 293 (March 1, 1993): pp. 94–119.

Draper, G. I. A. D. "The Implementation and Enforcement of the Geneva Conventions and of the two Additional Protocols of 1977." *Recueil des Cours* (The Hague) 3 (1979): pp. 1–54.

Dugard, John. "War Crimes in Internal Conflicts." *Israel Yearbook on Human Rights* 28 (1998).

———. "Bridging the Gap Between Human Rights and Humanitarian Law: The Punishment of Offenders." *IRRC*, no. 324 (September 1998): pp. 445–453. *http://www.icrc.org/icrceng.nsf/c1256212004ce24e4125621200524882/1daee6e828886a1f412566c70051c269?OpenDocument*

Duner, Bertil, ed. *An End to Torture: Strategies for its Eradication.* London: Zed Books, 1998.

Durand, Roger, and Jacques Meurant. *Préludes et pionniers. Les Précurseurs de la Croix-Rouge 1840–1860.* Genèvea: Société Henry-Dunant, 1991.

Ellis, Stephen. *The Mask of Anarchy: The Destruction of Liberia and the Religious Dimension of an African Civil War.* New York: New York University Press, 1999.

Falk, Richard. *Explorations on the Edge of Time. The Prospects for World Order.* Philadelphia, PA: Temple University Press, 1991.

————. *On Human Governance. Toward a New Global Politics.* Oxford, 1995.

————. *Religion and Humane Global Governance.* New York: Palgrave, 2001.

Falk, Richard, and Andrew Strauss. "Toward Global Parliament." *Foreign Affairs* (January/February 2001). *http://www.globalpolicy.org/ngos/role/globdem/globgov/2001/0418gap.htm*

Falk, Richard, and Jean Allain, eds. *Unlocking the Middle East.* Northampton, MA: Interlink Books, 2002.

FAO. *Near East Conference Endorses German Initiative for an International Alliance against Hunger and Poverty, Calls for Investment in Agriculture.* FAO Press Release 02/29, Teheran (March 13, 2002).

Federation Francaise des Clubs UNESCO/Ligue des Droits de l'Homme. *La conquête des droits de l'homme. Textes fondamentaux.* Paris: Le Cherche-Midi, 1988.

Fleck, Dieter, ed. *The Handbook of Humanitarian Law in Armed Conflicts.* Oxford: Oxford University Press, 1995.

Fox, Matthew. *A Spirituality Named Compassion.* Minneapolis, MN: Winston Press, 1979.

Freud, Sigmund. *Civilization and its Discontents.* Rev. ed. New York: Dover Publications, 1994.

Fromm, Erich. *The Anatomy of Human Destructiveness.* New York: Harper and Row, 1970.

————. *You Shall Be As Gods.* New York: Holt, Rinehart and Wilson, 1966.

Galli, Guido. *Humanitarian Cease-Fires in Contemporary Armed Conflicts: Potentially Effective Tools for Peacebuilding.* Dissertation for the Degree of Master of Arts in Post-War Recovery Studies. York, UK: The University of York, September 2001. *http://www.who.int/disasters/hbp/concept.htm*

Galli, Guido, and Jon Ebersole. *Humanitarian Cease-Fires Country List.*

Geneva: World Health Organization, 2001. *www.who.int/cha/disasters/hbt/hcfcntrs.htm*

Gangadean, Ashok. "Dialogue: the Key to Global Ethics." *GDI Anthology. Envisioning a Global Ethic. http://astro.temple.edu/~dialogue/Antho/ashok_an.htm*

Garreton, Robert. "Mission Impossible. The Massacres in Former Zaire." *Le Monde Diplomatique* (December 1997). (Available at: *http://MondeDiplo.com/1997/12/garreton.html*).

Gasser, Hans-Peter. "International Humanitarian Law: An Introduction." In *Humanity for All*, edited by Hans Haug. Geneva: ICRC, 1993.

Glover, Jonathan. *Humanity: A Moral History of the Twentieth Century.* London: Jonathan Cape, 1999.

Goldstone, Richard. "Exposing Human Rights Abuses—A Help or a Hindrance to Reconciliation?" *Hastings Constitutional Law Quarterly* 22, no. 3 (Spring 1995).

———. *For Humanity. Reflections of a War Crimes Prosecutor.* New Haven: Yale University Press, 2000.

Gourevitch, Philip. *We Wish to Inform You that Tomorrow We Will Be Killed With Our Families: Stories From Rwanda.* New York: Farrar Straus & Giroux, 1998.

Graditzky, Thomas. "Individual Criminal Responsibility for Violations of International Humanitarian Law Committed in Non-international Armed Conflicts." *International Review of the Red Cross,* no. 322 (March 1998): pp. 29–56. *http://www.redcross.org.au/ihl/articles/thomas_graditzky_individual ecrim.htm*

Greppi, Edoardo. "The Evolution of Individual Criminal Responsibility Under International Law." *International Review of the Red Cross,* no. 835 (1999): pp. 531–553. *http://www.icrc.org/Web/Eng/siteeng0.nsf/iwpList106/911763EAA63170C0C12 56 B66005D85D0*

Griffiths, Bede. *Return to the Center.* Springfield. Illinois: Templegate, 1977.

Grossman, Lt. Col. Dave. *On Killing. The Psychological Cost of Learning to Kill in War and Society.* Boston: Little, Brown, 1995.

Gutman, Roy, and David Rieff, eds. *Crimes of War. What the Public Should Know.* New York: W. W. Norton, 1999.

Hartung, William D. *And Weapons for All.* New York: Harper Collins, 1995.

———. "The New Business of War: Small Arms and the Business of

Conflict." *Ethics & International Affairs Annual Journal of the Carnegie Council on Ethics and International Affairs* 15, no. 1 (2001).

Hassan, Riffat. "A Muslim's Reflection on A New Global Ethics and Cultural Diversity." Presented at Conferentie "Kracht van Cultuur" (The Power of Culture), Amsterdam, November 8, 1996. *http:// kvc.minbuza.nl/uk/archive/amsterdam/ukverslag_hassan.html*

Hayner, Priscilla B. "Fifteen Truth Commissions—1974–1994. A Comparative Study." *Human Rights Quarterly* 16, no. 597 (1994). Also in N. J. Kritz, ed. *Transitional Justice: How Emerging Democracies Reckon With Former Regimes* (Washington: United States Institute of Peace Press) 1, no. 225 (1995).

Hayner, Priscilla B. *Unspeakable Truths: Confronting State Terror and Atrocity.* New York: Routledge, 2001.

Helton, Arthur C. *The Price of Indifference: Refugees and Humanitarian Action in the New Century.* Oxford: Oxford University Press, 2002.

Henkin, Alice H., ed. *Honoring Human Rights. From Peace to Justice.* Washington, D.C.: The Aspen Institute, 1998.

Henkin, Louis. *Age of Rights.* New York: Columbia University Press, 1996.

Hersch, Jeanne, ed. *Le droit d'être un homme.* Paris: UNESCO/Lattès, 1968.

———, ed. *Birthright of Man. An Anthology of Texts on Human Rights.* Paris: UNESCO, 1969.

Hieber, Loretta. *Lifeline Media: Reaching Populations in Crisis. A guide to developing media projects in conflict situations.* Geneva: Media Action International, 2001.

Hitchens, Christopher. *The Trial of Henry Kissinger.* New York: Verso, 2001.

Hoffman, Stanley. *The Ethics and Politics of Humanitarian Intervention.* Chicago: University of Notre-Dame, 1996.

Holbrooke, Richard. *To End a War.* New York: Knopf, 1999.

Hollingworth, Larry. *Merry Christmas, Mr. Larry.* London: Heinemann, 1996.

Homer-Dixon, Thomas. *Environment, Scarcity, and Violence.* Princeton: Princeton University Press, 1999.

———. "The Rise of Complex Terrorism." *Foreign Policy* (January–February 2002).

———. "Weapons of Mass Disruption." *Foreign Policy* (January–February 2002).

Huber, Max. *The Good Samaritan.* London: Gollancz, 1945.

Huizinga, J. *Homo Ludens. A Study of Play-Element in Culture.* Boston: The Beacon Press, 1955.

Huntington, Samuel P. *The Clash of Civilizations and the Remaking of World Order.* New York: Simon and Schuster, 1996.

Ignatieff, Michael. *The Warrior's Honour.* Canada: Penguin Books, 1998.

Independent Commission on Humanitarian Issues. *Famine. A man-made disaster? Foreword by David Owen.* London: Pan Books, 1986.

Independent Commission on Humanitarian Issues. *Modern Wars. The Humanitarian Challenge. Presented by Mohammed Bedjaoui. Foreword by Pierre Graber.* London: Pan Books, 1985.

International Committee of the Red Cross (ICRC). All cited ICRC documents are available at: *www.icrc.org*

————. "Agreement Between the International Criminal Tribunal for the Former Yugoslavia and the ICRC on Procedures for Visiting Persons held on the Authority of the Tribunal." *International Review of the Red Cross,* no. 311, pp. 238–242.

————. "Arms Availability and the Situation of Civilians in Armed Conflicts."

————. "Respect for and Protection of the Personnel of Humanitarian Organizations." Preparatory Document drafted by the International Committee of the Red Cross for the First Periodical Meeting on International Humanitarian Law, Geneva, January 19–23, 1998, pp. 1–7 (through "I.1. The environment in which humanitarian action takes place").

————. "Armed Conflicts Linked to the Disintegration of State Structures." Preparatory Document drafted by the International Committee of the Red Cross for the First Periodical Meeting on International Humanitarian Law, Geneva, January 19–23, 1998.

————. "Current Patterns of Conflict and Arms Availability." In *Arms Availability and the Situation of Civilians in Armed Conflict.* Geneva: ICRC, June 1, 1999.

————. *Handbook for Parliamentarians. Respect for IHL* (with IPU), 1999.

————. *Forum. War and Water.* Geneva.

————. *Strengthening Protection in War. A Search for Professional Standards.* Geneva, 2001.

————. *War and Accountability.* Geneva, 2002.

International Commission on State Sovereignty. *The Responsibility to Protect.* Ottawa, 2001.

International Federation of Red Cross and Red Crescent Societies. *World Disasters Report 2001.*

Jeannet, Stephane. "Non-Disclosure of Evidence Before International Criminal Tribunals: Recent Developments Regarding the International Committee of the Red Cross." *International and Comparative Law Quarterly* 50, no. 3 (August 3, 2001): pp. 643–656. (*www.3.oup.co.uk/iclqaj/hdb/Volume_50/Issue_03/pdf/500643.pdf*).

Jonas, Hans, trans. *Das Prinzip Verantwortung* (The Imperative of Responsibility: In Search of an Ethics for the Technological Age). Chicago: University of Chicago Press, 1984.

Joseph, James A. *The Charitable Impulse.* New York: The Foundation Carter, 1989.

Kaelin, Walter. "Flight in Times of War." *International Review of the Red Cross,* no. 843 (September 2001): pp. 629–649.

Kaplan, Robert D. *The Ends of the Earth.* New York: Random House, 1995.

———. *Warrior Politics. Why Leadership Demands a Pagan Ethos.* New York: Random House, 2001.

Keane, Fergal. *Season of Blood: A Rwandan Journey.* New York: Penguin, 1997.

Kent, Randoph C. *Anatomy of Disaster Relief. The International Network in Action.* London: Pinter, 1987.

King, Martin Luther Jr. *Strength to Love.* Cleveland: North Light Books, 1963.

Kiser, John W. *The Monks of Tibhirine. Faith, Love and Terror in Algeria.* New York: St Martin's Press, 2002.

Knightley, Phillip. *The First Casualty. From the Crimea to Vietnam: The War Correspondent as Hero, Propagandist, and Myth Maker.* New York: Harcourt, Brace Jovanovich, 1975.

Koskenniemi, Martti. *The Gentle Civilizer of Nations. The Rise and Fall of International Law 1870–1960.* Cambridge: Cambridge University Press, 2001.

Kung, Hans. *Projekt Weltethos.* Munich: Piper, 1990.

———, ed. *Ja zum Weltethos.* Munich: Piper, 1995.

———. *Global Responsibility: In Search of a New World Ethic.* London: SCM Press, 1991.

Kuper, Jenny. *International Law Concerning Child Civilians in Armed Conflict.* Oxford: Clarendon Press, 1997.

Lavoyer, Jean-Philippe. "Guiding Principles on Internal Displacement." *International Review of the Red Cross*, no. 324 (September 30, 1998).

Levie, Howard S. *The Law of Non-International Armed Conflict. Protocol 2 to the 1949 Geneva Conventions. A Record of Certain of the Proceedings of the 1974–1977 Geneva Diplomatic Conference.* Dordrecht: Martinus Nijhoff, 1987.

———. "History of the Law of War on Land." *International Review of the Red Cross*, no. 838 (June 2000): pp. 339–350.

Levine, Iain. "Promoting Humanitarian Principles: The Southern Sudan Experience." *Relief and Rehabilitation Network (RRN) Paper* (May 1997).

Lieven, Anatol. *Chechnya: Tombstone of Russian Power.* New Haven, CT: Yale University Press, 1998.

Lifton, Robert Jay, and Eric Markusen. *The Genocidal Mentality: Nazi Holocaust and Nuclear Threat.* New York: Basic Books, 1990.

Lotrionte, Catherine. "The Just War Doctrine and Covert Responses to Terrorism." *Georgetown Journal of International Affairs* 3, no. 1 (Winter/Spring 2002): pp. 85–93.

Lyman, Princeton N. *Partner in History. The U.S. Role in South Africa's Transition to Democracy.* Washington, D.C.: USIP, 2002.

Machel, Graça. "The Impact of Armed Conflict on Children: A Critical Review of Progress Made and Obstacles Encountered in Increasing Protection for War-affected Children." International Conference on War-Affected Children, Winnipeg, Canada, September 2000.

Mamdani, Mahmood. *When Victims Become Killers. Colonialism, Nativism, and the Genocide in Rwanda.* Princeton: Princeton University Press, 2001.

Maren, M. *The Road to Hell. The Ravaging Effects of Foreign Aid.* New York: The Free Press, 1997.

Maritain, Jacques, ed. *La loi naturelle ou loi non écrite.* Fribourg, Switzerland: Université de Fribourg, 1986.

Matthews, Dylan. *War Prevention Works. Fifty Stories of People Resolving Conflict.* Oxford: Oxford Research Group, 2001.

Mbaye, Kéba. *Les droits de l 'homme en Afrique.* Paris: Pedone, 1992.

Médecins sans frontières/Doctors Without Borders. *World in Crisis: The Politics of Survival at the End of the Twentieth Century.* London/New York: Routledge, 1997.

Melvern, Linda. *A People Betrayed: The Role of the West in Rwanda's Genocide.* London: Zed Books, 2000.

Meron, Theodor. "The Humanization of Humanitarian Law." *American Journal of International Law* 94, no. 2 (2000): pp. 239–278.

————. *War Crimes Law Comes of Age: Essays.* Oxford: Oxford University Press, 1999.

Moeller, Susan D. *Compassion Fatigue: How the Media Sell Disease, Famine, War, and Death.* New York: Routledge, 1998.

Moir, Lindsay. *The Law of Internal Armed Conflict.* Cambridge: Cambridge University Press, 2002.

Munro, Alan. "Humanitarianism and Conflict in a Post-Cold War World." *International Review of the Red Cross,* no. 835 (September 30, 1999): pp. 463–475.

Murphy, John F. "Civil Liability for the Commission of International Crimes as an Alternative to Criminal Prosecution." *Harvard HRJ* 12 (Spring 1999): pp. 1–56.

Mutua, Makau. "Savages, Victims, and Saviors: The Metaphor of Human Rights." *Harv Int'lL.J* 42, no. 201 (Winter 2001): pp. 201–245. *www.macconsortium.org/Past/SummerInstitute2001/Readings*

————. *Human Rights. A Political and Cultural Critique.* Philadelphia: University of Pennsylvania Press, 2002.

Nair, Ravi. "Confronting the Violence Committed by Armed Opposition Groups." *Yale HR L.J* 1, no. 2 (1998).

Neier, Aryeh. *War Crimes.* New York: Times Books, 1998.

Niebuhr, Reinhold. *Moral Man and Immoral Society.* Rev. ed. New York: Scribner, 1960.

O'Donnell, Daniel. "Trends in the Application of International Humanitarian Law by UN Human Rights Mechanisms." *International Review of the Red Cross,* no. 324 (September 30, 1998): pp. 481–503.

Organization for Economic Cooperation and Development (OECD)—Development Assistance Committee (DAC). Guidelines cited here are available at: *http://www.oecd.org/EN/document/0,,EN-document-notheme-2-no-24-5782-0,00.html*

————. *DAC Guidelines on Poverty Reduction* (2001).

————. *Helping Prevent Violent Conflict* (2001).

————. *DAC Guidelines on Gender Equality and Women's Empowerment in Development Cooperation* (1998).

————. *Donor Assistance to Capacity Development in Environment* (1995).

————. *Participatory Development and Good Governance* (1995).

Ouguergouz, Fatsah. *La Charte Africaine des Droits de l'Homme et des Peu-*

ples. Une Approche Juridique des Droits de l'Homme Entre Tradition et Modernité. Paris: PUF, 1993.

Owen, David. *Balkan Odyssey.* New York: Harcourt, 1997.

Palwankar, Umesh. "Measures available to States for fulfilling their obligation to ensure respect for international humanitarian law" *IRRC,* no. 298, pp. 9–25.

Panikkar, Raimundo, "Is the Notion of Human Rights a Western Concept?" *Diogenes* 120 (1982): pp. 75–102.

Peirce, G. A. B. "Humanitarian Protection for the Victims of War: The System of the Protecting Power and the Role of the ICRC." *Military Law Review* 90 (Fall 1980): pp. 89–162.

Pictet, Jean. *The Principles of International Humanitarian Law.* Geneva: ICRC, 1966.

———. *Development and Principles of International Humanitarian Law.* Dordrecht: Martinus Nijhoff, 1985.

Pirotte, Claire, Bernard Husson, and François Grunewald, eds. *Responding to Emergencies and Fostering Development. The Dilemmas of Humanitarian Aid.* London: Zed Books, 1999.

Power, Samantha. *A Problem from Hell. America and the Age of Genocide.* New York: Basic Books, 2002.

———. "Bystanders to Genocide. Why the United States Let the Rwandan Tragedy Happen." *The Atlantic Monthly,* September 2001. *http://www.theatlantic.com/issues/2001/09/power.htm*

Price, Richard M. *The Chemical Weapons Taboo.* Ithaca, NY: Cornell University Press, 1997.

Prins, Gwyn, and Hylke Tromp, eds. *The Future of War.* The Hague: Kluwer Law International, 2000.

Prunier, Gerard. *The Rwanda Crisis: History of a Genocide.* New York: Columbia University Press, 1997.

Ratner, Steven R., and Jason S. Abrams. *Accountability for Human Rights Atrocities in International Law. Beyond the Nuremberg Legacy.* Oxford: Oxford University Press, 2001.

Renner, Michael. *Fighting for Survival. Environmental Decline, Social Conflict, and the New Age of Insecurity.* New York: W. W. Norton, 1996.

Reno, William. *Warlords Politics and African States.* Boulder, CO: Lynne Riener, Publishers, 1999.

Rieff, David. "Case Study in Ethnic Strife." *Foreign Affairs* 76, no 2 (March/April 1997).

Roberts, Adam. "Humanitarian Issues in International Politics in the

1990s." *International Review of the Red Cross* (Geneva) 81, no. 833 (March 1999).

Rodley, Nigel S. *The Treatment of Prisoners Under International Law.* 2nd ed. Oxford: Oxford University Press, 2000.

Roth, Kenneth. "The Case of Universal Jurisdiction." *Foreign Affairs* (Sept./Oct. 2001): pp. 150–154.

Rottensteiner, Christa. "The Denial of Humanitarian Assistance as a Crime Under International Law." *International Review of the Red Cross,* no. 835 (1999): pp. 555–582.

Rufin, Jean-Christophe. *Le piège. Quand l'aide humanitaire remplace la guerre.* Paris: Lattes, 1986.

————. *Economie des guerres civiles.* Paris: Hachette, 1996.

Ryfman, Philippe. *La question humanitaire.* Paris: Ellipses, 1999.

Ryniker, Anne. "The ICRC's Position on 'Humanitarian Intervention'." *International Review of the Red Cross,* no. 482 (June 30, 2001): pp. 527–532.

Sassoli, Marco, and Antoine Bouvier. *How Does Law Protect in War? Cases, Documents and Teaching Materials on Contemporary Practice in International Humanitarian Law.* Geneva: ICRC, 1999.

Schiff, Ze'ev, and Ehud Ya'ari. *Israel's Lebanon War.* New York: Simon and Schuster, 1984.

Schweitzer, Albert. *Humanisme et Mystique.* Paris: Albin Michel, 1995.

Sen, Amartya. "East and West: The Reach of Reason." *The New York Review of Books* (July 20, 2000). *http://www.nybooks.com/articles/article-preview?article_id=20*

————. *Development as Freedom.* New York: Random House, 2000.

Senarclens, Pierre de. *L'humanitaire en catastrophe.* Paris: Presses de Sciences Po, 1999.

Shawcross, William. *Deliver Us From Evil. Peacekeepers, Warlords and a World of Endless Conflict.* New York: Simon & Schuster, 2000.

Shelton, Dinah. *Remedies in International Human Rights Law.* Oxford: Oxford University Press, 1999.

————, ed. *Commitment and Compliance. The Role of Non-Binding Norms in the International Legal System.* Oxford: Oxford University Press, 2000.

Shore, Bill. *Revolution of the Heart.* New York: Riverhead Books, 1995.

Silber, Laura, and Allan Little. *Yugoslavia: Death of a Nation.* New York: Penguin Books, 1997.

Silverstein, Ken. "Privatizing War. How Affairs of State are Outsourced to Corporations Beyond Public Control." *The Nation* (07/28—06/04/97). *http://past.thenation.com/issue/970728/0728silv.htm*

Singh, Nagendra. "Armed Conflicts and Humanitarian Laws of Ancient India." In *Études et essais sur le droit international humanitaire et sur les principes de la Croix-Rouge, en l'honneur de Jean Pictet*, Genève/La Haye, edited by C. Swinarski, p. 535. Comité international de la Croix-Rouge/Martinus Nijhoff, 1984.

Slim, Hugo. "Doing the Right Thing: Relief agencies, Moral Dilemmas and Moral Responsibility in Political Emergencies and War." *Disasters* 21 (Sept. 1997).

Smith-Christopher, Daniel L., ed. *Subverting Hatred*. New York: Orbis Books, 1998.

Smock, David R. *Interfaith Dialogue and Peacebuilding*. Washington, D.C.: USIP, 2002.

Starobinski, Jean. *Largesse*. Paris: Parti Pris, 1994.

Steiner, Henry J., and Philip Alston. *International Human Rights in Context. Law, Politics, Morals. Text and Materials*. Oxford: Clarendon Press, 1996.

Stremlau, John. T*he International Politics of the Nigerian Civil War*. Princeton, NJ: Princeton University Press, 1977.

———. *People in Peril. Human Rights, Humanitarian Action, and Preventing Deadly Conflict. A Report to the Carnegie Commission on Preventing Deadly Conflict*. New York: Carnegie Corporation of New York, 1998.

Sun Tzu. *The Art of War*. Oxford: Oxford University Press, 1963.

Swidler, Leonard. "The Dialogue Decalogue. Ground Rules for Interreligious, Intercultural Dialogue." *GDI Anthology. Envisioning a Global Ethic. http://astro.ocis.temple.edu/~dialogue/Antho/decalog.htm*

———. *Death or Dialogue*. Philadelphia: Trinity Press International, 1990.

———. "The Age of Global Dialogue." *Marburg Journal of Religion* 1, no. 2 (1996). *http://www.uni-marburg.de/religionswissenschaft/journal/mjr/swidler.html*

Tanguy, Joelle, and Fiona Terry. "On Humanitarian Responsibility." *Ethics & International Affairs* 13 (1999).

Taylor, Michael. *Not Angels but Agencies*. Geneva: World Council of Churches Publ., 1995.

Thich Nhat Hahn. *Being Peace*. California, U.S.: Parallax Press, 1987.

Thompson, Sir Robert. D*efeating Communist Insurgency. The Lessons of Malaya and Vietnam*. London: Chatto & Windus, 1967.

Tillion, Germaine. *Les ennemis complémentaires*. Paris: Editions de Minuit, 1960.

Toman, Jiri. *The Protection of Cultural Property in the Event of Armed Conflict. Commentary on the Hague Convention of May 14, 1954.* Paris: UNESCO Publishing/Dartmouth. Also in French.

UNESCO. *International Dimensions of Humanitarian Law*. Paris: UNESCO, 1988.

United Nations Documents. *Basic Principles on the Use of Force and Firearms by Law Enforcement Officials. (Adopted by the Eighth United Nations Congress on the Prevention of Crime and the Treatment of Offenders*, Havana, Cuba, August 27 to September 7, 1990.)

————. *Question of the Impunity of Perpetrators of Human Rights Violations (Civil and Political).* Revised final report prepared by Mr. Joinet pursuant to Sub-Commission decision, 1996/119. [E/CN.4/Sub.2/1997/20/Rev.1]

————. Secretary-General's Bulletin ("Observance by United Nations Forces of International Humanitarian Law") ST/SGB/1999/13, dated August 6, 1999, entering into force on August 12, 1999.

————. *Principles of Engagement for Emergency Humanitarian Assistance in the Democratic Republic of Congo.* (OCHA/CERB/2000/8, available at *http://coe-dmha.org/unicef/HPT_Session8Handout8_4.htm*)

————. *The Fall of Srebenica.* A/54/549, November 15, 1999.

————. *Report Of The Rwanda Genocide.* December 15, 1999.

————. *Report Of The Panel On United Nations Peace Operations.* A/55/305–S/2000/809, August 21, 2000.

————. *Report Of The Panel Of Experts Appointed Pursuant To Security Council Resolution 1306 (2000), Paragraph 19, In Relation To Sierra Leone.* S/2000/1195, December 20, 2000.

————. *Report Of the Security Council Mission To The Great Lakes Region,* May 15–26, 2001. S/2001/521, May 29, 2001. Report S/2001/521, May 29, 2001. Addendum S/2001/52/Add.1, May 30, 2001.

————. *Report of the Secretary-General to the Security Council on the Protection of Civilians in Armed Conflict.* S/2002/331, March 30, 2001.

U.S. Department of State. *Arms and Conflict in Africa.* July 1999.

Van Crefeld, Martin. *The Transformation of War.* New York: Free Press, 1991.

Veuthey, Michel. *Guérilla et droit humanitaire.* 2nd. ed. Geneva: ICRC, 1983.

————. "Les conflits armés de caractère non-international et le droit humanitaire." In *Current Problems of International Law,* edited by Antonio Cassese, pp. 175–266. Milan: Giuffrè, 1975.

———. "Implementation and Enforcement of Humanitarian Law and Human Rights Law in Non-International Armed Conflicts: the Role of the International Committee of the Red Cross." *The American University Law Review* (Washington D.C.) 33, no. 1, (Fall 1983): pp. 83–97.

———. "The Humanitarian Network: Implementing Humanitarian Law through International Co-operation." *Bulletin of Peace Proposals* (Oslo) 18, no. 2 (April 1987): pp. 133–146.

———. "The Contribution of International Humanitarian Law to the Restoration of Peace." In *A Framework for Survival. Health, Human Rights, and Humanitarian Assistance in Conflicts and Disasters. Health, Human Rights and Humanitarian Assistance in Conflicts and Disasters,* edited by Kevin M. Cahill, rev. ed. New York: A joint publication of Routledge and the Center for International Health and Cooperation, 1999, pp. 109–121.

———. "Remedies to Promote the Respect of Fundamental Human Values in Non-International Armed Conflicts." *The Israeli Yearbook on Human Rights* 30 (2001): pp. 37–77.

Vidal-Naquet. *La torture dans la république.* Paris: Minuit, 1972.

Vieira de Mello, Sergio. "La Conscience du Monde. L'ONU face à l'Irrationnel dans l'Histoire." Leçon inaugurale à l'Institut de Hautes Etudes Internationals (IUHEI) de Genève, le 2 novembre 2000.

Vigny, Jean-Daniel, and Cecilia Thompson. "Standards fondamentaux d'humanité: quel avenir?" *International Review of the Red Cross,* no. 840, pp. 917–939.

Walzer, Michael. *Just and Unjust Wars.* New York: Basic Books, 1977.

Warren, Kay B., ed. *The Violence Within. Cultural & Political Opposition in Divided Nations.* Boulder, CO: Westview Press, 1993.

Waters, Tony. *Bureaucratizing the Good Samaritan.* Boulder, CO: Westview Press, 2001.

Weeramantry, C. G. *The Lord's Prayer: Bridge to a Better World.* Liguori, MO: Liguori, 1998.

Weisbord, Marvin R. *Discovering Common Ground.* San Francisco: Berrett-Koehler Publ., 1992.

Wessels, Mike. "Child Soldiers." *Bulletin of Atomic Scientists* (Chicago) (Nov/Dec 1997). (*http://pangaea.org/street_children/africa/armies.htm*).

Wippman, David, ed. *International Law and Ethnic Conflict.* Ithaca: Cornell University Press, 1998.

Zahar, Marie-Joelle. "Protégés, Clients, Cannon Fodder: Civil-Militia Relations in Internal Conflicts." In Chesterman, Simon. *Civilians in War,* pp. 43–65. Boulder: Lynne Rienner, 2001.

Zartman, I. W., ed. *Collapsed States.* U.S.A.: Lynne Rienner Publ., 1995.

Zemmali, A. *Combattants et prisonniers de guerre en droit islamique et en droit international humanitaire.* Paris: Pedone, 1997.

NOTES TO CHAPTER SEVEN
RULES OF ENGAGEMENT: AN EXAMINATION OF RELATIONSHIPS AND EXPECTATIONS IN THE DELIVERY OF HUMANITARIAN ASSISTANCE
H. Roy Williams

1. See Donald Snow, *Distant Thunder: Patterns of Conflict in the Developing World* (Armonk: M. E. Sharpe, 1997), p. 193.

2. In an editorial, geoeconomist and strategy expert, Edward Luttwak, warns against the "usual mixture of useful, useless, and counterproductive aid" from the NGO community in Afghanistan and effectively repeating their performance in Kosovo; from E. Luttwak, "Keep a Lid on Aid Givers," *Los Angeles Times,* 28 November 2001, p. A19.

3. See also Nicola Weindorp and Peter Wiles, "Humanitarian Coordination: Lessons from Recent Field Experience," London: Overseas Development Institute (2001). *http://www.odi.org.uk/hpg/papers/ochacoordination.pdf*

4. Larry Minear, "Learning the Lessons of Coordination," in *A Framework for Survival: Health, Human Rights, and Humanitarian Assistance in Conflicts and Disasters,* ed. Kevin M. Cahill (New York: Routledge, 1999), pp. 298–316.

5. See Thomas G. Weiss, "A Research Note about Military-Civilian Humanitarianism: More Questions than Answers," *Disasters* 21, no. 2 (1997): 99–101.

6. Michael Pugh, "The Challenge of Civil-Military Relations in International Peace Operations," *Disasters* 25, no. 4 (2001): p. 349.

7. See Joelle Tanguy, "The *Médecins sans frontières* Experience," in

A Framework for Survival: Health, Human Rights, and Humanitarian Assistance in Conflicts and Disasters, ed. Kevin M. Cahill (New York: Routledge, 1999), pp. 226–244.

8. Rony Brauman explains MSF's transition to private funding stability in "The *Médecins sans frontières* Experience," in *A Framework for Survival: Health, Human Rights, and Humanitarian Assistance in Conflicts and Disasters,* ed. Kevin M. Cahill (New York: Basic Books, 1993), pp. 202–220.

9. For a discussion on the emerging private-public networks in global aid, see Mark Duffield, "Governing the Borderlands: Decoding the Power of Aid," *Disasters* 25, no. 4 (2001): 308–320.

10. Mark Walkup, "Policy Dysfunction in Humanitarian Organizations: The Role of Coping Strategies, Institutions, and Organizational Culture," *Journal of Refugee Studies* 10, no. 1 (1997): 37–60.

11. Ibid.

12. An example of this is the IRC's reporting of excess mortality in eastern Democratic Republic of Congo from 1998–2001. See Barbara Crosette, "World Briefing: Africa: Congo: The Uncountable Toll," *The New York Times,* 9 May 2001, sec. A, col. 5.

13. This issue and several others discussed in this chapter are addressed in Gyuri Fritsche's editorial, "Controlling Humanitarian Aid Cowboys in Afghanistan," *The Lancet* 356 (2001): 2002.

14. See Anne Marie Chaker, "Red Cross Gives Disaster Relief to Tony Enclave," *Wall Street Journal,* 7 February 2002, p. B1.

15. Fritsche, "Controlling Humanitarian Aid Cowboys in Afghanistan."

16. Larry Minear et al., "Humanitarian Action in the Former Yugoslavia: The UN's Role 1991–1993," *Thomas J. Watson Institute for International Studies and Refugee Policy Group: Occasional Paper #18* (1994): p. 51–58.

17. Rudy von Bernuth, "Remarks at World Hunger Program Eighth Annual Research Briefing and Exchange," Session 5, Brown University, April 5–7, 1995.

18. Ibid., 83–85.

19. See Scott Peterson, "Special Ops Tackle Aid Mission," *The Christian Science Monitor,* 1 March 2002, p. 1.

20. James Dao, "A Nation Challenged. Food Drops: 15-Hour Flight, 8-Second Job, Uncertain Success," *The New York Times,* 20 October 2001, sec. B, p. 4, col. 1.

21. See also Greg Jaffe, "Limited Engagement: In Afghan provinces, a few GIs struggle to bring aid, order—small 'civil affairs' teams have limited resources and demanding warlords—one SUV with two gears," *Wall Street Journal,* 28 February 2002, p. A1.

22. Joanna Macrae and Nicholas Leader, "Apples, Pears, and Porridge: The Origins and Impact of the Search for 'Coherence' Between Humanitarian and Political Responses to Chronic Political Emergencies," *Disasters,* 25, no. 4 (2001): pp. 290–307.

23. It is important to note that here, use of the word "coordination" has not been applied to the direct coordination of action.

24. See "About ICVA," *www.icva/ch/cgi-bin/browse.pl?doc= mandate*

25. See "InterAction's PVO Standards," *www.interaction.org/pvo standards/mission.html*

26. From "SCHR" flier, unpublished document; Joel McClellan, personal communication.

27. See "NGO VOICE," *www.oneworld.org/voice/str_gb.htm*

28. See "The People in Aid Code: The History of People in Aid and the Code of Best Practice," *www.peopleinaid.org/code/history.htm*

29. See "The Active Learning Network for Accountability and Performance in Humanitarian Action," *www.alnap.org*

30. See *www.sphereproject.org*

31. Louise Banham, "Talking at Cross Purposes? Can Donors Really Coordinate?" ID21 Communicating Development Research, *www .id21.org/soceity/s9blb1g1.htm*

32. Ibid.

Notes to Chapter Nine
The Sinews of Humanitarian Assistance:
Funding Policies, Practices, and Pitfalls
Joelle Tanguy

1. Attributed to Ernest Hemingway.

2. Global Humanitarian Assistance 2000, IASC/Development Initiative. Table A17.

3. 11.6 percent in 2001. ReliefWeb OCHA data.

4. Chronicle of Philanthropy, "Star Widens Refugee Group's Appeal," December 13, 2001; and "UN Looks to Donors for Aid but Efforts to Win Private Funds Spur Fears of Competition, Commercialism," September 9, 1999. *www.philanthropy.org*

5. Expression commonly used in the field and publicized by Michael Maren and David Rieff.

6. See MSF's annual "Top Ten Under-Reported Humanitarian Crises."

7. Shephard Forman, "Underwriting Humanitarian Assistance. Mobilizing Resources for Effective Action," Center on International Cooperation, New York University, January 1999; and in *A Framework for Survival: Health, Human Rights, and Humanitarian Assistance in Conflicts and Disasters,* ed. Kevin M. Cahill (New York: Routledge, 1999).

8. The Development Assistance Committee (DAC) is the principal body through which the OECD deals with issues related to cooperation with developing countries.

9. Judith Randel and Tony German, eds., "The Reality of Aid: An Independent Review of International Aid," *Earthscan Publications.*

10. See figure 9.1.

11. "Charity on the Rampage: The Business of Foreign Aid," *Foreign Aid* (Jan/Feb 1997).

12. White Paper on Globalization, "Global Development Assistance: The Role of NGOs and Other Charity Flows," commissioned by DFID from Development Initiatives, July 2000.

13. Only 2 percent of the American Red Cross operating expenses are allocated to "international services;" its focus is primarily national. Therefore, the organization does not feature prominently in our research.

14. The Philanthropy 400, developed by the Chronicle of Philanthropy, uses financial data gathered from U.S. nonprofits to determine which charities raised the most funds from individuals, foundations, and corporations.

15. The rest of SCF U.K. revenues come from general public appeals, legacies, volunteer branches and retail income, trusts and corporate sector contribution.

16. The funding is structured as a cooperative agreement and yields to the OFDA the right to vet the chief staffer of the DRC.

17. See Global Humanitarian Assistance 2000, chap. 3, p. 50.

18. Joelle Tanguy and Fiona Terry, "Humanitarian Responsibility and Committed Action," *Ethics & International Affairs* 13 (1999).

19. 80 percent in 2000 and 79 percent in 2001, as per MSF international activity report.

20. Another NGO, Samaritan's Purse U.S., describes itself as an inter-

national nonprofit Christian mission organization with a single-minded commitment to evangelism through relief aid and announces a 96 percent ratio, thanks to its 125 million in church and other private contributions, but close to 60 percent of those were in non-cash gifts, mostly goods, commodities, and Gospel booklets.

21. AAFRC Trust for Philanthropy: Giving U.S.A. 2001.

22. "The International Response to Conflict and Genocide: Lessons from the Rwanda Experience," chap. 9 in *Joint Evaluation of Emergency Assistance to Rwanda, 1995.* OECD-UN-ICRC-IFRC-NGO.

23. For an in-depth analysis, read Center of International Cooperation, "The Preparedness Challenge in Humanitarian Assistance," The Center of International Cooperation with Lester Salomon and Associates, Mimeo, New York University, August 1999.

24. For a discussion of the CNN effect, read Nik Gowing in his in-depth study and in *News Perspectives Quarterly* 11.

25. AAFRC Trust for Philanthropy: Giving U.S.A. 2001

26. "Global Development Assistance: The Role of NGOs and Other Charity Flows," DFID, July 2000, p. 17.

27. As scandals were threatening to discredit relief and development operators, the U.S. coalition of relief and development agencies, Inter-Action, among others, led to the development of standards in the areas of governance, finance and communications, management and human resources, program and public policy: the InterAction PVO Standards. Its members are required to comply with these standards and quite an extensive series of clauses concern ethical fundraising and related issues, focusing on the most sensitive practices mentioned above.

28. Elizabeth Harold Close, AmeriCares, "Letter to the Editor: 'Expired' Drugs Save Millions of Lives," *Wall Street Journal,* 3 December 1993.

29. Michael Maren, *The Road to Hell,* p. 265, quoting Pamela Winnick, an attorney investigating charities.

30. P. Berckmans, V. Dawans, G. Schmets, D. Vandenbergh, P. Autier, "Inappropriate Drug Donation Practices in Bosnia and Herzegovina, 1992 to 1996, *New England Journal of Medicine* 337 (December 18, 1997): pp. 1842–1845.

31. "Substandard Bosnia Drug Donations Challenged in U.S. Congress," *The Lancet* 351, no. 9098, p. 274.

32. Zbigniew Brzezinski, "Letter to the Editor: Old Scam in a New Era," *Wall Street Journal,* 5 June 1995.

33. Read Hammock and Charny in *From Massacres to Genocide,* ed. R. Rotberg and T. Weiss (World Peace Foundation, 1996).

34. Peter Shiras, "Big Problem, Small Print," in *From Massacres to Genocide,* ed. R. Rotberg and T. Weiss (World Peace Foundation, 1996).

35. Susan Moeller, *Compassion Fatigue: How the Media Sell Disease, Famine, War and Death* (New York: Routledge, 1999).

36. Maren, *The Road to Hell.*

37. Extract from InterAction PVO Standards, 2002.

38. Susan Moeller, "Relief Groups and the Press: A Delicate Balance," *Chronicle of Philanthropy* (March 1999).

39. Expression borrowed from Nik Gowing, in "The One Eye King of Real-Time TV News Coverage," *New Perspectives Quarterly* 11, no. 4.

40. Garrick Utley, "The Shrinking of Foreign News: From Broadcast to Narrowcast," *Foreign Affairs* (March/ April 1997).

41. Joelle Tanguy, "The Media and Humanitarian Crises," *Tikkun Magazine* (1998).

42. Expression borrowed from Peter Shiras, op. cit.

43. From *Harper's* Index, *Harper's* Magazine, January 2002. Source: Tyndall Report/ *Harper's* research.

44. David Shaw, "Foreign News Shrink in Era of Globalization," *Los Angeles Times,* 27 September 2001.

45. The Tyndall Report (*www.tyndalreport.com*) monitors U.S. networks' weekday nightly newscasts. Published by ADT Research.

46. Claude Moisy, "The Foreign News Flow in the Information Age," Harvard University Shorenstein Center Research & Discussion Papers, November 1996.

47. The Tyndall Report (*www.tyndalreport.com*).

48. From Tyndall Report, cited in InterPress Service, December 4, 1992.

49. "Save us from this African folly," by Simon Jenkins, Opinion piece, *The New York Times,* November 16, 1996.

REFERENCES TO CHAPTER NINE
THE SINEWS OF HUMANITARIAN ASSISTANCE: FUNDING POLICIES, PRACTICES, AND PITFALLS
Joelle Tanguy

On Funding of Humanitarian Assistance

Center of International Cooperation. "The Preparedness Challenge in Humanitarian Assistance." The Center of International Cooperation with Lester Salomon and Associates, mimeo, New York University, August 1999.

Development Initiatives. "Global Humanitarian Assistance 2000." An independent report commissioned by the IASC from Development Initiatives, May 2000. *http://www.devinit.org/ghaprelims.pdf*

Development Initiatives. "White Paper on Globalization. Global Development Assistance: The Role of NGOs and Other Charity Flows," commissioned by DFID from Development Initiatives, July 2000.

Forman, Shephard. "Underwriting Humanitarian Assistance. Mobilizing Resources for Effective Action." Center on International Cooperation, New York University, January 1999. Also in Cahill, Kevin M., ed. *A Framework for Survival. Health, Human Rights and Humanitarian Assistance in Conflicts and Disasters.* New York: Routledge, 1999. ISBN: 0415922348.

Forman, Shepard, and Rita Parhard. "Paying for Essentials: Resources for Humanitarian Assistance." Center on International Cooperation, New York University, September 1997. *http://www.cic.nyu.edu/pubs/PayingEssentialsPrint.html*

Lancaster, Carol. "Transforming Foreign Aid: United States Assistance in the Twenty-first Century." *Institute for International Economics,* August 2000. See also Carol Lancaster, "Foreign Economic Aid." *Foreign Policy in Focus,* December 2000.

McDermott, Anthony. *The New Politics of Financing the UN.* Oslo: International Peace Research Institute, 1999. ISBN 0312222246.

Overseas Development Institute. "The State of the International Humanitarian System." Overseas Development Institute Briefing Paper, March 1998. *http://www.odi.org.uk/briefing/1_98.html*

Owen, Lord David, M.D. "Reflections from the Donor: Obligations and Responsibilities of All Nations." In *A Framework for Survival. Health, Human Rights and Humanitarian Assistance in Conflicts and Disasters,* edited by Kevin M. Cahill. New York: Routledge, 1999. ISBN: 0415922348.

Stremlau, John. "People in Peril: Human Rights, Humanitarian Action and Preventing Deadly Conflict." Report to the Carnegie Commission on Preventing Deadly Conflicts, *Journal of Humanitarian Assistance,* May 1998. *http://www.jha.ac/articles/a032.htm*

West, Katarina. "Humanitarian Action in a new security environment." Institute for Security Studies Western European Union, Paris, April 1998. *www.weu.int/institute/*

On Standards, Coordination, and Accountability

Edwards, Michael, and David Hulme. "NGOs—Performance and Accountability: Beyond the Magic Bullet." *Earthscan*, 1995.

Hilhorst, Dorothea. "Being Good at Doing Good." Presented at conference hosted by the Dutch Ministry of Foreign Affairs, October 2001. *http://www.hapgeneva.org/pdf/ La%20Hague%20Being%20good%20at%20doing %20goo d.pdf*

Mapping Accountability in Humanitarian Assistance, Active Learning Network for Accountability and Performance in Humanitarian Action (ALNAP), May 2000. *www.odi.org.uk/alnap/alnappubs.html*

Maren, Michael. *The Road to Hell: The Ravaging Effects of Foreign Aid and International Charity.* New York: Simon & Schuster, 1997. ISBN: 0743227867.

1994 Code of Conduct for the International Red Cross and Red Crescent Movement in Disaster Relief (RRN Network Paper 7). *www .odihpn.org/report.asp?ReportID= 2141*

ODI. "Mainstreaming the Organisational Management of Safety and Security." HPG Briefing 2, ODI Publications, March 2001. *publications@odi.org.uk*

People in Aid Code of Best Practice in the Management and Support of Aid Personnel (RRN Network Paper 20). *www.odihpn.org/ report.asp?ReportID= 2128 and www.peopleinaid.org.uk*

Sphere Project: Humanitarian Charter and Minimum Standards in Disaster Response. *www.sphereproject.org*

Terry, Fiona. "The Limits and Risks of Regulation Mechanism for Humanitarian Action." *Humanitarian Exchange*, October 2000.

The Reality of Aid: An Independent Review of Poverty Reduction and Development Assistance. *Earthscan. www.oneworld.org/eurostep and www.icva.ch*

Stockton, Nicholas. "Performance Standards and Accountability in Realizing Rights: The Humanitarian Case." Talk given at Overseas Development Institute, March 1999. *http://www.odi.org.uk/speeches/ sumstockton.html*

On Media and Humanitarian Assistance

Girardet, Edward. "Media Must Do More in Crises." *Reuters AlertNet ViewPoints*, April 2001. *www.alertnet.org*

Gowing, Nik. "Real Time Television Coverage of Armed Conflicts and Diplomatic Crises: Does It Pressure or Distort Foreign Policy Decisions?" Working paper #94-1, The Joan Shorenstein Barone Centre on the Press, Politics and Public Policy, John F. Kennedy School of Government, Harvard University, 1994.

————. "The One-Eyed King of Real-Time News Coverage." *New Perspectives Quarterly* (Center for the Study of Democratic Institutions), September 22, 1994.

Hammock, John C., and Joel R. Charny. "Emergency Response as Morality Play." In *From Massacres to Genocide,* edited by R. Rotberg and T. Weiss. World Peace Foundation, 1996.

Hess, Stephen. *International News and Foreign Correspondents.* Washington: Brookings, 1996.

McElroy, Andy (IFRC). "Western Media Plays Follow the (Government) Leader." *Reuters AlertNet ViewPoints,* February 2001. *www.alertnet.org*

Moeller, Susan. *Compassion Fatigue: How the Media Sell Disease, Famine, War and Death.* New York: Routledge, 1999.

————. "Relief Groups and the Press: a Delicate Balance." *Chronicle of Philanthropy,* March 1999.

Moisy, Claude. "The Foreign News Flow in the Information Age." Harvard University Shorenstein Center Research & Discussion Papers, November 1996.

Shiras, Peter. "Big Problem, Small Print." In *From Massacres to Genocide,* edited by R. Rotberg and T. Weiss. World Peace Foundation, 1996.

Tanguy, Joelle. "The Media and Humanitarian Crises." *Tikkun Magazine,* 1998.

The Tyndall report *(www.tyndalreport.com)* monitors U.S. networks' weekday nightly newscasts. Published by ADT Research.

Utley, Garrick. "The Shrinking of Foreign News: From Broadcast to Narrowcast." *Foreign Affairs,* March/April 1997.

APPENDIXES

On December 10, 1948, the General Assembly of the United Nations adopted and proclaimed the Universal Declaration of Human Rights, the full text of which appears in the following pages. Following this historic act, the Assembly called upon all Member countries to publicize the text of the Declaration and "to cause it to be disseminated, displayed, read, and expounded principally in schools and other educational institutions, without distinction based on the political status of countries or territories."

Preamble

Whereas recognition of the inherent dignity and of the equal and inalienable rights of all members of the human family is the foundation of freedom, justice, and peace in the world;

Whereas disregard and contempt for human rights have resulted in barbarous acts which have outraged the conscience of mankind, and the advent of a world in which human beings shall enjoy freedom of speech and belief and freedom from fear and want has been proclaimed as the highest aspiration of the common people;

Whereas it is essential, if man is not to be compelled, to have recourse, as a last resort, to rebellion against tyranny and oppression, that human rights should be protected by the rule of law;

Whereas it is essential to promote the development of friendly relations between nations;

Adopted and proclaimed by General Assembly resolution 217 A (III) of December 10, 1948

Whereas the peoples of the United Nations have in the Charter reaffirmed their faith in fundamental human rights, in the dignity and worth of the human person, and in the equal rights of men and women, and have determined to promote social progress and better standards of life in larger freedom;

Whereas Member States have pledged themselves to achieve, in cooperation with the United Nations, the promotion of universal respect for and observance of human rights and fundamental freedoms;

Whereas a common understanding of these rights and freedoms is of the greatest importance for the full realization of this pledge;

Now, therefore, THE GENERAL ASSEMBLY proclaims this UNIVERSAL DECLARATION OF HUMAN RIGHTS as a common standard of achievement for all peoples and all nations, to the end that every individual and every organ of society, keeping this Declaration constantly in mind, shall strive by teaching and education to promote respect for these rights and freedoms and by progressive measures, national and international, to secure their universal and effective recognition and observance, both among the peoples of Member States themselves and among the peoples of territories under their jurisdiction.

Article 1. All human beings are born free and equal in dignity and rights. They are endowed with reason and conscience and should act toward one another in a spirit of brotherhood.

Article 2. Everyone is entitled to all the rights and freedoms set forth in this Declaration, without distinction of any kind, such as race, color, sex, language, religion, political or other opinion, national or social origin, property, birth or other status. Furthermore, no distinction shall be made on the basis of the political, jurisdictional, or international status of the country or territory to which a person belongs, whether it be independent, trust, non-self-governing, or under any other limitation of sovereignty.

Article 3. Everyone has the right to life, liberty, and security of person.

Article 4. No one shall be held in slavery or servitude; slavery and the slave trade shall be prohibited in all their forms.

Article 5. No one shall be subjected to torture or to cruel, inhuman, or degrading treatment or punishment.

Article 6. Everyone has the right to recognition everywhere as a person before the law.

Article 7. All are equal before the law and are entitled without any discrimination to equal protection of the law. All are entitled to equal protection against any discrimination in violation of this Declaration and against any incitement to such discrimination.

Article 8. Everyone has the right to an effective remedy by the competent national tribunals for acts violating the fundamental rights granted him by the constitution or by law.

Article 9. No one shall be subjected to arbitrary arrest, detention, or exile.

Article 10. Everyone is entitled in full equality to a fair and public hearing by an independent and impartial tribunal, in the determination of his rights and obligations and of any criminal charge against him.

Article 11. 1. Everyone charged with a penal offence has the right to be presumed innocent until proved guilty according to law in a public trial at which he has had all the guarantees necessary for his defense.

2. No one shall be held guilty of any penal offence on account of any act or omission which did not constitute a penal offence, under national or international law, at the time when it was com-

mitted. Nor shall a heavier penalty be imposed than the one that was applicable at the time the penal offence was committed.

Article 12. No one shall be subjected to arbitrary interference with his privacy, family, home, or correspondence, nor to attacks upon his honor and reputation. Everyone has the right to the protection of the law against such interference or attacks.

Article 13. 1. Everyone has the right to freedom of movement and residence within the borders of each state.

2. Everyone has the right to leave any country, including his own, and to return to his country.

Article 14. 1. Everyone has the right to seek and to enjoy in other countries asylum from persecution.

2. This right may not be invoked in the case of prosecutions genuinely arising from non-political crimes or from acts contrary to the purposes and principles of the United Nations.

Article 15. 1. Everyone has the right to a nationality.

2. No one shall be arbitrarily deprived of his nationality nor denied the right to change his nationality.

Article 16. 1. Men and women of full age, without any limitation due to race, nationality, or religion, have the right to marry and to found a family. They are entitled to equal rights as to marriage, during marriage and at its dissolution.

2. Marriage shall be entered into only with the free and full consent of the intending spouses.

3. The family is the natural and fundamental group unit of society and is entitled to protection by society and the State.

Article 17. 1. Everyone has the right to own property alone as well as in association with others.

2. No one shall be arbitrarily deprived of his property.

Article 18. Everyone has the right to freedom of thought, conscience, and religion; this right includes freedom to change his religion or belief, and freedom, either alone or in community with others and in public or private, to manifest his religion or belief in teaching, practice, worship, and observance.

Article 19. Everyone has the right to freedom of opinion and expression; this right includes freedom to hold opinions without interference and to seek, receive, and impart information and ideas through any media and regardless of frontiers.

Article 20. 1. Everyone has the right to freedom of peaceful assembly and association.

2. No one may be compelled to belong to an association.

Article 21. 1. Everyone has the right to take part in the government of his country, directly or through freely chosen representatives.

2. Everyone has the right of equal access to public service in his country.

3. The will of the people shall be the basis of the authority of government; this will shall be expressed in periodic and genuine elections which shall be by universal and equal suffrage and shall be held by secret vote or by equivalent free voting procedures.

Article 22. Everyone, as a member of society, has the right to social security and is entitled to realization, through national effort and international cooperation and in accordance with the organization and resources of each State, of the economic, social, and cultural rights indispensable for his dignity and the free development of his personality.

Article 23. 1. Everyone has the right to work, to free choice of employment, to just and favorable conditions of work, and to protection against unemployment.

2. Everyone, without any discrimination, has the right to equal pay for equal work.

3. Everyone who works has the right to just and favorable remuneration ensuring for himself and his family an existence worthy of human dignity, and supplemented, if necessary, by other means of social protection.

4. Everyone has the right to form and to join trade unions for the protection of his interests.

Article 24. Everyone has the right to rest and leisure, including reasonable limitation of working hours and periodic holidays with pay.

Article 25. 1. Everyone has the right to a standard of living adequate for the health and well-being of himself and of his family, including food, clothing, housing, and medical care and necessary social services, and the right to security in the event of unemployment, sickness, disability, widowhood, old age, or other lack of livelihood in circumstances beyond his control.

2. Motherhood and childhood are entitled to special care and assistance. All children, whether born in or out of wedlock, shall enjoy the same social protection.

Article 26. 1. Everyone has the right to education. Education shall be free, at least in the elementary and fundamental stages. Elementary education shall be compulsory. Technical and professional education shall be made generally available, and higher education shall be equally accessible to all on the basis of merit.

2. Education shall be directed to the full development of the human personality and to the strengthening of respect for human rights and fundamental freedoms. It shall promote understanding, tolerance, and friendship among all nations, racial or religious groups, and shall further the activities of the United Nations for the maintenance of peace.

3. Parents have a prior right to choose the kind of education that shall be given to their children.

Article 27. 1. Everyone has the right freely to participate in the cultural life of the community, to enjoy the arts, and to share in scientific advancement and its benefits.

2. Everyone has the right to the protection of the moral and material interests resulting from any scientific, literary, or artistic production of which he is the author.

Article 28. Everyone is entitled to a social and international order in which the rights and freedoms set forth in this Declaration can be fully realized.

Article 29. 1. Everyone has duties to the community in which alone the free and full development of his personality is possible.

2. In the exercise of his rights and freedoms, everyone shall be subject only to such limitations as are determined by law solely for the purpose of securing due recognition and respect for the rights and freedoms of others and of meeting the just require-ments of morality, public order, and the general welfare in a democratic society.

3. These rights and freedoms may in no case be exercised con-trary to the purposes and principles of the United Nations.

Article 30. Nothing in this Declaration may be interpreted as im-plying for any State, group, or person any right to engage in any activity or to perform any act aimed at the destruction of any of the rights and freedoms set forth herein.

Common Article 3, 1949 Geneva Conventions

In the case of armed conflict not of an international character occurring in the territory of one of the High Contracting Parties, each Party to the conflict shall be bound to apply, as a minimum, the following provisions:

1. Persons taking no active part in the hostilities, including members of armed forces who have laid down their arms and

those placed hors de combat by sickness, wounds, detention, or any other cause, shall in all circumstances be treated humanely, without any adverse distinction founded on race, color, religion or faith, sex, birth or wealth, or any other similar criteria.

To this end, the following acts are and shall remain prohibited at any time and in any place whatsoever with respect to the above-mentioned persons:

a. violence to life and person, in particular murder of all kinds, mutilation, cruel treatment, and torture;

b. taking of hostages;

c. outrages upon personal dignity, in particular humiliating and degrading treatment;

d. the passing of sentences and the carrying out of executions without previous judgement pronounced by a regularly constituted court, affording all the judicial guarantees which are recognized as indispensable by civilized peoples.

2. The wounded and sick shall be collected and cared for.

An impartial humanitarian body, such as the International Committee of the Red Cross, may offer its services to the Parties to the conflict.

The Parties to the conflict should further endeavor to bring into force, by means of special agreements, all or part of the other provisions of the present Convention.

The application of the preceding provisions shall not affect the legal status of the Parties to the conflict.

THE CENTER FOR INTERNATIONAL HEALTH AND COOPERATION AND THE INSTITUTE OF INTERNATIONAL HUMANITARIAN AFFAIRS

THE CENTER FOR INTERNATIONAL HEALTH and Cooperation (CIHC) was founded by a small group who believed that health and other humanitarian endeavors sometimes provide the only common ground for initiating dialogue, understanding, and cooperation among people and nations shattered by war, civil conflicts, and ethnic violence. The Center has sponsored symposia and published books that reflect this philosophy, including: *Silent Witnesses; A Framework for Survival: Health, Human Rights, and Humanitarian Assistance in Conflicts and Disasters; A Directory of Somali Professionals; Clearing the Fields: Solutions to the Land Mine Crisis; Preventive Diplomacy: Stopping Wars Before They Start;* and *Tropical Medicine: A Clinical Text;* as well as this book and other volumes in the Fordham University Press International Humanitarian Affairs series.

The Center and its Directors have been deeply involved in trying to alleviate the wounds of war in Somalia and the former Yugoslavia. A CIHC amputee center in northern Somalia was developed as a model for a simple, rapid, inexpensive program that could be replicated in other war zones. In the former Yugoslavia, the CIHC was active in prisoner and hostage release, in legal assistance for human and political rights violations, and facilitated discussions between combatants. The Center directs the International Diploma in Humanitarian Assistance (IDHA) in partnership with Fordham University in New York, the University of Geneva in Switzerland, and the Royal College of Surgeons in Ireland. The CIHC cooperates with other centers in offering specialized training courses for humanitarian negotiators and international human rights lawyers. The Center has offered staff support in recent years in crisis management in East Timor, Aceh, Kosovo, Palestine, Albania, and other trouble spots.

The Center has been afforded full consultative status at the United Nations. In the United States, it is a fully approved public charity.

The CIHC is closely linked with Fordham University's Institute of International Humanitarian Affairs (IIHA). The Directors of the CIHC serve as the Advisory Board of the Institute. The President of the CIHC is the University Professor and Director of the Institute, and two of the CIHC officers, Larry Hollingworth and Michel Veuthey, are adjunct professors of Fordham. The Institute offers courses in various aspects of international humanitarian affairs and sponsors symposia on cutting edge topics in this field.

Directors

Kevin M. Cahill, M.D.
(President)
Lord David Owen
Boutros Boutros-Ghali
Peter Tarnoff
Jan Eliasson
Peter Hansen

Francis Deng
Joseph A. O'Hare, S.J.
Abdulrahim Abby Farah
Lady Helen Hamlyn
Eoin O'Brien, M.D.

ABOUT THE AUTHORS

Kevin M. Cahill, M.D., is University Professor and Director of The Institute of International Humanitarian Affairs at Fordham University; President and Director of the Center for International Health and Cooperation; Professor and Chairman, Department of Tropical Medicine, Royal College of Surgeons in Ireland; Clinical Professor of Medicine, New York University; Director, The Tropical Disease Center, Lenox Hill Hospital; and Chief Medical Advisor, Counterterrorism, New York Police Department.

Abdulrahim Abby Farah is a Director of the Center for International Health and Cooperation. He is a former Undersecretary-General of African Affairs at the United Nations, and had served as Somalia's Ambassador to Ethiopia and the United Nations.

Joshua Friedman is an award-winning journalist and teacher. He won a Pulitzer Prize for his coverage of the Ethiopian famine. He has been the chief foreign affairs and United Nations reporter for *Newsday*. He has also served as a distinguished Professor at the Columbia University School of Journalism. He is the former Chairman, and the current Executive Committee Member of The Committee for the Protection of Journalists.

Paul Grossrieder is the Director-General of the International Committee of the Red Cross (ICRC). He had previously served as Deputy Director of Operations of the organization and was Head of the ICRC Delegation in Israel.

S. W. A. Gunn, M.D., is President of the International Association of Humanitarian Medicine. He was Chief of Emergency Services at the World Health Organization in Geneva, Switzerland. Professor Gunn is President of the Mediterranean Council for the Prevention and Treatment of Burns and Fire Disasters, and is the author of the *Multilingual Dictionary of Disaster Medicine and International Relief.*

Pamela Lupton-Bowers is Head of Training and Development at the International Federation of the Red Cross and Red Crescent Societies based in Geneva, Switzerland. She has worked extensively in management development and team building with IFRC teams across Africa, Asia, and Europe. She previously led a team of corporate trainers in a global multinational corporation and has taught people management and cross-cultural communication at universities in England and the United States.

Ibrahim Osman is Director of Monitoring and Evaluation for the International Federation of Red Cross and Red Crescent Societies (IFRC) in Geneva, Switzerland. He was Secretary-General of the Sudanese Red Crescent Society, Head of the Africa Department of the League of Red Cross and Red Crescent Societies and Under-Secretary General of the IFRC. Prior to joining the IFRC, he was a member of the Sudan Parliament and held several ministerial positions in the Sudanese government.

Joelle Tanguy is a well-known consultant in the organization, funding, and management of international humanitarian organizations. She was the Executive Director of Doctors Without Borders U.S.A. She had led relief and refugee operations in, among other crisis areas, Somalia, Bosnia, Zaire, Uganda, and Armenia.

Michel Veuthey is the Geneva Representative and Academic Director of the Center for International Health and Cooperation's International Diploma in Humanitarian Assistance (IDHA). He also directs the Summer Course with the International Institute of Humanitarian Law. He is an Adjunct Professor at the Fordham University School of Law and Board Member of MSF–Switzerland

and the Geneva Fund. Prior to joining the CIHC, he had served for thirty years with the ICRC in many positions including Assistant to the President.

H. Roy Williams is President of the Center for Humanitarian Cooperation. He previously served as Director of the United States Office of Foreign Disaster Assistance in the United States Agency for International Development. He also was Regional Director for the International Organization for Migration working in Thailand and Malaysia, Chief of Operation in Geneva, and Vice President for Operations and Planning at the International Rescue Committee.

INDEX

Acceptable risk, 39
Active Learning Network for Accountability and Performance in Humanitarian Action (ALNAP), 162
Africa
  annual humanitarian assistance, 21
  average annual humanitarian assistance, 24
  border disputes, 250–251
  disaster assistance per person, 22
  effort to create unity, 243–244
  faces the reality of an interdependent world, 247–248
  non–intervention in internal affairs of states, 246–247
  political instability and the military, 248–249
  problem of underdevelopment, 244–245
African Charter on Human and Peoples' Rights (1981), 122
African Commission on Human Rights and Peoples' Rights, 130
American Red Cross, 213
AmeriCares, 229–230, 231
Americas
  annual humanitarian assistance, 21
  disaster assistance per person, 22

Amin, Mohammed, 188
Amnesty, 210
Annan, Kofi, 117
Asia
  annual humanitarian assistance, 21
  average annual humanitarian assistance, 24
  disaster assistance per person, 22
Assessment, 39
Authoritarian leadership for assistance, 63

Bandler, R., 69
Bangladesh, 21
Battle of Bethiingen, 7
Battle of Solferino (1859), 7, 118
Battle of Tsushima, 118
Behavioral flexibility, 71
Belbin Team Type Inventory, 74
Bilateral cooperation, 44
Biological Weapons Convention, 45
Bioterrorism, 39
Borderless movement, 11
Born, Friedrich, 10
Bridges among civilizations, 116–117
Bruno, Giordano, 5

Cambodia, 133–134
Caracas, 6
CARE, 144, 212

Catastrophe theory, 39
Catholic Relief Services, 195, 212
Center for International Health
    and Cooperation, 51–54
Center for Research on the Epide-
    miology of Disasters, 29
Charter of Fundamental Rights of
    the European Union (2000),
    122
Child sponsorship, 228–229
China, 21
Christian charity, 5, 6
CNN, 197, 198–199
Cognitive differences, 72
Cognitive preferences, 71
Commission on Human Rights,
    123
Committee to Protect Journalists,
    193
Complex disasters
    assistance and costs, 28(t)
    assistance as a percentage of
        needs covered, 31(t)
    assistance by continent, 29(t)
    assistance per person, 30(t)
    average humanitarian assis-
        tance, 25
    defined, 33–34, 37
    demand for higher caliber work-
        ers, 64
    increase in and dangers of,
        187–188
    longevity and permanence of re-
        lief operations, 63–64
    numbers affected, 27(t)
Compulsive personality, 103
Consolidated Appeals Process
    (CAP), 220
    distribution by agency, 222(t)
    funding rates, 221(t)
Conventional arms, 39
Convention Against Torture and

Other Cruel, Inhuman, or De-
    grading Treatment, 122
Convention for Protection of
    Human Rights and Funda-
    mental Freedoms of the
    Council of Europe, 122
Convention on the Prevention and
    Punishment of the Crime of
    Genocide, 121
Convention on the Rights of the
    Child (1989), 122
Crimes against humanity, 39–40

Danieli, Yael, 186
Daughters of Charity, 6
Declaration on the Right to Devel-
    opment (1986), 123
Decolonization, 11
Deportation, 40
Development aid, decline of, 208
Disappearance/forced disappear-
    ance, 40
Disarmament, 40
Disaster medicine, 38
Disasters
    assistance as percentage of cost,
        25(t)
    assistance per continent, 23(t)
    average assistance per affected
        person by continent, 33(t)
    cost of, 20
    cost of assistance, 22(t)
    cost per person, 22
    dangers to workers and journal-
        ists, 185–186
    defined, 32–33, 37
    epidemiology, 40
    management, defined, 38
    man-made, 37, 249–251
    natural, defined, 33, 36
    natural in Africa, 251–255
    numbers affected, 21(t)

preparedness, defined, 37
relief, basic tenets of, 50
sources of data, 29–32
trends of numbers affected, 19–20
trends of those affected, 18, 19(t)
Doctors without borders, 11–12, 126(t), 212, 217
Drought, 251–252
Dunant, Henry, 3, 7

Embargo, 40
EM–DAT, 29, 30, 31
Emergence relief situation model, 67
Emotional intelligence, 71–72
Environmental pollution, 41
Ethiopia, 188–190, 195
Ethiopian drought (1973–1974; 1984–1985), 253–254
Ethnic cleansing, 41
Europe
    annual humanitarian assistance, 21
    average annual humanitarian assistance, 24
    disaster assistance per person, 22
European Commission, 131
European Committee for the Prevention of Torture and Inhuman or Degrading Treatment or Punishment, 131
European Convention for the Prevention of Torture and Inhuman or Degrading Treatment or Punishment, 122
European Court, 131
ExxonMobil, 213

Financial Tracking System, 29
Flore, Joachim de, 5

Forgiveness and reconciliation, denial of, 134–135
Forman, Shepard, 207
Francis of Assisi, Saint, 5, 116
Frankel, Marvin, 134–135
Frankl, Viktor, 133
Fundamental Principles of the Red Cross/Crescent, 123
Funding, 189
    accountability, 257–258
    crisis driven, 220
    distortion from emotional appeals for, 232–233
    government greatest source, 201–205
    sources of, 227–228

Geneva Conventions, 8, 10, 44, 119, 120, 121(t)
Genocide, 41
Gifts in kind, 229–232, 230(t)
    inappropriateness of, 231
Greeks, 3, 4, 6
Grinder, J., 69
Groupthink, 100–102
Guerilla warfare, 41
Gujerat, 63

Hague Regulations (1907), 118, 119
Hazard, 39
Health, 38
Hersey and Blanchard Situation Leadership model, 92, 93(t)
High Commissioner for Human Rights, 45
High Commissioner for Refugees (UNHCR), 221, 223
Holocaust, 10
Human dignity
    denial of, 132–133
    recognition of, 116

Humanitarian Accountability Project, 238
Humanitarian actions, 6–7
  basic principles, 7–8
  case of the U.S.A., 194–196
  conflicts on the periphery, 12–13
  defined, 200–201
  and military operations, 14
  peacekeeping, 14
  politicization of, 14–15
  postwar, 10
  UN instruments for, 124(t)
  World War I, 8
  World War II, 9–10
Humanitarian assistance
  as a percentage of GNP, 209(t)
  average annual, 24
  bilateral as a share of bilateral ODA, 210(t)
  by regions, 26(t)
  character and importance of teams, 59–62
  comparison for complex and natural disasters, 26–27
  comparisons, 27–28
  contributions from non–OECD countries, 203–204
  coordination of workers, 256–257
  cost per person, 24(t)
  for complex disasters, 25
  from multilateral to bilateral, 208–211
  from NGOs, 204–205
  growth of, 20–21
  impact of training, 51–52
  importance of training, 49–50
  in U.S. dollars, 202(t)
  multilateral and bilateral, 202
  need for professionalism, 224–225

  per capita, 203(t)
  and political influence, 226–227
  poor response to appeals, 257
  problem of complex resource flows, 205–207
  recruiting staff, 258
  self regulation and accountability, 238–240
  top ten donors, 204(t)
  to UN appeals, 205(t)
  trends, 18–19, 20(t)
Humanitarian Charter, 163
Humanitarian law, 8, 9
  during the Cold War, 10–12
  mechanisms, 127–129
  Protecting Power, 128
  States Party, 128
  and the USSR, 11
  to limit violence in war, 117–119
  and war on terrorism, 15–16
Humanitarian medicine, 38
Humanitarian missions
  a team based model, 65–67
Humanitarian organizations
  deal with decolonization, 11
  role in helping the press, 183
Humanitarian relief
Humanitarian values
  means of achieving, 135–141
Humanitarian workers
  motivations, 68
  and political responsibility, 240
  problem of turnover, 64–65
  unevenness of, 185
Human rights, 41, 120–123
Human Rights Court, 130
Human Rights Mechanisms, 129–131
Human Rights Watch, 210
Human Right to Health, 123
Human Right to Peace, 123

Incident/accident, 41
InterAction, 157–158, 163, 171, 212
Interagency Gifts–in–Kind Standards, 232
Inter-Agency Standing Committee (IASC), 34
Inter-American Convention on Human Rights (1969), 122
Inter-American Convention to Prevent and Punish Torture (1985), 122
Internally displaced persons, 41–42
International Committee of the Red Cross, 7, 8, 9, 9–10, 44, 119–120, 128–129, 186, 217–220, 218(t)
International Council of Voluntary Agencies (ICVA), 157, 163
International Court of Justice, 120
International Covenant on Civil and Political Rights, 121
International Covenant on Economic, Social, and Cultural Rights, 121
International Criminal Court, 129
International Diploma in Humanitarian Assistance, 50, 55(t), 56–58, 67
International Disaster Management Information Network, 45
International Federation of Red Cross and Red Crescent Societies, 45–46, 162
International health, 38
International Humanitarian Law, 119, 131–132
International Military Tribunal of Nuremberg, 119
International networking, 258

International Red Cross Movement, 45
International Rescue Committee (IRC), 144
Interpersonal relationships, 71–72

Justice for war crimes, denial of, 133–134

Kant, I., 116
King, Martin Luther, Jr., 140–141
Kurdistan, 14

Larrey, Baron, 7
Las Casas, Bartholomew de, 116
Law of nations, 116
Lazarists, 6
Leadership
  accommodating motivations, 99–100
  communication skills, 96–99
  decision making, 100–103
  personality style, 102–105
  situational management, 92–96
  styles, 90–92
League of Red Cross Societies, 9
Limiting violence in war
  international Humanitarian Law, 117–119
  taboos, 114
  the Golden Rule, 115–116

Malhuret, Claude, 14–15
Martens Clause, 140
Measures of effectiveness, 42
Media
  decline of international coverage, 236–237
  and humanitarian crises, 235–236
  inadequate reporting of crises, 234–235

response to humanitarian crises, 233–234

and the Ethiopian drought, 253

Ministry Watch, 212

Miscommunication, 69–70

Mitigation, 39

Moeller, Susan, 232

Myers Briggs Type Indicator, 74

Narcissistic personality, 103–104

NBC, 188

Neuro–linguistic programming (NLP), 69–70

Neutrality in humanitarian actions, 123, 126–127

Newsday, 174

The New York Times, 174

NGOs

competition among for fund-raising, 150

differences among, 143–145

growth of influence, 191

and individual's motivations, 145

influence and motivations of donors, 148, 150–151

leadership problems, 146–147

as members of consortia, 156–158, 160–161(t)

proliferation of, 211–214

question of their independence, 214–217

relationship with press and public, 154–156

relationship with the military, 152–154

sources of failure to meet expectations, 163–167

the organization vs. the individual, 145–46

The Triangle of Response, 147–149

Nonprofit agencies funding rations, 214(t)

North–South, 42

Occupational Personality Questionnaire, 74–75

Oceania

annual humanitarian assistance, 21

average annual humanitarian assistance, 24

disaster assistance per person, 22

Office for the Coordination of Humanitarian Affairs, 45

Office for the Coordination of Humanitarian Assistance (OCHA), 220

Organization for Coordination of Humanitarian Assistance (OCHA), Organization of African (OAU), 29, 30

Organization of American States Commission on Human Rights, 130

Oxfam, 210, 212

Pacifism, 9

Paranoid personality, 104

Pare, Ambroise, 7

Peace of God, 114

People in Aid Code of Best Practice, 159–162

Pictet, Jean, 140

Post traumatic stress disorder, 42

Poverty, 5–6, 132

Preferential styles of interpersonal relationships, 73–77

Press

covering Kosovo, 177–179, 181–185

editors functions, 174–175

and humanitarian workers,
171–173
reduces coverage of humanitar-
ian issues, 196–199
reporters' concerns, 175–176
rules of interviewing, 176–177
Prisoner of conscience, 42
Prisoners of war, 10, 42
Private voluntary organizations
(PVO), 192
Private Voluntary Organization
Standards, 158

Red Cross, 7, 45
Red Cross/Crescent, 125(t)
Refugee Convention, 10
Refugees, 251
African, 255–256
defined, 42–43
Relief-Web, 29–30
Religious organization effect on
individual motivation, 68
Resettlement, 43
Rieff, David, 209
Right brain/left brain dominance,
72, 73(t)
Right to intervene, 43
Risk, 39
Rufin, Jean-Christophe, 12
Rwanda, 14

Sahelian drought (1973), 252–253
Saint Petersburg Declaration
(1868), 118
Salvation Army, 213
Santo Domingo, 6
Satellite phones, 179–181
Save the Children, 210, 212
Save the Children Fund, 9
Save the Children U.S.A., 190
Second Lateran Council, 114
Self-awareness, 71

September 11, 2001, 15
Seven Years' War, 7
Shirer, William, 180
Situational management, 92–96
Somalia, 14, 50
Somalia drought (1974–1975),
254–255
Somaliland, analysis of its disaster
situation, 259–267
South African Truth and Reconcil-
iation Commission, 134
Sphere Minimum Standards in Di-
saster Response, 162
The Sphere Project, 163, 238
Standard operating behaviors, 78,
81–84
States Party, 128
Steering Committee for Humani-
tarian Response (SCHR), 158,
163
Sustainable development, 43

Team Management Systems Index,
74
Teams
balance in, 76
barriers to effectiveness, 70–72
building rapport, 69
communication, 76
contribution inclusiveness, 76
decision making, 106–108(t)
feedback, 76, 87–89
identifying objectives, 84–85
identifying with differences, 79
method of operation, 86
mistakes in formation of,
109–110
orientation, 78–79
performance, 80–81
profiles of members, 85–86
resolving differences, 80
role of the leader, 89–90

Terrorism, 43
Third Lateran Council, 114–115
Truce of God, 114
Tuckman, B. W., 78
Turkey and journalists, 193–194
Tutu, Desmond, 134

Union of Soviet Socialist Republics, 9
United Nations, 10
  Consolidated Appeal Process
    (CAP), 220–224
  and NGO staff security, 152
  as source of program funding,
    151–152
United Nations Charter, 120
United Nations High Commission
  for Refugees (UNHCR), 9,
  184
United Nations International Children's Emergency Fund (UNICEF), 184
United Nations Resolution 688, 43

Universal Declaration of Human
  Rights, 121
Utley, Garrick, 234

Victims of war, neutrality of, 7
Vietnam War, 119
Vincent de Paul, Saint, 5–6
Vitoria, Francisco de, 116
Voluntary Organizations in Cooperation in Emergencies
  (VOICE), 158–159, 163
Vulnerability, 39
Wall Street Journal, 174
War crimes, 43–44
Washington Post, 174
Waugh, Evelyn, 180
Weapons of mass destruction, 44
World Food Program (WFP), 221
World Food Summit, 123, 195
World Health Organization
  (WHO), 44–45
World Vision, 188, 189–190, 210,
  212, 217

Yugoslavia, 14